Westby-Nunn's
Company Secretarial Handbook

Westby-Nunn's
Company Secretarial Handbook

Eleventh edition

Mark Stamp LL B (Soton) LL M (Wisc) LL M (Cantab)
Solicitor

Anne Marshall BA LL B (Melb)
Solicitor

Consultant Editor
Christopher N Gorman MA LL M (Cantab)

LONGMAN

© Longman Group UK Ltd 1992

ISBN 0 85121 9063

Published by

Longman Law, Tax and Finance
Longman Group UK Limited
21–27 Lamb's Conduit Street, London WC1N 3NJ

Associated Offices:

Australia, Hong Kong, Malaysia, Singapore, USA

Printed in Great Britain by
Biddles of Guildford Ltd

Contents

CONTENTS vii

Preface

Since the previous edition of this work in 1988 the flow of companies legislation has continued its steady, seemingly remorseless progress, with one major statute — the Companies Act 1989 — and a number of significant statutory instruments, notably those relating to the new Stock Exchange transfer regime (TAURUS). The text of this new edition of Westby-Nunn reflects these legislative changes as well as other relevant changes in law and practice since 1988.

The principal objective of the work remains to provide a reasonably practical guide to the requirements of the Companies Acts — and in particular those of 1985 and 1989 — and related matters for company secretaries and others engaged in company administration. It does not purport to be a comprehensive treatment of companies legislation currently in force. In particular, it does not cover the more arcane provisions — for this, company secretaries should continue to have recourse to the standard works on company law or to their professional advisers. It is designed, however, to provide ready assistance on a day-to-day basis and a signpost in cases of difficulty, and to be of direct practical relevance in dealing with a number of commonly encountered situations.

I have been principal co-editor of the last four editions of Westby-Nunn. On this occasion however I have acted as consultant editor only, with the detailed preparation of the new edition being undertaken by my colleagues Mark Stamp and Anne Marshall. I am grateful to them for assuming this not inconsiderable burden. Both they and I would of course welcome any suggested changes or improvements for future editions.

October 1992   Christopher N Gorman

Table of Cases

Table of Statutes

Table of Statutory Instruments

Chapter 1

Introduction

1.1 General

1.1.1 References

The statutory provisions which govern the formation and conduct of registered companies are contained mainly in the Companies Act 1985 as amended by the Companies Act 1989, referred to in this book as 'the Act' and 'the 1989 Act' respectively. Unless otherwise stated, references to sections or Schedules relate to the Act. Most of the statutory provisions relating to the winding-up of registered companies have now been moved to the Insolvency Act 1986, although a few of them remain in Part XX of the Act. References in this book to regulations (eg 'reg 46') are, unless the contrary is stated, to those contained in Table A in the Schedule to the Companies (Tables A to F) Regulations 1985 (SI 1985 No 805) as very slightly amended by the Companies (Tables A to F) (Amendment) Regulations 1985 (SI 1985 No 1052) (see 1.3.4). Where company forms are referred to (eg Form 395), these indicate the official number normally derived from the Companies (Forms) Regulations 1985 (SI 1985 No 854). (Wherever possible the official form number is now the same as the number of the relevant section of the Act.)

Unless otherwise stated, references to 'the Secretary of State' are to the Secretary of State for Trade and Industry, and references to 'the Registrar' are to the Registrar of Companies.

1.1.2 Essential materials

Every company secretary should have a copy of the Act. He may also, according to circumstances, need other statutes such as the Insolvency Act 1986 and the Financial Services Act 1986. If any securities of any company with which he is concerned are dealt

1

in on a stock exchange or investment exchange or anyone makes a market in them, he will need the Company Securities (Insider Dealing) Act 1985 (see 8.9.3). If any company with which he is concerned carries on business under a name other than its own name, he will need the Business Names Act 1985. Occasionally he may need the Companies Consolidation (Consequential Provisions) Act 1985.

In the case of a company whose securities are admitted to the Official List of The Stock Exchange a company secretary should have a copy of *Admission of Securities to Listing*, published by the Council of The Stock Exchange and commonly known as the Yellow Book, and if any such securities are dealt in on The Stock Exchange's Unlisted Securities Market he should have a copy of The Stock Exchange's relevant booklet, *Unlisted Securities Market*.

1.1.3 Delivery of documents to Registrar of Companies

Regulations may be made prescribing requirements as to size, durability and legibility of documents delivered to the Registrar (s 706) and the Registrar may accept for registration any material other than a document (such as information on microfilm) of a kind approved by him (s 707).

A person persistently in default in relation to the requirements of the Act as to the delivery of documents to the Registrar may be disqualified for up to five years (or in certain circumstances fifteen years) from holding office or from being concerned or taking part in any way in the promotion, formation or management of a company (Company Directors Disqualification Act 1986, ss 1 to 5). Any person acting in contravention of such an order may be fined or imprisoned and may incur personal responsibility for the company's debts and other liabilities (1986 Act, ss 13 and 15). The Secretary of State is required to maintain a register of such disqualification orders for the time being in force and such register is open to inspection on payment of the prescribed fee (1986 Act, s 18). Additional penalties will now apply to delays in lodging company accounts (see 7.2.3).

1.1.4 The Companies Registry

The address of the Registrar of Companies (or, colloquially, the Companies Registry) for England and Wales is Companies Registration Office, Companies House, Crown Way, Maindy, Cardiff

CF4 3UZ (telephone Cardiff (0222) 388588) although company searches, delivery of documents and certain other procedures (including the special 'same day' procedure for registration, re-registration and change of names of companies) may be effected at Companies House, 55–71 City Road, London EC1Y 1BB (telephone 071-253 9393).

In this book, to 'file' a document means to deliver it to the Registrar of Companies for registration.

1.1.5 Scottish companies

This book deals principally with English law: in most but not all respects Scottish company law which applies to companies registered in Scotland is the same or very similar. The address of the Registrar of Companies for Scotland is Companies Registration Office, 102 George Street, Edinburgh EH2 3DJ (telephone 031-225 5774/5).

1.2 The Secretary

Every company must have a secretary (s 283 (1)). There can be joint secretaries (see s 290(1)).

1.2.1 Appointment of secretary

The directors of a *public* company (see 1.4.4) must take all reasonable steps to secure that the secretary or each joint secretary is a person who appears to them to have the requisite knowledge and experience to discharge the functions of secretary and who is qualified in one of the following ways:

(1) on 22 December 1980 he was secretary or assistant or deputy secretary of the company
(2) for at least three of the five years before his appointment as secretary he was secretary of a public company
(3) he is a member of:
    The Institute of Chartered Accountants in England and Wales,
    The Institute of Chartered Accountants of Scotland,
    The Institute of Chartered Accountants in Ireland,
    The Chartered Association of Certified Accountants,
    The Institute of Chartered Secretaries and Administrators,
    The Institute of Cost and Management Accountants, or

The Chartered Institute of Public Finance and
Accountancy.

(4) he is a barrister, advocate or solicitor called or admitted in any part of the United Kingdom.

(5) by virtue of his holding or having held any other position or being a member of any other body he appears to the directors capable of discharging those functions (s 286).

Subject to the above rules, any person may be appointed secretary, including a corporation, save that the secretary may not be (*a*) a person who is also the company's sole director (s 283(2)) or (*b*) a corporation the sole director of which is sole director of the company (s 283(4)(*a*)). In addition, since an officer of a company or a partner or employee of an officer may not be its auditor (s 27 1989 Act), and for this purpose 'officer' includes a director, manager or secretary (s 744), it follows that, for example, the auditor may not also be the secretary. There is nothing to prevent the company's solicitor from being the secretary.

The statement of particulars to be delivered on application for registration of a company (Form 10) must contain the name and relevant particulars of the first secretary, or the first joint secretaries, and on the company's incorporation he or they are deemed to have been appointed as such (s 13(5)). Any appointment by the Articles is void unless the person appointed is also named in the statement of particulars (s 10(5)). Each subsequent appointment of a person to the office of secretary is usually made by the directors of the company in exercise of the power conferred on them by the company's Articles (eg reg 99); though it seems that they may make the appointment even if the Articles do not specifically confer such a power on them.

Where there is more than one director, the secretary may also be a director of the company; but where a provision in the Act requires something to be done by or to a director *and* the secretary, it cannot be done by or to the same person acting as both director and secretary (s 284).

An assistant or deputy secretary is not one of the principal officers of the company (see the definition of 'officer' in s 744). However if the office of secretary is vacant, or there is for any other reason no secretary capable of acting, anything required to be done by or to the secretary may be done by or to his deputy or assistant, or, if there is no such deputy or assistant capable of acting, by or to any officer of the company authorised generally or specially in that behalf by the directors (s 283(3)). In other circumstances a deputy or assistant secretary can perform a function of the secretary if the Articles permit and provided that the function is not required by statute to be carried out by the secretary.

Every appointment of a secretary must be recorded in the register of directors and secretaries and notified to the Registrar of Companies (see 8.8).

1.2.2 Change of secretary

A secretary appointed by the directors may be dismissed by them, but if such dismissal breaks his contract of service he may have a claim against the company for breach of that contract. The termination of a secretary's appointment must be recorded in the register of directors and secretaries and notified to the Registrar of Companies (see 8.8).

1.2.3 Status of secretary

The secretary is an officer of the company (s 744) with ministerial and administrative functions; but he does not have, by virtue of his office, managerial functions, although in practice he is frequently given, expressly or impliedly, considerable managerial authority and responsibility. As the chief administrative officer of the company he has ostensible authority to enter into contracts connected with the administrative side of the company's affairs, eg for the employment of staff or the hiring of cars to meet customers (*Panorama Developments (Guildford) Ltd v Fidelis Furnishing Fabrics Ltd* [1971] 2 QB 711); but depending on the circumstances and any course of dealing his authority may not extend to concluding managerial contracts, eg the borrowing of money, for which he would have to be given authority by the board of directors.

The secretary may or may not be an employee of the company: this is important in the event of a receiver being appointed or the company being wound up, for only if he is an employee is he entitled to rank as a preferential creditor in respect of his remuneration. If he is engaged by the company full-time with regular hours he will probably be an employee and a preferential creditor; but if, for example, he is a practising solicitor or accountant who acts as secretary and does the work in his own time, he will not be an employee and therefore not a preferential creditor (*Cairney v Back* [1906] 2 KB 746).

1.2.4 Liabilities of secretary

Many important duties are imposed on secretaries by the Act, and in many cases serious penalties may be incurred if these duties are not carried out. Some of the penalising sections make the secretary liable only if he is knowingly or wilfully a party to the default, and it is not possible to make any general statement as to what degree of inaction constitutes this form of default; but in most cases where a secretary had called the attention of his directors to the fact that a certain duty had to be performed and had continued to remind them that it had not been performed, he would probably be deemed to have done what was within his power to carry out the duty.

Like all other employees of the company, a secretary may be liable to the company for damage resulting from his own negligence; and any provision in the Articles or any contract with the company which purports to exempt any director, manager or officer of the company from liability in respect of negligence, default, breach of duty or breach of trust is void (s 310). However, the company can purchase and maintain insurance for the secretary against such liability, or indemnify him against the costs of litigation in which he is exculpated (s 310(3)). In addition, the court can relieve him from responsibility in certain cases (s 727).

Failure to draw the attention of the directors to the company's insolvency or likely insolvency, and the consequences of continuing in business, can amount to negligence, but mere silence and omission do not necessarily bring the secretary within the provisions of s 213 of the Insolvency Act 1986 ('fraudulent trading') (*Re Maidstone Buildings Provisions Ltd* [1971] 1 WLR 1085).

A secretary may incur liability to third parties in respect of contracts entered into ostensibly on behalf of the company, if sufficient care is not taken; though, if such contracts are made in the name of the company and it is made clear that the secretary is acting only as the company's agent, he should avoid personal liability. Care should be taken in signing bills of exchange and cheques. The words 'for and on behalf of ____ ____ Limited' should always be written under the secretary's signature. It is not sufficient to use the formula 'John Smith, secretary of ____ ____ Limited'. The word 'Limited' must not be omitted (*Atkins & Co v Wardle* (1889) 58 LJQB 377) (see further 2.3). The above of course applies equally in the case of a public company.

1.3 Memorandum and Articles

The secretary should acquire a thorough knowledge and understanding of the company's Memorandum and Articles of Association, for upon these documents the conduct of the company's business and many of the rights, duties and liabilities of directors and members of the company depend.

1.3.1 The Memorandum

Every company must have a Memorandum of Association, which must state the name of the company, whether the registered office is to be situated in England and Wales, Wales or Scotland, the objects of the company, that the liability of members is limited (if it is), and the amount of the share capital (if any) (s 2). (The country in which the registered office is to be situated could, in the case of companies incorporated before the Companies Act 1985, be stated as 'England' alone since England includes Wales.) A company whose Memorandum of Association states that its registered office is to be situated in Wales may have its Memorandum and Articles, and may deliver documents to the Registrar of Companies, in Welsh but accompanied by a certified English translation (s 21).

In the Memorandum the clause setting out the objects of the company is important, for a company is able to pursue only those objects which are either expressly set out in or are reasonably incidental to its Memorandum. A company is permitted to state in its Memorandum that its object is 'to carry on business as a general commercial company' and this will permit the company to carry on any trade or business whatsoever (s 3A). Although the company is then deemed to have power to do all such things as are incidental or conducive to the carrying on of any trade or business, there is room for interpretation as to whether certain actions (such as making charitable donations) would be permitted. For certainty, therefore, it may still be advisable exhaustively to list the company's objects.

In construing the objects clause of the Memorandum certain general principles apply. In *Cotman v Brougham* [1918] AC 514, a provision for each object to be treated as a main object was held by the House of Lords to be effective; and one empowering the company to carry on any ancillary business which 'in the opinion of the directors' could be advantageously carried on was upheld in *Bell Houses Ltd v City Wall Properties Ltd* [1966] 2 QB

656. In *Introductions Ltd v National Provincial Bank Ltd* [1970] Ch 199 a borrowing provision in the objects clause was, however, held to be a power rather than an object and accordingly, despite a *Cotman v Brougham* and a *Bell Houses* provision, exercisable only for the purposes of its true business objects. Even where a transaction is within the scope of an express object, it may be ultra vires (see 1.3.2 below) if no reasonable person could have concluded that it was entered into for the benefit of the company (*Charter-bridge Corporation v Lloyds Bank Ltd* [1970] Ch 62). See further *Re Halt Garage* (1964) Ltd [1982] 3 All ER 1016, *Rolled Steel Products v British Steel Corporation* [1985] 2 WLR 908 (CA) and *Rosemary Simmons Memorial Housing Association Ltd v United Dominions Trust Ltd* [1986] 1 WLR 1440.

1.3.2 Ultra vires

The doctrine of ultra vires provides that any act of a company outside its permitted objects is void and cannot be enforced by or against third parties. The Act now attempts to abolish this doctrine in relation to third parties although it expressly retains the doctrine with regard to shareholders so that they are still able to bring an action against directors for ultra vires acts.

Section 35(1) provides: 'The validity of an act done by a company shall not be called into question on the ground of lack of capacity by reason of anything in the company's memorandum.' This section is subject to three exceptions:

(1) A shareholder is able to obtain an injunction against the company in respect of acts proposed to be done outside the objects clause. However, no injunctive proceedings can be brought in respect of an act that is required to be done in fulfilment of a legal obligation arising from a previous act of the company. Accordingly, if, for example, a company enters into a contract to purchase land, being an act outside its objects clause, then a shareholder will not be able to obtain an injunction to prevent the company completing the purchase.

(2) An act outside a company's objects clause is able to be ratified by a special resolution of shareholders and if shareholders' approval is obtained in advance no injunctive proceedings will be able to be brought.

(3) Where it is a director of a company or its holding company

or a person connected with him is the person dealing with
the company.

Section 35A(1) provides additional relief to

> 'a person dealing with a company in good faith, in respect
> of whom the power of the board of directors to bind the
> company, or authorise others to do so, is deemed to be free
> of any limitation under the company's constitution.'

A person is treated as dealing with a company if he is a party
to any transaction or other act to which the company is a party
which includes being the recipient of a gift from the company.

Section 35A(2)(b) provides that a person shall not be regarded
as acting in bad faith by reason only of his knowing that an act
is beyond the powers of the directors under the company's constitution. Therefore, in order for a person to lose the protection of
s 35A, it will be necessary for the company to show that he has
actual knowledge of the company's or directors' lack of capacity
and that, armed with this knowledge, it can be proved that he
acted otherwise than in good faith. For example, if the third party
knew that the directors knew that they were acting outside their
authority derived from the company's constitution this may deprive
him of the protection of s 35A.

Section 35A protects third parties from lack of authority derived
from 'any limitation under the company's constitution', which
includes limitations deriving from a resolution of the company in
general meeting or from any agreement between the members or
of any class of members (ie written resolutions and those requiring
to be filed pursuant to s 380(4)(c) and (d)). Accordingly, s 35A will
be of no assistance in the following cases:

(1) Where the act is illegal: for instance, where the directors
authorise the company to give financial assistance in connection with the purchase by the company of its own shares
contrary to s 151.

(2) Where the directors act in breach of their fiduciary duties
and it is claimed that a third party has received the company's
property in knowledge of the breach of duty and is a
constructive trustee.

(3) Where the limitation arose from a resolution of the board
itself. So that, for example, if the board passes a resolution
prohibiting the finance director from entering into contracts
for more than £1,000 and the finance director does so then

s 35A will not be relevant in determining whether the third party can enforce the contract because this is not a limitation under the company's constitution. In these circumstances the rights of a third party dealing with the company will depend upon the rules of ostensible authority (see *Freeman & Lockyer v Buckhurst Park Properties (Mangal) Ltd* [1964] 2 QB 480).

The distinction between objects and powers (see 1.3.1 above) remains relevant for the purpose of ratification. If the directors are acting outside the objects of the company then their action can be ratified only by a special resolution (s 35(3)). Furthermore, if the directors wish to be relieved from personal liability in respect of the unauthorised transaction this must be done by separate resolution so that shareholders have the opportunity to affirm the act without, necessarily, releasing the directors from liability. If, however, the directors are acting within the objects but outside their powers then, since it is not a matter relating to corporate capacity, the transaction concerned can be ratified by an ordinary resolution.

1.3.3 Alteration of Memorandum

General While the Articles may be altered at will by means of a special resolution, the method of altering the Memorandum will vary according to the nature of the alteration. The following is a summary of the points most likely to be encountered. As to certain general restrictions on amendments under s 16, see 1.3.5.

Name Should it be desired to change the name of a company, it is necessary to obtain the sanction of the shareholders by special resolution. The prior consent of the Registrar to the new name is not required, but the provisions of s 28 should be borne in mind (and see 2.1 and 2.3).

A copy of the resolution must be filed with the Registrar and the fee prescribed by the regulations for the time being in force under s 708 must be paid (currently £40).

The Registrar will in due course enter the new name on the register and issue a certificate of incorporation on change of name. The change of name takes effect from the date of issue of this certificate. The Memorandum itself remains unaltered; but since the resolution will 'evidence' a change in the Memorandum the filing requirements of s 18 will apply (see 6.6.5).

Registered office The situation of the registered office may be changed at the will of the company, within the limits of the country named in the Memorandum, without altering that document. Notice of the change must be given to the Registrar within 14 days (s 287(2)) (Form 287).

In order to change the country of domicile mentioned in the Memorandum, it would be necessary to obtain Parliamentary sanction, but, if such a change were decided on, it would probably be found less expensive to reconstruct the company.

Objects The objects may be altered by a special resolution (s 4).

Where, however, a resolution altering the objects is passed, application to the court may be made, by a minority holding 15 per cent of the share capital, within 21 days of the date of the resolution, for the alteration to be cancelled. It should, however, be remembered that acts outside the objects clause may now be ratified by 75 per cent of shareholders present at the meeting. Accordingly whilst a minority could seek to prevent a change in the objects of the company, they would be unable to stop the majority ratifying ultra vires actions. Such proceedings are therefore unlikely to be brought in practice and the objects of a company are generally regarded as freely alterable.

Where a company desires to sell or dispose of its undertaking to another company, and it is proposed to put the selling company into liquidation, it is not necessary that the Memorandum of the selling company should authorise the sale; but where the selling company is to continue business, such authority is necessary if the result of the sale or disposition is a change in the nature of the company's activities. If, for instance, a manufacturing company sells its undertaking for shares in another company and continues to carry on business as a mere shareholding concern, it would be necessary for the Memorandum to authorise the transaction.

Limited liability Sections 49 to 52 of the Act provide for limited companies being re-registered as unlimited and unlimited companies being re-registered as limited. No public company may apply under s 49 to be re-registered as an unlimited company (s 49(3)).

Capital For alteration of the share capital as shown in the Memorandum see 4.12.

Alteration of non-essential contents of Memorandum It was formerly the custom to include in the Memorandum many matters which could lawfully be provided for by the Articles, eg class rights of shareholders; and s 17 provides that any condition contained in the Memorandum, which could lawfully have been contained in the Articles, may be altered by special resolution. This general rule is subject, however, to the following modifications:

(1) it does not apply where the Memorandum itself provides for or prohibits the alteration of all or any of such conditions;

(2) it does not authorise any variation or abrogation of the special rights of any class of members;

(3) where such a special resolution is passed, application may be made to the court by members (but not debenture holders) as if the resolution altered the objects of the company and in that event the procedure laid down by s 4 for dealing with such applications will apply. It is not necessary, however, to give notice of a special resolution for this purpose to debenture holders;

(4) no alteration can increase a member's liability to contribute to share capital unless he consents; and all alterations are subject to s 459 (power of court to grant relief where members are unfairly prejudiced).

1.3.4 *The Articles*

The Articles of Association provide the machinery for the conduct of the company's affairs, laying down regulations, eg for the summoning and holding of meetings of members, the appointment, retirement and powers of directors, the keeping of accounts, and the issuing of shares. In SI 1985 No 805 (as very slightly amended by SI 1985 No 1052) there is a model set of Articles of Association known as Table A. This forms the Articles of a company registered after 30 June 1985 if no special Articles are registered; and, even where special Articles are registered, those regulations of Table . A apply which are not expressly excluded or contradicted by the special Articles (s 8).

Table A, as it appears in that statutory instrument, differs from the forms of Table A which appeared in various Companies Acts prior to 1985, and care must be taken to ascertain which form of Table A, if any, is applicable to a particular company. Companies formed before 1 July 1985 are not governed by Table A in SI 1985 No 805 unless they take steps to adopt that version of Table A (Companies Consolidation (Consequential Provisions) Act 1985 s 31(8)). Companies formed under the Acts of 1862, 1908, 1929 or 1948 may still be governed by the version of Table A adopted when the company was formed, unless it has been excluded or a later version of the Table has been adopted. Many provisions in older versions of Table A are, however, overridden by the Act. Considerable care must, therefore, be taken in applying earlier versions of the Table.

Part II of the 1948 Table A (restrictions on transfer of shares, number of members etc) applied only to private companies and was repealed for new companies by the Companies Act 1980; it will however, unless excluded, continue to apply to private companies registered before 22 December 1980.

1.3.5 Alteration of Articles

Section 9 of the Act empowers every company to alter or add to its Articles by a special resolution.

In exercising this power, the functions of the Articles must be borne in mind. Thus, the Articles cannot be altered so as to permit the company to do what is ultra vires (*Guinness v Land Corporation of Ireland Ltd* (1882) 22 Ch D 349); and the court may restrain the company from making an alteration which necessarily causes a breach of contract (*British Murac Syndicate Ltd v Alperton Rubber Co Ltd* [1915] 2 Ch 186). The Articles cannot be altered so as to deprive the shareholders of their statutory rights (*Re Peveril Gold Mines Ltd* [1898] 1 Ch 122); or to oppress a minority without benefiting the company (*Menier v Hooper's Telegraph Works* (1874) 9 Ch App 350); but it is for the company, and not for the court, to decide what is likely to benefit the company (*Shuttleworth v Cox Bros & Co (Maidenhead) Ltd* [1927] 2 KB 9) although the courts sometimes apply a more objective test (eg *Greenhalgh v Arderne Cinemas Ltd* [1951] Ch 286).

Section 16 provides that no member of a company is bound by an alteration of the Memorandum or Articles which requires him to increase his holding of shares or increases his liability to pay money to the company, unless (*a*) the alteration is made before he becomes a member, or (*b*) he agrees in writing to be bound. Further a member who considers the alteration unfairly prejudicial may apply to the court (ss 17 and 459). Apart from these provisions, an alteration of the Articles may be retrospective in effect (*Allen v Gold Reefs of West Africa Ltd* [1900] 1 Ch 656); but this will not eg enable the company to acquire a lien over shares after they have been transferred for value by a debtor (*M'Arthur (W & A) Ltd (Liquidator) v Gulf Line Ltd* [1909] SC 732).

Notice of intention to alter the Articles must indicate the nature of the alteration, and, as in the case of any other special resolution, a copy must be filed with the Registrar (see 6.6.5). If the resolution is for the adoption of new Articles, a print of such Articles identified by the signature of an officer of the company, usually the chairman or secretary, must also be delivered. In any event, by s 18, a special resolution altering the Articles which is filed with the Registrar must be accompanied by a printed copy of the Articles as altered which should have endorsed thereon a certificate signed by a director or the secretary that the print is a true copy of the Articles as altered. Small alterations may be dealt with by a rubber stamp or typed or by permanently affixing the new version to a copy of the original in such manner as to obscure the amended words.

1.3.6 Certificate of incorporation

When the Memorandum and Articles have been registered with the Registrar and other preliminary requirements have been fulfilled (see Chapter 2) a certificate of incorporation is issued by the Registrar (s 13(1)). The company comes into existence on the date of issue of this certificate and the certificate is conclusive evidence that the requirements of the Act have been fulfilled (s 13(7)).

1.3.7 Copies of Memorandum and Articles

If any member of the company so requires, he must be sent a copy of the Memorandum and Articles (s 19). A fee of not more than 5p may be charged. Every copy of the Memorandum issued must contain all alterations made prior to the date of issue and every copy of the Articles must embody or annex special resolutions for the time being in force which will include those altering the Articles (ss 20 and 380(2)).

1.4 Technical Terms

In studying the Memorandum and Articles and the Act and applying their provisions, the secretary must understand certain technical terms. Many of these will be explained in the text as they are encountered; but some are so important and frequent that they are explained here.

1.4.1 Members

The term 'member' is defined by s 22, which states that the subscribers to the Memorandum of a company shall be deemed to have agreed to become members of the company, and on its registration shall be entered as members in its register of members; and that every other person who agrees to become a member of the company, and whose name is entered in the register of members, shall be a member of the company.

'Member' is not synonymous with 'shareholder'. A company limited by guarantee, for instance, may have members who hold no shares. Moreover, a person who possesses a share warrant (see 4.6), though he is a shareholder, is not a member, except to the extent that he may be deemed to be so under the Articles (s 355(5)).

If the number of members of a company other than a private company limited by shares or guarantees (see 1.4.2 below) is reduced below two and the company carries on business for more than six months while the number is so reduced, every person who is a member of the company during the time that it carries on business after those six months and knows it has only one member is liable (jointly and severally with the company) for the payment of the debts of the company contracted during that time (s 24).

1.4.2 Single member companies

Under the Companies (Single Member Private Limited Companies) Regulations 1992, a company may be formed by one person and may have one member, and any enactment which provides to the contrary is deemed to be automatically modified as necessary. If the membership of a company falls to one, that event must be recorded on the register of members, as must any subsequent increase of the membership to more than one (s 352A). Certain other consequences result from a company being or becoming a single member company: the quorum at meetings will be one member; contracts with sole members who are also directors must be recorded in writing or in board minutes for the meeting next following the making of the contract; and decisions of the sole member in respect of the company other than at general meetings must also be recorded in writing and the written record maintained by the company.

1.4.3 Companies and bodies corporate

The Act refers sometimes to 'companies' and sometimes to 'bodies corporate'. Where the term 'company' is used, it usually means a company formed and registered under the Act or a previous Companies Act (s 735(1)). There are, however, many other types of corporate bodies, which, though they are not directly governed by the Act, are referred to in it, such as companies formed by Royal Charter or by special Act of Parliament or incorporated or formed outside Great Britain. All these as well as companies formed and registered under the Act or earlier Companies Acts are included in the phrase 'bodies corporate'. In some places in the Act 'company' includes any such body corporate, eg in the definition of 'subsidiary' and 'holding company' in s 736. This also applies in the Company Securities (Insider Dealing) Act 1985 (s 11 of that Act) (see 8.9.3).

1.4.4 Public and private companies

A public company is a limited company with a share capital (whether limited by shares or guarantee) whose Memorandum states that it is to be a public company and which has been registered or re-registered at the Companies Registry as a public company on or after 22 December 1980, the date on which the provisions of the Companies Act 1980 relating to classification of companies came into effect (s 1(3)). A public company must satisfy minimum capital requirements explained below. The name of a public company must end with 'public limited company' or its Welsh equivalent (or certain abbreviations thereof) (see 2.3).

Any company which is not a public one is a private one (s 1(3)). Most companies are private ones. Since the Companies Act 1980 it is no longer necessary for the Articles of a private company to restrict the right to transfer shares, put a basic limit of fifty on the number of members and prohibit any offering of its shares or debentures to the public (provisions included in Part II of the 1948 Act, Table A, and see 1.3.5) although it may include any of such matters in its Articles if it wishes and the prohibition on a private limited company offering its securities to the public is now set out in s 81 (which section will be repealed once Part V of the Financial Services Act comes into force, whereupon s 170 of that Act will have the same effect).

A company can be initially formed as a public company only if its share capital as stated in its Memorandum is at least 'the authorised minimum', a figure which is currently £50,000 but can be varied by statutory instrument (ss 11 and 118). Further, a company registered as a public one on its original incorporation must not do business or exercise any borrowing powers until the Registrar has issued it with a certificate under s 117 (or it has re-registered as a private company). This certificate is obtained only if the Registrar is satisfied that the company has *allotted* share capital in nominal amount of at least the authorised minimum and there is delivered to him an application and statutory declaration (Form 117) stating this and certain other matters. (Shares allotted under an employees' share scheme are taken into account for this purpose only if paid up as to at least a quarter of nominal amount and the whole of any premium.)

The share capital requirements are more onerous where an 'old public company' proposes to re-register as a public company. (An old public company is one which was a public company within the meaning which that expression had before 22 December 1980 but which has not taken action since that date to re-register as a public company within the new meaning of that expression, or to become a private company.) In such circumstances reference should be made to s 3 of the Companies Consolidation (Consequential Provisions) Act 1985.

If a private company (other than an old public company) proposes to re-register as a public company, the share capital requirements are more stringent still (s 45). Not only must the company have an allotted share capital in nominal amount of at least the authorised minimum but:

(1) each of the company's allotted shares must be paid up at least as to one quarter of its nominal amount and the whole of any premium;

(2) if any of the company's shares have been fully or partly paid up, as to nominal amount or premium, by an undertaking to do work or perform services, the undertaking must have been performed or otherwise discharged; and

(3) if shares have been allotted as fully or partly paid up, as to nominal amount or premium, otherwise than in cash and the consideration for the allotment is or includes any other undertaking, *either* the undertaking must have been performed or otherwise discharged *or* there must be a contract under which it is to be performed within five years.

For the purposes of these three requirements one can disregard:

(a) shares allotted before 22 June 1982 provided they and any shares to be disregarded under (b) below do not exceed in nominal value one-tenth of the company's allotted share capital (such allotted share capital not including for this purpose shares to be disregarded under (b)); and

(b) shares allotted pursuant to an employees' share scheme if they would prevent the share capital requirements being satisfied.

Any shares so disregarded do not count in deciding whether the allotted share capital reaches the authorised minimum.

1.4.5 Holding companies and subsidiaries

The Act often refers to holding companies and subsidiaries. The meaning of these terms is contained in s 736. There is also a new term 'subsidiary undertaking' introduced in the 1989 Act. This term is explained in paragraph 1.4.6 below.

A company is a *subsidiary* of another company if its holding company:

(1) holds a majority of the *voting rights* in it, or

(2) is a member of it and has the right to appoint or remove a majority of its board of directors, or

(3) is a member of it and controls alone, pursuant to an agreement with other shareholders or members, a majority of the *voting rights* in it, or

(4) it is a subsidiary of a company which is itself a subsidiary of the *holding company*.

Voting rights mean the rights conferred on shareholders to vote at general meetings of the company on all or substantially all matters: accordingly, votes attaching to securities such as preference shares, which confer voting rights only where the matters to be decided relate to the interest of preference shareholders, are disregarded.

References to the right to appoint or remove 'a majority' of the board of directors mean directors together holding a majority of the rights to vote at meetings of the board; again on all, or substantially all matters. A company is not regarded as having 'the right to appoint a director' if that right is exercisable only with the consent or concurrence of another person. However, a company is deemed to have the right to appoint a director if that person's appointment flows necessarily from his appointment as a director of the holding company or if the directorship is held by the holding company itself.

Rights which are exercisable only in certain circumstances are regarded as 'voting rights' only when either the circumstances have arisen (for so long as they continue) or when the circumstances are within the control of the person allegedly having the rights. Rights which are normally exercisable but temporarily incapable of exercise (eg when shares are disenfranchised by virtue of failure to comply with notices pursuant to section 212 of the Act—see 4.3.3 below) shall continue to be taken into account.

Any rights exercisable in a fiduciary capacity are to be treated as not exercisable by a suspected holding company.

On the other hand, rights exercisable by any person as a nominee for the suspected holding company (except where the suspected holding company is concerned only in a fiduciary capacity) are generally to be treated as held or exercisable by the suspected holding company; and shares held or powers exercisable by, or by a nominee for, a subsidiary of the suspected holding company (not being a subsidiary concerned only in a fiduciary capacity) are to be treated as held or exercisable by the suspected holding company. Rights attaching to shares held by way of security are generally treated as held by the person providing the security.

A body corporate is the *wholly owned subsidiary* of another body corporate if it has no members except that other and that other's wholly-owned subsidiaries and persons acting on its or their behalf (s 736(2)).

For the purposes of the definition of a subsidiary, the expression 'company' includes any body corporate (eg a statutory, chartered or foreign company may be a subsidiary of a registered company) (s 736(6)).

1.4.6 Parent and subsidiary undertakings

Prior to the 1989 Act, a company was required to produce consolidated accounts only for itself and its subsidiaries. Now, however, the requirement is for consolidated accounts in respect of a parent company and its *subsidiary undertakings* (s 227(2)). The definitions of *parent* and *subsidiary undertakings* are contained in ss 258 and 259 and Schedule 10(A) of the Act.

An *undertaking* is defined as a body corporate or partnership, or an unincorporated association carrying on a trade or business with or without a view to profit (s 259(1)). Accordingly, a joint venture established by way of partnership will be an undertaking and it will fall to all corporate partners to determine whether it is also a *subsidiary undertaking* which should be consolidated in its group accounts.

Section 258 provides that an undertaking is a *parent undertaking* in relation to another undertaking, or a *subsidiary undertaking*, in any one of the situations described below:

(1) If it holds the majority of the voting rights in the undertaking: this calculation is the same as for the equivalent test to determine whether a company is a 'subsidiary' (see 1.4.5 *above*). In the case of undertakings which are not companies, the expression is defined as the right under the undertaking's constitution to direct the overall policy of the undertaking or to alter its constitution.

(2) If it has the right to appoint or remove a majority of the subsidiary undertaking's board of directors: again, this is the same calculation as the equivalent test for determining whether a company is a 'subsidiary'. For undertakings which are not companies, a 'director' is the person performing the equivalent function for that undertaking.

(3) If it has the right to exercise a 'dominant influence' by virtue of the undertaking's Memorandum or Articles or by virtue of a 'control contract' (being a contract which lawfully confers such a right which is authorised by the Memorandum and Articles of the undertaking and lawful in the relevant jurisdiction): this means the right to give directions with respect to the operating and financial policies of the undertaking which its directors are bound to comply with, regardless of whether it is in the best interests of the undertaking.

(4) If it is a member and controls alone, pursuant to an agreement with other shareholders or members, a majority of the voting rights in the undertaking.

An undertaking is also a parent undertaking in relation to a subsidiary undertaking if it has a 'participating interest' in the subsidiary undertaking and it actually exercises a dominant influence over it, or it and the subsidiary undertaking are managed on a unified basis. A 'participating interest' is defined in section 260 as an interest in shares (which in relation to an undertaking which does not have a share capital means an interest conferring rights to share in the profits or losses of the undertaking or giving rise to an obligation to contribute to the debts or expenses of the undertaking in a winding-up) which it holds, on a long-term basis for the purpose of securing a contribution to its activities via the exercise of control of influence arising from that interest. A holding of 20 per cent or more of the shares of an undertaking is deemed to be a participating interest unless the contrary is shown. An 'interest' in shares for these purposes includes an interest in convertible securities or in options.

As for the determination of whether a company is a subsidiary of another company, interests held in a fiduciary capacity are not included, nor are security interests in the circumstances described above. In addition, a parent undertaking is deemed to hold the rights held by any of its subsidiary undertakings. The following examples may be of assistance.

Example A

C is a company with an issued share capital of 100 ordinary shares, all of one class. A and B each hold 50 shares and are parties to an agreement which provides that A will have the right to approve budgets and otherwise settle the financial policy of C and to appoint its managing director and auditors. C will be a subsidiary undertaking of A.

Example B

The facts are the same as example A but B has the right to appoint seven out of 12 directors. C will be a subsidiary undertaking of both A and B.

Example C

C is a company with an issued share capital of 100 ordinary shares, all of the same class. B holds 30 shares. C holds 30 shares. C agrees with B always to vote in accordance with B's directions. A is a subsidiary undertaking of B.

Example D

C is a company with an issued share capital of 1,000 shares. A holds 200 shares and B holds 800 shares. A in fact, over a period of years, has determined the financial policy of the company and performed all of its management functions. C is a subsidiary undertaking of A.

Example E

A and B are in partnership on terms that each contribute equally to its capital and share equally in its profits. A, however, manages partnership affairs and controls partnership finances. The partnership is a subsidiary undertaking of A.

Chapter 2

Incorporation

2.1 Formation

A company comes into legal existence upon the issue of a certificate of incorporation, which is obtained by filing with the Registrar of Companies the following documents:

(1) A Memorandum of Association.
(2) Articles of Association (if desired), signed by each subscriber to the Memorandum and attested by at least one witness.
(3) A statement of the first registered office and the names and particulars of the first directors and secretary, signed by or on behalf of the subscribers to the Memorandum of Association, containing a consent to act signed by each person named as a director or secretary (Form 10) (s 10 and Sched 1).
(4) A statutory declaration, by a solicitor engaged in the formation of the company or by a person named in the statement of particulars (see (3) above) as a director or secretary of the company, as to due compliance with the requirements of the Act (Form 12) (s 12(3)).

Registration fees in accordance with the regulations for the time being in force must be paid when the documents are lodged.

Before any documents are filed, a search should be made at the Companies Registry to ascertain whether there is already a company registered with the same name or one very similar. The registration of a company with the same name as one already registered is prohibited (s 26(1)(c)) and if a company is registered with a name which in the opinion of the Secretary of State is too like the name of an existing company the Secretary of State may within a year of its formation require the new company to change its name (s 28(2)). Certain minor matters (eg, 'The' at the beginning of a name and 'Company' or 'Limited' (or abbreviations thereof) at the end of a name) are disregarded in determining whether two names are the same or too like one another (ss 26(3) and 28(2)).

2.2 Registered Office

Every company must at all times have a registered office to which all communications and notices may be addressed (s 287(1)).

The Memorandum of Association states in which part of Great Britain the registered office is to be situated (ie England and Wales, Wales or Scotland). The intended situation of a company's registered office on incorporation must be specified in the statement of particulars to be delivered on application for registration (Form 10) and notice of any change in the situation of the registered office must also be given to the Registrar within fourteen days of the change (s 287(2)) (Form 287). For publication of the address of the registered office on business letters and order forms, see 2.4.

2.3 Name

The name of a company must be painted or affixed and kept painted or affixed outside every office or place of business in a conspicuous position and in easily legible letters (s 348(1)). In addition, the name must be mentioned in legible letters in all business letters, notices and other official publications of the company, and in all bills of exchange, promissory notes, endorsements, cheques and orders for money or goods which purport to be signed by or on behalf of the company, and in all invoices, receipts and letters of credit of the company (s 349). A company with 'Cyfyngedig' as its name's last word must also publicise in English the fact that the company is limited (s 351(4)). Similarly, a public company which ends its name 'Cwmni Cyfyngedig Cyhoeddus' must publicise in English the fact that it is a public limited company (s 351(3)).

Officers of the company may incur criminal penalties if these provisions are not observed. Further, where the default consists of signing a bill of exchange, promissory note, cheque or order for money or goods on which the company's name is not given correctly, the officer signing will be personally liable for the amount thereof if payment is not made by the company (s 349(4)). In *Durham Fancy Goods Ltd v Michael Jackson (Fancy Goods) Ltd* [1968] 2 QB 839, it was held, however, that the plaintiff, who had himself incorrectly prepared a form of acceptance in the name of 'M Jackson (Fancy Goods) Ltd' for signature by a director—the M should have read Michael—was estopped from enforcing personal liability under s 349 (contrast *Maxform SpA v Mariani* [1979] 2 Lloyd's Rep 385). Note that a default will be committed under these provisions if the *full* name of the company is not included, so that the omission of the word 'Limited' may render an officer liable (*Atkins & Co v Wardle* (1889) 58 LJQB 377, *British Airways Board v Parish* [1979] 2 Lloyd's Rep 361); though liability will not be incurred merely by abbreviating 'Limited' to 'Ltd' (*Stacey & Co v Wallis* (1912) 106 LT 544) or 'Company' to 'Co' (*Banque de l'Indochine et de Suez SA v Euroseas Group Finance Co Ltd* [1981] 3 All ER 198). Signature of a cheque with the omission of an ampersand in the company's name can result in personal liability under s 349 (*Hendon v Adelman* (1973) 117 SJ 631).

If an existing company knows in time of the formation of a new company with the same or a very similar name it may ask the Secretary of State to exercise his power under s 28(2) to require the new company to change its name. Otherwise action may be taken for an injunction to restrain the new company from allowing its name to remain on the register in the offending form and to restrain it from passing off (*Exxon Corporation v Exxon Insurance Consultants International Ltd* [1981] 1 WLR 624): a similar remedy is available where an unincorporated partnership or an individual attempts to deceive the public by adopting a name similar to that of an existing company. Arrangements can be made with the Registrar, however, for the name of an existing company to be adopted by another company (whether existing or newly formed) subject to the existing company first, or simultaneously, changing its name.

A public company (which is necessarily a limited company) must have at the end of its name 'Public Limited Company' or the abbreviation 'plc' (which abbreviation can be rendered in upper or lower case letters, or with the 'p' in upper case and the 'l' and 'c' in lower case, and with or without intervening spaces or full stops) or, if its Memorandum states that its registered office is to be situated in Wales, their Welsh equivalents 'Cwmni Cyfyngedig Cyhoeddus' or 'CCC' (ss 25 and 26). A private limited company must normally have as the end of its name 'Limited' or 'Ltd' or, if its Memorandum states that its registered office is to be situated in Wales, 'Cyfyngedig' or 'cyf' (ss 25 and 26).

However, a private company limited by guarantee need not comply with the above, provided its objects are the promotion of commerce, art, science, education, religion, charity or any profession, and anything incidental or conducive to any of those objects, and its Memorandum or Articles:

(1) require it to apply its profits in promoting its objects;
(2) prohibit payment of dividends to members; and
(3) require it on a winding-up to transfer surplus assets to a body with similar objects or charity (s 30).

(The same applies to a company which on 25 February 1982 was a private company limited by shares with a name which, by virtue of a licence under s 19 of the former Companies Act 1948, did not include 'Limited' provided its objects and Memorandum or Articles satisfy the above conditions.) A statutory declaration must be filed at the Companies Registry as provided in s 30(4) before a company may be formed or may change its name as permitted by s 30.

By s 351(1)(*d*), a limited company exempt from the obligation to use the word 'Limited' (or an equivalent) as part of its name must state that it is a limited company on all business letters and order forms.

A company may not be registered with a name:

(1) which includes otherwise than at its end 'Limited', 'Unlimited' or 'Public Limited Company' or their Welsh equivalents or their abbreviations;
(2) the use of which would in the opinion of the Department of Trade be a criminal offence;
(3) which in the Department's opinion is offensive; or
(4) except with the Department's approval, which (*a*) would in its opinion be likely to give the impression that the company is connected with Her Majesty's Government or any local authority or (*b*) includes any word or expression specified in the Company and Business Names Regulations 1981 (SI 1981 No 1685 as amended by SI 1982 No 1653) (such as Royal, United Kingdom, England, Insurance, Chamber of Commerce and University) (s 26).

The Department may also direct a company to change its name within a specified period of not less than six weeks if the Department is of the opinion that the name by which a company is registered gives so misleading an indication of the nature of its activities as to be likely to cause harm to the public (s 32). Application may be made to the court within three weeks to set aside the direction. An overseas company may be restrained from carrying on business in Great Britain under its corporate name if registration under that name would not have been permitted had it been a British company (s 694).

2.4 Particulars on Business Letters, Order Forms etc

A company must also state in legible characters on its business letters and order forms (in addition to its name, and the fact that it is limited if it has 'Cynfyngedig' at the end of its name, or is exempt from ending its name with 'Limited' or 'Cynfyngedig'— see above):

(1) the country in which it is registered, ie England and Wales, Wales or Scotland;
(2) its registered number;
(3) the address of its registered office; and
(4) if it is an investment company within the meaning of s 266 the fact that it is such (s 351).

Appropriate wording for the country of registration of a company registered in England and Wales (unless it is a company whose Memorandum states that its registered office is to be in Wales) is 'Registered in England and Wales'. However, the Registrar would not object to 'Registered in Cardiff', 'Registered in England' or 'Registered in London' (*Law Society's Gazette*, 23 March 1977, p 243).

Further, a public company which ends its name with the Welsh equivalent of 'public limited company' (or its abbreviation) (see 2.3) must state that it is a public limited company in English in legible characters on all its prospectuses, bill-heads, letter paper, notices and other official publications and similarly in a conspicuous notice at every place where it carries on business (s 351).

2.5 Business Names

Trading by a company under a name other than its corporate name (called below a business name) is controlled by the Business Names Act 1985 (except where a company merely adds to its corporate name an indication that its business is carried on in succession to a former owner of the business, eg 'X Limited, successor to J Smith'). A company may not, without the written approval of the Secretary of State trade in Great Britain under a business name which would be likely to give the impression that the business is connected with Her Majesty's Government or a local authority or includes a word or expression specified in the Company and Business Names Regulations 1981 (SI 1981 No 1685 as amended by SI 1982 No 1653) save that:

(1) a company which acquires a business may carry it on under its former lawful business name for a year; and

(2) a company may continue to carry on a business indefinitely under the name under which it lawfully carried it on immediately before 26 February 1982 (s 2 of that Act).

2.6 Currency of Share Capital

A company may have its share capital in sterling or in another currency or in several currencies (*Re Scandinavian Bank Group plc* [1987] 2 WLR 752).

2.7 Seal and Documents under Seal

A company need not have a corporate seal (s 36A(3)), but if it does, its full name must be engraved on the seal in legible characters (s 350). A document signed by a director and the secretary (or two directors) of a company and expressed to be executed by the company has the same effect as if executed under the corporate seal (s 36A(4)). A document executed by a company (whether under seal or otherwise) which makes it clear on its face that it is intended to be a deed has effect as such and shall be presumed (unless a contrary intention is proved) to be delivered on execution. If favour of a purchaser in good faith for valuable consideration, this presumption is irrebuttable, unless the document is under seal (see 2.11 below for further explanation).

If the seal is to be used, the regulations in the Articles or Table A should be observed, although any provision that deeds must be sealed will no longer be of any legal force. Any additional requirements (eg three directors) as to the application of the seal, however, should be followed.

Articles commonly provide that the seal is to be used only by authority of the board of directors and that every document to which the seal is affixed must be signed by one director and the secretary or by two directors (see reg 101) although modern Articles often provide for the sealing of share and debenture certificates without signature or with facsimile signatures. If the Articles provide that affixation of the seal must be attested by the signatures of, eg, a director and the secretary, it is not permissible for someone who is not a director to sign on behalf of a director pursuant to a power of attorney, unless—as would be unusual—the Articles allow this (*TCB Ltd v Gray* [1986] 1 All ER 587). In no circumstances should the seal be used unless authority has previously been obtained from a properly constituted meeting of the board of directors or a committee duly authorised in that behalf. The authority may however be a general one authorising affixation of the seal to a category of documents: a separate authority is not needed for each specific transaction.

A minute of the resolution of the board or committee, authorising the execution of a deed or other document under seal, must be entered in the minute book.

A document or proceeding requiring authentication by the company may be signed by a director, secretary, or other authorised officer, and need not be under seal (s 41).

If Articles permit it, a company whose objects include the transaction of business in foreign countries may have for use out of the United Kingdom an official seal which is a facsimile of its common seal with the addition on its face of the names of the jurisdictions in which it is to be used (s 39). A company may also, by writing under its common seal or executed as above, empower an attorney to execute deeds on its behalf elsewhere than the United Kingdom (s 38). In addition, s 40 provides that a company may have, for use for sealing securities issued by it and documents creating or evidencing securities so issued, an official seal which is a facsimile of its common seal with the addition on its face of the word 'Securities'. See further 4.5.1.

2.8 Contracts

Of necessity a company must make all contracts through the medium of an agent. If a contract is of such a nature that, if made between individuals, the law would require it to be in writing under seal, it should be signed by a director and the secretary or two directors (as described in 2.11) or made under the common seal of the company. If, however, the law would require the contract if between individuals to be in writing signed by the parties to be bound, it may be made on behalf of the company in writing signed by any person acting under its authority, express or implied. If the contract, if made between individuals, could be made orally, then it may be made orally on behalf of the company by any person acting under its authority, express or implied (s 36).

It is not always essential for the validity of a contract made on behalf of a company that the company should be described with complete accuracy (*F Goldsmith (Sicklesmere) Ltd v Baxter* [1970] Ch 85).

2.9 Commencement of Business

A private company may commence business as soon as a certificate of incorporation has been issued; but a company originally formed as a public company may not do business or exercise any borrowing powers until the Registrar has issued it with a certificate under s 117 (or it is re-registered as a private company). The Registrar issues this certificate on receipt of an application (which incorporates a statutory declaration) (Form 117), if satisfied that the company fulfils the share capital requirements for a public company (see 1.4.4).

Pre-incorporation contracts are not binding on, and cannot be ratified by, a company although they can be taken over by novation. However, by s 36C a pre-incorporation contract will, unless otherwise agreed, impose personal liability on the person purporting to act for the company in entering into it: for an illustration see *Phonogram Ltd v Lane* [1982] QB 938.

A company which does not commence business within one year after its incorporation or which being a public company originally formed as such is not issued with a certificate under s 117 within that time may be wound up by the court (Insolvency Act 1986, s 122).

2.10 Transfers of Non-cash Assets by Subscribers

In certain circumstances s 104 imposes requirements relating to expert valuation where a public company contracts with a subscriber to its Memorandum. These requirements apply if:

(1) the company was originally formed as a public company;
(2) the contract is for the transfer by the subscriber of non-cash assets during the first two years in which the company is entitled to do business; and
(3) the consideration to be given by the company equals or exceeds one tenth of its issued share capital.

2.11 Execution of Documents by a Company

Contracts may be executed by a company under hand or under seal. It will be necessary to execute documents under seal where:
(1) There is no consideration passing from the company under the relevant contract.
(2) Where statute or the articles require a particular document to be under seal.
(3) Where it is intended to increase the limitation period. Actions under a sealed document can be brought 12 years from the date of the contract whereas it is only six years in the case of contracts under hand.

2.11.1 Documents under hand

In respect of documents that do not have to be under seal, the procedure for execution is relatively simple. On the assumption that the board meeting approves the document it will give named director(s) power the sign the agreement on behalf of the company. A suggested form of resolution is as follows:

> IT IS RESOLVED THAT the agreement between X limited and the Company relating to the purchase by the Company of the business known as 'Danny's Shoes' be hereby approved and that any director be authorised to sign the same on behalf of the Company with power to make such amendments to the agreement [other than in relation to price] as he may, in his absolute discretion, think fit.

Where a person is signing on behalf of a company the appropriate attestation clause on a document would be:

Signed by [   ]
for and on behalf of [Limited]

2.11.2 Documents under seal

A company may seal a document in one of two ways. It can either affix the company seal in the presence of appropriate witnesses or use the procedure set out in s 36A, described below.

Section 36A(4) provides that a document signed by a director and the secretary or two directors and expressed (in whatever form of words) to be executed by the company has the same effect as if executed under the common seal.

Using this method of execution will give rise to a rebuttable presumption that, provided that the document makes it clear on its face that it is intended to take effect as a deed, it will take effect on execution (s 36A(5)).

In addition there is an irrebuttable presumption in favour of a purchaser that a document is duly executed by the company if it purports to be signed by a director and a secretary or two directors. Furthermore, where it makes clear on its face that it is intended by the persons making it to be a deed there is an irrebuttable presumption that it is delivered upon being executed (s 36A(6)). A 'purchaser' is defined as a 'purchaser in good faith for valuable consideration and includes a lessee, mortgagee or other person who for valuable consideration acquires an interest in property'. Accordingly, if it is not intended for the document to be immediately delivered upon execution and the document leaves the control of the company—such as some form of escrow arrangement—the use of the company seal may, in some circumstances, be preferred.

The appropriate board resolution for a document being executed under s 36A:

IT IS RESOLVED THAT [   ] be executed as a deed and signed by any two directors or any director and the secretary.

The form of attestation where a company is executing a document in accordance with s 36A is:

Signed as a deed by [name of company]   [signature]
acting by [name of director] a director
and [name of director or secretary]   [signature]
[a director or secretary]

Chapter 3

Issue of Shares

3.1 Authority to Allot and Pre-emption Rules

Sections 80 and 89 to 96 deal with authority to allot shares and rights of pre-emption of existing shareholders. The following explanation of these provisions is necessarily a summary. The application of the sections and the preparation of resolutions and other drafting affected thereby will often require professional advice. Particularly complex problems can arise in connection with, eg, convertible loan stocks. Listed companies will have to bear in mind the views expressed by institutional investors' representative bodies on resolutions under ss 80 and 95.

3.1.1 Authority to allot shares

A company's Articles usually give the power to allot shares to the directors. However by s 80 the directors may not allot relevant securities unless they are authorised to do so in the way explained below by a resolution of the company in general meeting (which may be an ordinary resolution) or by the Articles. 'Relevant securities' means:
   (1) shares in the company other than those which under its Memorandum are taken by the subscribers or shares allotted pursuant to an employees' share scheme; and
   (2) any right to subscribe for, or convert any security (such as loan stock) into, shares within (1) above.
Moreover, for the purposes of s 80 'allotment' is deemed to occur when any such right is granted, following which actual allotment of the shares pursuant to that right is not regarded as an allotment for the purposes of s 80.

A s 80 authority may be given for a particular transaction or be general; it may be subject to conditions or unconditional. Whether contained in the Articles or not, the authority must state

33

the maximum amount of relevant securities which may be allotted under it: in the case of the grant of rights described in paragraph (2) above the maximum to be stated is the number of shares which can be allotted pursuant to the rights. Also, whether contained in the Articles or not, the authority must state the date on which it will expire or, in the case of an elective resolution passed by a private company only, that it is for an indefinite period (s 80A(2)(*a*) and 6.10.3 below). An authority in respect of a public company may not last beyond five years from its grant. An allotment can be made after the expiry of an authority if it is pursuant to an offer or agreement made by the company before such expiry and the authority allows the company to make an offer or agreement which would or might require such an allotment. An authority can be revoked or varied by the company in general meeting and also renewed under similar rules any number of times.

A resolution to give, vary, revoke or renew a s 80 authority may, even if it alters a company's Articles, be an ordinary resolution. But whether the resolution is ordinary or special it must be filed at the Companies Registry (ss 80(8) and 380).

An allotment of relevant securities which contravenes s 80 is not void or voidable but may involve the directors in criminal liability.

3.1.2 Pre-emption rules

By ss 89 to 96, except with the sanction of a special resolution, any 'equity securities' which a company proposes to allot wholly for cash must be offered first to its existing equity shareholders pro rata. There are detailed provisions relating to the manner in which the offer is made and the period for which it must remain open.

To decide what are 'equity securities' one must first consider the meaning for these purposes of 'relevant shares': a share will be a relevant share unless (i) its right to participate in both dividends and capital is limited to specified amounts or (ii) it is held by a person who acquired it pursuant to an employees' share scheme or, if it has not been allotted, it is to be allotted pursuant to such a scheme (s 94(5)). 'Equity securities' are then defined as relevant shares (except subscribers' shares or bonus shares) or a right to subscribe for, or convert any securities into, relevant shares (s 94(2)). A similar rule to that explained above in connection with s 80 applies in construing the meaning of allotment in ss 89 to 96. An offer required by s 89 must be made to holders of relevant shares and to holders of 'relevant employee shares', ie shares which would be relevant shares if they were not held by a person who acquired them pursuant to an employees' share scheme.

There are provisions which apply where a company's Memorandum or Articles contain similar pre-emption rights (s 89(2) and (3)). Section 91(1) enables a private company to exclude s 89 by its Memorandum or Articles.

Under s 95 where directors have a general s 80 authority they may be given power by the Articles or by special resolution to allot equity securities pursuant to that authority as if:

(1) the pre-emption rule in s 89(1) did not apply; or

(2) it applied with such modifications as the directors determine.

There are broadly similar powers of disapplying the pre-emption rule in relation to particular allotments but in this case there is a requirement that disapplication be recommended by the directors and certain information circulated to shareholders. There are transitional provisions to cover the case where a company was at the time when the rules became applicable to it (in 1980 to 1982) subject to an obligation inconsistent with them.

3.2 Consideration for an Allotment of Shares

Subject as mentioned below, shares, including any premium on them, may be paid up in money or money's worth (including good-will and know-how) (s 99(1)).

Shares taken by a subscriber to the Memorandum of a public company in pursuance of his undertaking in the Memorandum, and any premium on them, must be paid up in cash (s 106).

A public company may not accept as payment for its shares, whether as to nominal amount or premium, an undertaking that work will be done or services performed (s 99(2) and (3)). Except in pursuance of an employees' share scheme, a public company may not allot a share unless at least a quarter of the share's nominal value and the whole of any premium is paid up (s 101). A public company may not allot shares as fully or partly paid, as to nominal amount or premium, otherwise than in cash if the consideration is or includes an undertaking which will or may be performed more than five years after the allotment (s 102). If any of these rules are broken, the shareholder is liable to pay to the company in cash immediately the amount involved or the deficiency, as the case may be, with interest.

Except where the consideration for the allotment is wholly or partly the acquisition of shares in another company pursuant to an offer made to all its shareholders (or all its shareholders of a class) or the acquisition of all the assets and liabilities of another company, a public company must not allot shares as fully or partly paid, as to nominal amount or premium, otherwise than in cash unless the consideration for the allotment has been valued, a report on such value has been obtained in accordance with the detailed requirements of ss 108 to 110 from a person qualified to be the company's auditor and a copy of the report has been sent to the proposed allottee (s 103). Infringement involves the allottee in liability to pay to the company the amount involved in cash with interest. A copy of any such report must also be filed at the Companies Registry with the relevant return of allotments (s 111).

Under s 113 the court has limited powers to grant relief from liabilities imposed by the above rules.

3.3 Applications and Allotment

3.3.1 Applications

Where shares are offered to the public, the offering document is usually accompanied by a form of application for shares. Even where shares are allotted otherwise than as a result of an offer to the public, the prospective allottee should be asked to complete a form of application (see Appendix 5) as written evidence that he agrees to become a member of the company. Only if a person agrees to become a member of a company *and* his name is entered in the register of members will he be a member (s 22). A separate application form is not however needed if the allottee has agreed in another document (eg a subscription agreement) to become a member.

A form of application for shares will constitute a written offer to take shares, and no binding contract will exist until the company notifies the applicant that his offer is accepted (eg by posting to him a certificate or letter of allotment in respect of the shares).

See 3.7.6 as to rules relating to the revocation of an application for shares where the prospectus provisions of the Act apply and a prospectus is issued generally. In other circumstances (for example where Part IV of the Financial Services Act 1986 applies—see 3.4 and 3.5) an application may be withdrawn at any time before the posting of, eg, the letter of allotment (*Re Imperial Land Co of Marseilles, Harris' Case* (1872) 7 Ch App 587) unless by a collateral contract the applicant agrees for consideration that his application shall not be withdrawn (as will usually be the case).

An application for shares will lapse if allotment is not made within a reasonable time (*Ramsgate Victoria Hotel Company v Montefiore* (1866) 4 H&C 164).

An allotment of shares must be made by a properly recorded resolution passed at a properly convened and constituted meeting of directors or of a duly authorised committee. Where the shares are offered otherwise than by an offer by an issuing house, the secretary should prepare lists of applicants showing the number of shares for which each has applied. In appropriate cases the directors will determine which, if any, of the applications should be rejected. Again, where the prospectus provisions of the Act apply and a prospectus is issued generally, special rules apply as to when allotments may be made or applications revoked (see 3.7.6) and as to minimum subscription (see 3.7.7). See 3.8.1 as to partial subscription.

3.3.2 Letter of allotment

To each applicant to whom the directors decide to allot shares a letter of allotment (Appendix 5) or share certificate should be forwarded at the earliest possible date. If the allottee is to have the power to renounce the allotment in favour of another person, a renounceable letter of allotment will be the appropriate document of title.

According to the ordinary law of contract, a letter of allotment, being an acceptance of the applicant's offer to take shares, must be unconditional and must not vary the terms of the application. Thus, no binding contract exists if a smaller number of shares is allotted than the number for which application is made, unless the applicant has agreed to accept a smaller number (*Re Barber* (1851) 20 LJ Ch 146). Usually the form of application is worded to cover this contingency; but care should be taken to see that the words are not struck out by the applicant.

If the number of shares applied for exceeds that to be allotted, care must be taken in carrying out the provisions of the offer with regard to the amount received. Normally, the amount paid will be applied towards the payment of the amount due on allotment and the balance returned to the applicant. The letter of allotment has to be altered or completed accordingly.

Before letters of allotment or certificates are posted, particulars should be entered in a list of applications and allotments.

3.3.3 *Letter of regret*

Where an issue is over-subscribed, letters of regret should be sent to those applicants to whom shares are not allotted, accompanied by cheques for the amounts paid on application or the return of the applicants' cheques. A form such as the following may be adopted:

LETTER OF REGRET

—— PUBLIC LIMITED COMPANY
(Incorporated under the Companies Act 1985)
Offer of .... Ordinary
Shares of .... each at .... per Share

Dear Sir or Madam,

I refer to your application for Ordinary Shares in this Company and regret to inform you that in view of the over-subscription of the Offer, you have not been successful in obtaining an allotment of shares.

A cheque for £....., the sum paid by you on application, is enclosed.

Yours faithfully,

Secretary

Companies whose securities are listed on The Stock Exchange are required to issue letters of regret preferably at the same time as, but in any event not later than three business days after, allotment letters and if it is impossible to issue letters of regret at the same time as allotment letters, to insert in the press a notice to that effect so that the notice appears on the morning after the allotment letters are posted.

3.3.4 *Return of allotments*

Within one month of an allotment of shares, the secretary must file with the Registrar a return of allotments, stating the number and nominal amount of the shares allotted, particulars of the allottees and the amount paid or due and payable on each share, on Form 88(2) (s 88). Where shares are allotted on renounceable documents, the return of allotments must be delivered within one month of, in the case of a rights issue, receipt of acceptances and, in other cases, allotment of the shares. 'Receipt of acceptances' means each day on which the company (or its registrar) receives provisional allotment letters completed and accompanied by a remittance for the subscription monies. A person acquires the unconditional right to be included in the company's register of members in respect of the shares on that date and accordingly allotment takes place on that date (s 738(1)). Allotment does not take place on the closing date for acceptances (except as regards acceptances received on that date) or on the last date for renunciation. However, particulars of the allottees need not be filed until after the renunciation period has expired: Form 88(2) should be filed within the one month referred to above with a note on the back of the Form explaining that details of the allottees will be delivered after the end of the renunciation period. Such details should then be filed as soon as possible on a continuation Form 88(2), cross-referenced to refer to the original Form.

A return need not be filed in respect of the shares subscribed for in the Memorandum.

If shares are being allotted at intervals, a return of allotments should be made within one month of the first allotment and should include all shares allotted up to the date of filing. A further return will then be required within one month of the next allotment.

Where allotments are wholly or partly for a consideration other than cash, a contract in writing, constituting the title of the allottee, must be filed, together with a return stating the number and nominal amount of the shares so allotted, the extent to which they are to be treated as paid up, and the consideration for which they have been allotted. If no such written contract exists, particulars of the verbal contract must be filed, stamped with the same stamp as would have been required had the contract been in writing (s 88) (Form 88(3)).

If default is made in complying with these provisions, every director, manager or secretary who is knowingly a party to the default will be liable to a fine; but the court may in certain circumstances grant relief from the penalty.

3.4 Offers of Securities

There are two régimes relating to offers of shares or debentures to the public: on the one hand the régime for listed securities laid down in Part IV of the Financial Services Act 1986 and in listing rules made by The Stock Exchange as competent authority for Part IV (see 3.5) and on the other hand the prospectus provisions of the Act (see 3.7) which are now confined to unlisted securities. (These are in addition to the rules laid down by Part I of the Financial Services Act 1986 as to who may carry on investment business including offering securities, for which see 4.19.) In due course Part V of the Financial Services Act (see 3.6) will supersede in respect of offers of unlisted securities, the prospectus provisions of the Act.

3.5 Listed Securities

3.5.1 General

Shares and debt securities of a company, warrants to subscribe for shares and certificates conferring rights in respect of shares can be admitted to the Official List of The Stock Exchange only in accordance with Part IV of the Financial Services Act 1986 ('the FSA') (FSA, s 142). The Council of The Stock Exchange is the competent authority for the purposes of Part IV and as such makes listing rules which are incorporated in the Yellow Book (see 1.1.2). An application to list securities must be made in such manner as the listing rules require and must have the consent of the issuer of the securities (FSA, s 143(1) and (2)). No application for listing may be made in respect of securities issued by a private company (FSA, s 143(3)).

3.5.2 Listing particulars

If securities are to be admitted to the Official List, listing particulars in respect of them must be prepared in accordance with the requirements in the Yellow Book, must be submitted to and approved by The Stock Exchange and must be published (FSA, s 144), subject to certain exceptions (see 3.5.7).

In addition to the detailed requirements set out in the Yellow Book (see 3.5.6), listing particulars must contain all such information as investors and their professional advisers would reasonably require, and reasonably expect to find there, to make an informed assessment of the assets and liabilities, financial position, profits and losses and prospects of the issuer and of the rights attaching to the securities (FSA, s 146(1)). The information to be included is that which is within the knowledge of any person responsible for the listing particulars, or which it would be reasonable for him to obtain by making enquiries (FSA, s 146(2)). In determining what information is required to be included under s 146 regard shall be had:

(1) to the nature of the securities and the issuer;
(2) to the nature of the persons likely to consider acquiring them;
(3) to the fact that certain matters may reasonably be expected to be known to professional advisers whom those persons may reasonably be expected to consult; and
(4) to information available to investors or their professional advisers by virtue of, eg, the continuing obligations of listed companies as to publication of information (FSA, s 146(3)).

Besides this overriding duty and the detailed requirements in the Yellow Book, listing particulars must comply with the general law as to, eg, misrepresentation, defamation and copyright.

If significant changes or new matters arise before dealings in the securities begin, the issuer must in accordance with the Yellow Book prepare, submit to The Stock Exchange for its approval and publish supplementary listing particulars (FSA, s 147).

The Stock Exchange may authorise the omission of information from listing particulars if:

(1) its disclosure would be contrary to the public interest;
(2) its disclosure would be seriously detrimental to the issuer and its omission would not mislead an investor as to facts which it is essential for him to know in order to make an informed assessment; or
(3) in the case of debt securities specified by listing rules, its disclosure is unnecessary for persons of the kind expected normally to buy or deal in the securities (FSA, s 148).

On or before the date of publication of listing particulars a copy of them must be filed at the Companies Registry for England and Wales, Scotland or Northern Ireland according to the issuer's country of incorporation or, if the issuer is incorporated elsewhere, at any of those Registries (FSA, s 149).

3.5.3 Responsibility for listing particulars

For the purposes of Part IV of the FSA the persons responsible for listing particulars in respect of a company are:

(1) the company itself,

(2) its directors,

(3) anyone who has authorised himself to be named, and is named, in the particulars as a director or as having agreed to become a director,

(4) anyone who accepts, and is stated in the particulars as accepting, responsibility for the particulars or part of them, and

(5) anyone else who has authorised the contents of the particulars or part of them (FSA, s 152(1)).

If a person accepts responsibility for or authorises only part, he is responsible under (4) or (5) above for only that part and only if it is in (or substantially in) the form and context to which he agrees (FSA, s 152(3)). There are provisions for the division of responsibility on takeovers (FSA, s 152(4)) and for The Stock Exchange to excuse a person from responsibility by reason of a conflict of interests (FSA, s 152(5)).

3.5.4 Compensation for false or misleading particulars

Persons responsible for listing particulars are liable to pay compensation to anyone who acquires the securities and suffers loss in respect of them as a result of any untrue or misleading statement in the particulars or the omission of anything required to be included (FSA, s 150). This is in addition to other remedies which may be available at common law.

A person is not liable under s 150 if he satisfies the court that he reasonably believed when the particulars were submitted to The Stock Exchange, having made reasonable enquiries, that the statement was true and not misleading (or the omission was proper) and:

(1) that he continued in that belief until the securities were acquired; or

(2) that they were acquired before a correction could be brought to the attention of likely buyers; or

(3) that before the securities were acquired he had taken all reasonable steps to bring a correction to their attention; or

(4) that he continued in that belief until after dealings had begun and that the securities were acquired after such a lapse of time that he ought to be reasonably excused (FSA, s 151(1)).

There is a similar defence for, eg, directors where statements are included in listing particulars in reliance on experts (FSA, s 151(2)).

Publication of a correction before the securities are acquired can also be a defence (FSA, s 151(3)).

3.5.5 *The Yellow Book requirements*

The listing rules in the Yellow Book incorporate the requirements of three EEC Directives relating to, respectively, the admission of securities to official listing, listing particulars and interim reports by companies and also The Stock Exchange's own additional requirements.

For listing to be granted:

(1) The issuer must fulfil certain conditions set out in Chapter 2 of Section 1 of the Yellow Book.

(2) The application procedure prescribed by Chapter 1 of Section 2 of the Yellow Book must be followed. (The procedure varies according to whether the applicant is a new applicant or already listed.)

(3) With certain exceptions, listing particulars must, as already explained, be prepared, approved by The Stock Exchange and published.

The application form for listing includes a declaration that all applicable conditions for listing are met and that all information required to be included in the listing particulars is included.

Proofs of listing particulars submitted to The Stock Exchange must, to help The Stock Exchange check them, be marked to show where each of the items of information required by the Yellow Book is given. As listing particulars can be published only if they have been approved by The Stock Exchange, the *final* version of them must be submitted to and formally approved by The Stock Exchange.

3.5.6 *Detailed contents of listing particulars*

The detailed contents of listing particulars are prescribed in

Section 3 of the Yellow Book. Chapter 1 of Section 3 lays down the following important, overriding principles:

(1) The detailed information required by Chapter 2 of Section 3 must be included in a form that can be understood and analysed as easily as possible.

(2) Subject to 1 above, the information need not follow the same layout or order as Chapter 2. (Indeed it will rarely be desired to follow that layout.)

(3) Where an item of information required by Chapter 2 is inappropriate to the issuer's field of activity or legal form, the item must be adapted appropriately so that equivalent information is given. Thus item 7.1 in Chapter 2 refers to trends in production, sales and stocks, the state of the order book and trends in costs and selling prices. These will have to be adapted for a company which is not a manufacturer.

(4) Negative statements are needed only where indicated in Chapter 2. So item 3.6(a) requires one to state 'Amount of any outstanding convertible debt securities'. If the issuer has no such securities it is not necessary to state this. On the other hand, item 3.15 requires information on significant legal or arbitration proceedings 'or an appropriate negative statement'. If therefore there are no such proceedings, this should be stated.

(5) The Stock Exchange may require disclosure of such additional information as it considers appropriate in any particular case.

The Stock Exchange's power to authorise omission of information which is not required by the listing particulars directive (ie which represents an additional requirement of The Stock Exchange) is not limited to the three cases explained at 3.5.2, but The Stock Exchange will normally have regard to similar criteria, as explained in the Yellow Book.

Chapter 1 of Section 3 specifies which of the lengthy list of detailed items of information in Chapter 2 will be needed in any particular circumstances. Thus a new applicant for listing, seeking listing for shares, will need to include all the items in Chapter 2 except item 5.2 (which is an alternative to item 5.1) and the items in Part 8 of Chapter 2 (which apply only to debt securities). A listed issuer seeking listing for shares may omit some items, notably item 5.1 (an accountants' report covering three years), but must include item 5.2 (three years' summary figures). On a rights issue of shares by an issuer whose shares are already listed further items may be omitted.

Various combinations of requirements apply on an issue of debt securities, depending on whether the securities are or are not Euro-currency securities, debt securities or convertible debt securities; whether the issuer is a new applicant; whether the issue is by way of rights by an issuer whose shares are already listed; whether the issuer of debt securities will or will not be the issuer of the shares into which they will be converted; and whether the securities are guaranteed.

In the Yellow Book 'convertible debt securities' means debt securities convertible into shares, debt securities exchangeable for shares and debt securities accompanied by warrants to subscribe or purchase shares. The expression therefore includes certain securities which would not come within its ordinary meaning and does not include debt securities convertible into other debt securities (which would be within the ordinary meaning of the expression).

Special requirements are laid down in Section 10 of the Yellow Book for property companies, mineral companies, investment trusts and investment companies.

3.5.7 Exemptions

1 Eurobonds Relaxed requirements set out in Section 7 of the Yellow Book apply to a selective marketing of euro-currency securities. A euro-currency selective marketing is a 'placing' of euro-currency securities with a syndicate of dealers with a view to their reselling them as principals otherwise than through The Stock Exchange. In addition, The Stock Exchange may permit all or part of the provisions of Section 7 to apply to debt securities if nearly all of them, because of their nature, are normally bought and traded by a limited number of investors who are particularly knowledgeable in investment matters.

2 Equivalent document published within twelve months If the securities to be listed:
  (1) have been the subject of a public issue, or
  (2) are issued in connection with a take-over offer, or
  (3) are issued in connection with a merger or various other transactions,
and, not more than 12 months previously, a document has been published in the United Kingdom containing, in The Stock Exchange's opinion, equivalent information to that otherwise

required, then listing particulars containing only the following may be acceptable:

(1) any material changes since the previous document or a negative statement,

(2) a statement that application has been made to list a given number of specified securities,

(3) any other information which The Stock Exchange considers appropriate, and

(4) a responsibility statement.

The listing particulars and the previous document must be published and made available to the public as explained in the Yellow Book.

3 Capitalisation issues, conversions etc   Listing particulars are not needed (although certain details have to be published) where the securities to be listed are:

(1) shares allotted by a capitalisation issue to holders of listed shares; or

(2) shares resulting from the conversion or exchange of convertible debt securities, if the issuer of those shares already has its shares listed; or

(3) shares resulting from the exercise of the rights conferred by warrants, if shares of the issuer are already listed; or

(4) shares issued in place of shares already listed, provided that the nominal value of the shares so issued does not exceed the nominal value of the shares in place of which they are issued.

4 Share issues below ten per cent and employees' shares   Listing particulars are also not needed (although certain details—fewer than those referred to in paragraph 3 above—have to be published) where the securities are:

(1) shares which would increase the shares of a class already listed by less than ten per cent (there is no exemption for further issues, however small, of debt securities of a class already listed); or

(2) shares allotted to employees if shares of the same class are already listed.

5 Public utilities etc   Certain relaxations, for which reference should be made to the Yellow Book, apply to debt securities which have a state guarantee and to debt securities issued by public utilities, state monopolies etc.

6 Issuers transferring from the Unlisted Securities Market   These may be allowed exemption from some of The Stock Exchange's additional requirements, eg an accountants' report.

7 Foreign issuers   Section 8 of the Yellow Book explains that The Stock Exchange may allow special treatment to foreign issuers who are already subject to regulatory standards and controls which The Stock Exchange considers satisfactory.

3.5.8 Publication of listing particulars

For companies, the requirements as to publication of listing particulars are set out in Chapter 3 of Section 2 of the Yellow Book. These involve, depending on the circumstances, insertion of the full listing particulars or of a formal notice in newspapers and/or making the listing particulars available to the public in certain places.

3.5.9 Advertisements etc

Where listing particulars are, or are to be, published in connection with an application for listing, no advertisement or other information of a kind specified by listing rules may be issued unless the contents of the advertisement or other information have been submitted to The Stock Exchange and The Stock Exchange has either approved the contents or authorised the issue of the advertisement or information without such approval (FSA, s 154). This rule applies to 'mini-prospectuses' (short-form prospectuses published at the same time as listing particulars). Failure to include material facts in a mini-prospectus will not give rise to liability if the mini-prospectus and the listing particulars read together are not misleading (FSA, s 154(6)).

3.5.10 Continuing obligations

Section 5 of the Yellow Book sets out certain continuing obligations which are binding on listed issuers (FSA s 153). These combine the obligation in the Interim Reports directive for companies whose shares are listed to publish half-yearly reports, certain obligations in the Admissions directive and The Stock Exchange's own requirements (previously in the Listing Agreement).

3.6 Unlisted Securities — The Proposed Régime

Part V of the FSA, when it is brought into force, will apply
to offers of shares and debt securities of a company, warrants to
subscribe for them and certificates conferring rights in respect of
the foregoing if they are neither listed nor the subject of an
application for listing in accordance with Part IV. For brevity,
such securities are called simply 'securities' in this section 3.6, as
they are in Part V of the FSA. They will include securities dealt
in on The Stock Exchange's Unlisted Securities Market, commonly
called 'the USM'.

The provisions which will apply when Part V is in force are
outlined below.

3.6.1 Offers on admission to an approved exchange

An advertisement may not be issued in the United Kingdom
offering securities on the occasion of their admission to dealings
on an approved exchange (or on terms that they will be issued
if so admitted) unless a prospectus has been submitted to and
approved by the exchange and filed at the Companies Registry
or the advertisement is such that no agreement can be entered
into under it until a prospectus has been submitted, approved and
delivered (FSA, s 159(1)). However, this does not apply if:

(1) a prospectus has been filed in the previous twelve months
    (FSA, s 159(2)), or
(2) the securities have been *listed* in the previous twelve months
    (FSA, s 161(1)),

and (in either case) the exchange certifies that it is satisfied that
likely buyers will have sufficient information.

An advertisement offers securities if:

(1) it invites a person to enter into an agreement for or with
    a view to subscribing for or otherwise acquiring or
    underwriting them, or
(2) it contains information calculated to lead directly or indirectly
    to a person entering into such an agreement (FSA, s 158(4)).

An 'advertisement' includes every form of advertising, whether
inter alia in a publication, by the display of notices, by means
of circulars or other documents, by films, sound broadcasting or
television, by the distribution of recordings, or in any other manner
(FSA, s 207(2)).

3.6.2 Other offers of securities

An advertisement offering securities may not be issued in the United Kingdom if a 'primary' or 'secondary' offer is involved, unless a prospectus relating to the securities and expressed to be in respect of the offer has been filed or the advertisement is such that no agreement can be entered into until a prospectus has been filed.

An advertisement offering securities otherwise than as explained in 3.6.1 will be a *primary* offer if the intended agreement is to subscribe or underwrite new securities. It will be a *secondary* offer if the intended agreement is to acquire existing securities and the advertisement is issued (or caused to be issued) by:

(1) a person who has acquired the securities from the issuer with a view to issuing such an advertisement; or

(2) a person who, with a view to issuing such an advertisement, has acquired the securities otherwise than from the issuer but *without* their having been:

   (a) admitted to dealings on an approved exchange, or

   (b) held by a person who acquired them as an investment and without intending that such an advertisement would be issued; or

(3) a person who is or has been in the previous twelve months a controller of the issuer and who is acting with the consent or participation of the issuer in issuing the advertisement (FSA, s 160(3)).

In the absence of evidence to the contrary a person is presumed to have acquired securities with a view to issuing the advertisement if he issues it within six months after issue of the securities or before the price for which he acquired them has been satisfied (FSA, s 160(4)).

A controller means a person who, either alone or with certain associates, is entitled to exercise, or control the exercise of, 15 per cent or more of the voting power at any general meeting of the issuer or its holding company (FSA, s 207(5)).

However a prospectus is not needed if one has been filed in respect of an offer of the same securities in the previous six months by a person making a primary offer or a previous secondary offer (FSA, s 160(5)).

3.6.3 Exemptions and exceptions

Exemptions from the need for a prospectus on any advertisement of an offer otherwise falling within ss 159 and 160 FSA can be made by statutory instrument, eg where the advertisements are of a private character, deal with investments only incidentally or are issued to persons sufficiently expert to understand any risks involved, but no such exemptions have been announced at the time of writing (FSA, s 160A).

In addition, s 161 FSA provides that ss 159 and 160 do not apply if:

(1) the offer is conditional on the securities being admitted to listing in accordance with Part IV FSA;
(2) the advertisement is a mere 'box advertisement';
(3) other securities of the issuer are already dealt in on an approved exchange and the exchange certifies that investors will have sufficient information available to them; or
(4) a statutory instrument gives an exemption on the grounds that overseas law provides equivalent protection.

3.6.4 Requirements as to a prospectus

A prospectus must contain such information and comply with such other requirements as may be laid down by statutory instrument, save that the Secretary of State may direct that the rules of an approved exchange in respect of prospectuses shall apply instead if it appears to him that they provide equivalent protection (FSA, s 162). It is anticipated that such a direction will be made in respect of the USM.

In addition, there is a general duty to provide all information needed for an informed assessment: this requirement is in equivalent terms to that which is explained at 3.5.2 in relation to listed securities (FSA, s 163).

Unlike listing particulars (which need to be approved by The Stock Exchange) or a prospectus prepared pursuant to 3.6.1 above (which needs to be approved by the approved exchange), a prospectus prepared pursuant to 3.6.2 above does not have to be approved by any authority (this is currently the position with respect to prospectuses prepared in accordance with Schedule 13 to the Act).

An approved exchange empowered by the Secretary of State has similar powers to authorise the omission of information from a prospectus as The Stock Exchange has in the case of listing particulars (see 3.5.2) (FSA, s 165).

If significant changes or new matters arise while an agreement can be entered into pursuant to the offer, a supplementary prospectus must be filed in a similar way to supplementary listing particulars (FSA, s 164).

3.6.5 Responsibility and compensation

Sections 166 to 168 of the FSA lay down similar rules to those explained at 3.5.3 and 3.5.4 in relation to listed securities.

3.6.6 Other rules

The Secretary of State may make rules:
(1) regulating the terms on which a person may offer securities by an advertisement to which Part V applies, and
(2) otherwise regulating the conduct of such a person to ensure that the addressees of the offer are treated equally and fairly (FSA, s 169).

However no such rules have been made to date.

3.7 Unlisted Securities—The Existing Régime

Until Part V of the FSA is brought into force the prospectus provisions of the Companies Act will continue to apply to offers of shares or debt securities of a company which are not the subject of an application for listing. These are summarised below.

3.7.1 What is a prospectus?

Section 744 defines a prospectus as any prospectus, notice, circular, advertisement, or other invitation, offering to the public for subscription or purchase any shares or debentures of a company. The key phrase is 'to the public'; for if the offer is not made to the public, the document will not be a prospectus as defined by the Act; though, on the other hand, if it is made to the public, it will be a prospectus as so defined, whatever form it may take, and even if it bears the words 'private and confidential'.

The offer can be made by the company itself by means of a direct invitation to the public: but it is frequently made, eg, by an issuing house by means of an 'offer for sale' (see below) or 'placing' of the shares or debentures. A prospectus can be issued only in relation to a public company: a private limited company cannot invite public subscriptions (s 81).

Section 59 provides that any reference in the Act to offering shares or debentures to the public is to be read, subject to any provision to the contrary, as including a reference to offering them to any section of the public, whether selected as members or debenture holders of the company concerned or as clients of the person issuing the prospectus or in any other manner. This means that the statutory requirements as to prospectuses cannot be avoided by limiting the offer to a specified section of the public.

On the other hand, if an offer or invitation can properly be regarded, in all the circumstances, as not being calculated to result, directly or indirectly, in the shares or debentures becoming available for subscription or purchase by persons other than those receiving the offer or invitation, or otherwise as being a domestic concern of the persons making and receiving it, it is not required to be treated as made to the public (s 60(1)). Similarly a provision in a company's Articles prohibiting invitations to the public to subscribe for shares or debentures shall not be taken as prohibiting the making to members or debenture holders of an invitation which would fall within s 60(1) (s 60(2)).

An offer of or invitation to subscribe for shares or debentures of a private company will, unless the contrary is proved, be regarded as being a domestic concern of the persons making and receiving it if it is made to:

(1) an existing member of the company,
(2) an existing employee of the company,
(3) a member of the family of such a member or employee, or
(4) an existing debenture holder (s 60(3) and (4)).

For these purposes the members of a person's family are:

(a) the person's husband or wife, widow or widower and children (including stepchildren) and their descendants, and
(b) any trustee of a trust the principal beneficiary of which is that person or any of those relatives (s 60(5)).

An offer or invitation will also, unless the contrary is proved, be regarded as being such a domestic concern if it is to subscribe for shares or debentures to be held under an employees' share scheme. An offer or invitation is to be regarded as being such a domestic concern under the above rules even if it is renounceable, provided that it can be renounced only in favour of persons mentioned in paragraphs (1) to (4) above or, where there is an employees' share scheme, persons entitled to hold shares or debentures under the scheme (s 60(7)).

Finally, an offer of 'short-dated debentures' (debentures to be repaid within five years of the date of issue) to a person whose ordinary business is to buy or sell shares or debentures is not deemed an offer to the public (FSA s 195).

It is necessary to judge each case on its merits and determine, having regard to all the circumstances, whether or not an offer is made to the public.

Where a company allots shares or debentures to an issuing house, which then offers the shares or debentures for sale to the public, the offer would not, without s 58, be a prospectus issued by the company; but s 58 provides that if a company allots or agrees to allot its shares or debentures with a view to all or any of them being offered for sale to the public, any document by which the offer for sale to the public is made is deemed for all purposes to be a prospectus issued by the company (s 58(1)). Moreover, unless the contrary is proved, the fact that an offer for sale is made within six months after an allotment, or that at the time of the offer for sale the whole consideration to be received by the company in respect of the shares or debentures had not been so received, is evidence that the allotment was made with a view to the subsequent offer for sale.

3.7.2 Registration of prospectus

Every prospectus issued by or on behalf of a company or in relation to an intended company must be dated, and the date, unless the contrary is proved, is taken as its date of publication (s 63). On or before the date of publication a copy must be delivered to the Registrar of Companies for registration (s 64). This copy must be signed by every person named in the prospectus as a director or proposed director or by his agent authorised in writing, and in the case of an offer for sale deemed to be a prospectus under s 58, must also be signed by two directors or no fewer than half the partners of the issuing house (or their agents). The copy filed must have endorsed on or attached to it (a) any requisite consent of a person as an expert and (b) in the case of a prospectus 'issued generally' (ie to persons who are not existing members or debenture holders of the company (s 65(1)) a copy of, or memorandum in respect of, any contract required to be mentioned in the prospectus (see Sched 3, para 11), and any statement concerning adjustments made in compliance with Sched 3, para 21.

In addition, every prospectus must on its face state that a copy has been delivered for registration to the Registrar as required by s 64, and specify (or refer to statements in the prospectus specifying) any documents required to be endorsed on or attached to the copy filed (s 64(3)).

3.7.3 Form and contents of prospectus

Generally, every prospectus issued by or on behalf of a company or by or on behalf of any person who is or has been engaged or interested in the formation of the company must comply with Sched 3 (s 56(1)).

It is unlawful to issue any application form for shares or debentures unless it is issued with such a prospectus (s 56(2)), except:

(1) in connection with a bona fide invitation to a person to enter into an underwriting agreement, or

(2) in relation to shares or debentures which are not offered to the public.

The foregoing provisions do not apply:

(1) to the issue to existing members or debenture holders of a prospectus or application form relating to shares in or debentures of the company, whether an applicant for them will or will not be able to renounce in favour of others, or

(2) to the issue of a prospectus or application form relating to shares or debentures in all respects uniform with ones previously issued and currently listed on The Stock Exchange (s 56(5)).

Any condition requiring an applicant for shares or debentures to waive compliance with the foregoing provisions or purporting to affect him with notice of any contract, document or other matter not specifically referred to in the prospectus is void (s 57).

Schedule 3 requires (subject to minor exceptions) the inclusion in a prospectus of specified details relating to various matters listed in Part I of the Schedule and also the following reports:

(1) A report by the company's auditors with respect to (a) the profits or losses of the company in respect of each of the preceding five financial years; (b) the assets and liabilities of the company at the last date to which accounts have been made up; and (c) the rates of dividend, if any, paid by the company in respect of each class of shares for each of those five years. For details see Sched 3, Pt II, para 16.

Where the company has subsidiaries, the report must also deal with the combined profits and losses of the subsidiaries so far as they concern members of the company, or with the profits or losses of each subsidiary individually so far as they concern members of the company, or instead of dealing separately with the company's profits or losses, deal as a whole with the profits or losses of the company and (so far as they concern members of the company) with the combined profits or losses of the subsidiaries. Assets and liabilities of subsidiaries must also be dealt with in one of these three ways (ibid).

(2) If all or part of the proceeds of the issue of the shares or debentures are to be applied in the purchase of any business, a report by named accountants on the profits or losses of the business in respect of each of the preceding five financial years and on the assets and liabilities at the last date to which the accounts of the business were made up (Sched 3, Pt II, para 17).

If all or part of the proceeds of the issue are to be applied in any manner resulting in the acquisition by the company of shares in any other body corporate, and that other body corporate will become a subsidiary of the company, a similar accountants' report must be made indicating a number of particulars concerning the other body corporate and its subsidiaries (Sched 3, Pt II, para 18).

These accountants' reports must be made by persons qualified for appointment as auditors of companies (see 9.1), and must not be made by an officer or servant, or partner or employee of an officer or servant, of the company, its subsidiary or holding company or another subsidiary of its holding company; for this purpose 'officer' includes a proposed director but not an auditor (Sched 3, Pt II, para 22(2)).

3.7.4 Reports of experts in prospectuses

A prospectus must not be issued including a statement purporting to be made by an expert unless (a) he has given and has not, before delivery of a copy of the prospectus for registration, withdrawn his written consent to its issue with the statement included in the form and context in which it is included; and (b) a statement that he has given and not withdrawn his consent appears in the prospectus. For this purpose 'expert' includes engineer, valuer, accountant and any other person whose profession gives authority to a statement made by him (s 62).

3.7.5 Liability for false statements and omissions in prospectuses

Where a prospectus includes any untrue statement, any person who authorised its issue is liable to criminal penalties, unless he proves that the statement was immaterial or that he had reasonable ground to believe and did up to the time of the issue of the prospectus believe that the statement was true (s 70(1)). But a person is not deemed to have authorised the issue of a prospectus merely because he consented to the inclusion of a statement made by him as an expert (s 70(2)).

In addition, civil liability to pay compensation may be incurred by directors of the company, persons who authorised themselves to be named as directors or proposed directors, promoters, experts and other persons who have authorised the issue of the prospectus. All such persons are prima facie liable to those who subscribe for shares or debentures on the faith of the prospectus, for the loss or damage which they sustain by reason of any untrue statement included in it or in any report or memorandum appearing on its face or by reference incorporated in or issued with it (ss 67 and 71(b)).

In order to escape from this prima facie liability the person sued must establish one of the defences set out in s 68.

Whether or not a statement in a prospectus is a mis-statement for the purpose of imposing a liability under the above provisions is a question of fact; but a statement is deemed to be untrue if it is misleading in the form and context in which it is included (s 71(a)).

The non-disclosure of a material fact, which renders the terms of the prospectus misleading, may give rise to an action for deceit if the non-disclosure is deliberate or reckless.

Any person who takes shares or debentures on the faith of a prospectus which does not comply with or contravenes s 56 (eg by omitting something required by Sched 3) is entitled to recover damages from the persons responsible for its issue, but only if he is able to prove that the facts omitted were of a material nature and that actual damage has been suffered through the omission. But no person responsible for the issue of the prospectus shall be liable for such non-compliance or contravention if:

(1) as regards any matter not disclosed, he proves that he was not cognisant of it; or

(2) he proves that the non-compliance or contravention arose from an honest mistake of fact on his part; or

(3) the non-compliance or contravention was in respect of matters which, in the opinion of the court dealing with the case, were immaterial or was otherwise such as ought (in the court's opinion, having regard to all the circumstances) reasonably to be excused (s 66(1)).

A company can now be held liable for damages to a subscriber of shares as a result of, inter alia, misrepresentations in a prospectus (s 111A). This reverses the principle drawn from the case of *Houldsworth v City of Glasgow Bank* (1880) 5 App Cas 317.

3.7.6 Date of allotment and revocation of application

No allotment may be made of a company's shares or debentures pursuant to a prospectus issued generally (ie, to persons who are not existing members of the company or holders of its debentures), and no proceedings may be taken on applications made pursuant to such a prospectus, until the beginning of the third day after that on which the prospectus is first so issued or such later time (if any) as may be specified in the prospectus (s 82(1)). The beginning of that third day, or that later time, is called 'the time of opening of the subscription lists' (s 82(2)). The day on which the prospectus is first issued generally means the day when it is first so issued as a newspaper advertisement or, if it is not so issued as a newspaper advertisement before the third day after that on which it is first issued generally in some other way, then it means the day on which it is first issued generally in any way (s 82(3)).

To calculate for these purposes the third day after another day, any day which is a Saturday or Sunday or is a bank holiday in any part of Great Britain is disregarded (s 82(4)).

The validity of an allotment is not affected by a contravention of the above rule but the company and every officer in default is liable to a fine (s 82(5)).

Where a prospectus is issued generally an application for shares or debentures cannot be revoked until after the expiration of the third day after the time of the opening of the subscription lists, unless, before that date, some person has given public notice with a view to avoiding liability for mis-statements in the prospectus (s 82(7)).

3.7.7 Minimum subscription

Where shares are first offered to the public for subscription, no allotment may be made unless the minimum subscription has been applied for and the sum payable on application in respect of such minimum has been paid to and received by the company (s 83(1)). A sum is treated as paid to and received by the company if a cheque for it has been received in good faith by the company and the directors have no reason to suspect that the cheque will not be paid.

The minimum subscription means the amount stated in the prospectus as the minimum amount which, in the opinion of the directors, must be raised by the issue of share capital to provide for the matters specified in para 24 Sched 3, which are:

(1) the purchase price of any property purchased or to be purchased which is to be paid in whole or in part out of the proceeds of the issue;

(2) preliminary expenses and underwriting and other commissions payable in respect of subscriptions;

(3) the repayment of money borrowed for the above purposes; and

(4) working capital.

It is not necessary to include in this minimum amount sums borrowed to provide the company with working capital, or the purchase price of property to be provided otherwise than out of the proceeds of the shares offered to the public; but if any of the four items described are to be provided otherwise than by means of the issue, the amount and sources thereof must be shown in the prospectus.

If, for instance, a company has contracted to purchase an existing business for an agreed sum of £700,000 on terms that (a) the agreed price shall be paid as to £400,000 in cash to be raised by an issue of shares and as to £300,000 by the allotment of fully paid shares of that nominal value, and (b) the preliminary expenses and underwriting expenses shall be payable by the vendors of the business, it is necessary to state in the prospectus the amount of the purchase price and the preliminary expenses and underwriting commission; but only the cash portion of the purchase price (£400,000) need be included in the minimum subscription.

Any amount payable otherwise than in cash cannot be counted towards the minimum subscription (s 83(3)).

If the minimum subscription is not subscribed or the sum payable on application in respect of it is not received within 40 days after the first issue of the prospectus, all money received from applicants must be repaid to them forthwith without interest (s 83(4)). If any such money is not returned within 48 days after the issue of the prospectus, the directors are jointly and severally liable to repay it with interest at the rate of five per cent per annum from the 48th day (except that a director is not so liable if he proves that the default was not due to any misconduct or negligence by him) (s 83(5)).

3.7.8 *Allotment where stock exchange listing expected*

Where a prospectus, whether issued generally or not, states that application has been or will be made for permission for the shares or debentures offered to be listed on any stock exchange, allotments made will be void if (*a*) the permission has not been applied for before the third day after the first issue of the prospectus, or (*b*) the permission has been refused before the expiration of three weeks from the date of the closing of the subscription lists or such longer period (not exceeding six weeks) as may, within those three weeks, be notified to the applicant for permission by or on behalf of the stock exchange (s 86(1) and (2)). But permission is not deemed to be refused if it is intimated that the application for it, though not at present granted, will be given further consideration (s 86(8)).

Where permission has not been applied for or has been refused as mentioned above the company must forthwith repay without interest all money received from applicants, and, if such money is not repaid within eight days after the company becomes liable to repay it, the directors are jointly and severally liable to repay it with interest at the rate of five per cent per annum from the expiration of the eighth day, except that a director is not liable if he proves that the default was not due to any misconduct or negligence on his part (s 86(5)).

All money received from applicants in such cases must be kept in a separate bank account so long as the company may become liable to repay it (s 86(6)); and any condition requiring or binding any applicant to waive compliance with the section is void (s 86(7)).

Where an underwriter has agreed to take shares offered by the prospectus, he is, for the purposes of the section, deemed to have applied for the shares in pursuance of the prospectus (s 86(9)).

Section 87 applies the above rules where shares are offered for sale.

3.8 Rules Applicable to any of the Régimes

The following rules apply whether an issue of securities is made under the régime for listed securities or under the existing or future régime for unlisted securities.

3.8.1 Partial subscription

Share capital of a public company offered for subscription must not be allotted unless it is subscribed for in full or the offer states that it may be allotted even if it is not subscribed for in full (s 84). In the case of an issue of unlisted securities under the present régime, this is in addition to the provisions discussed at 3.7.7.

3.8.2 Underwriting commission

Where shares are offered to the public, the issue is often underwritten. In effect, the company or the vendors of the shares insure against the risk of the public not applying for them by paying a premium to underwriters, who, in consideration thereof, agree to take up such of the shares as are not applied for by the public. The premium payable to the underwriters usually takes the form of a commission or percentage of the price at which the shares are issued, but such commission can be paid by the company only if authorised by its Articles.

The rate of commission is a matter for arrangement between the company or the vendors of the shares and the underwriters save that commission paid by the company must not exceed any limit fixed by the company's Articles or ten per cent of the price of the shares, whichever is the less (s 97). When para 16 of Sched 16 of the Financial Services Act 1986 is brought into force, the ten per cent limit will be liable to alteration so far as unlisted securities are concerned by statutory instrument under s 169.

Where the listed securities régime applies, certain details have to be given in the listing particulars as to the underwriting arrangements eg the identity of the underwriters, their remuneration and whether any of the securities are 'underwritten firm'. (Securities are 'underwritten firm' where it is agreed that a certain number of them are to be allotted to the underwriters irrespective of the number for which the public apply.) Similar requirements will no doubt be included in the rules to be made by the Secretary of State for unlisted securities under s 169 and in the meantime apply to such securities under s 97.

Underwriting commission is a commission paid as consideration for an agreement to subscribe for shares; but sometimes (eg on a 'placing') a commission is paid to persons who procure subscriptions from others and here the same principles apply.

3.8.3 Brokerage

The above restrictions relating to underwriting commission do not apply where brokerage (usually a small sum per share) is paid to persons (such as banks and stockbrokers) through whom successful applications are made. Nothing in ss 97 and 98 affects the power of a company to pay such brokerage as it was formerly lawful to pay and it was held in *Metropolitan Coal Consumers' Association v Scrimgeour* [1895] 2 QB 604 that the payment by a company of a reasonable amount of money by way of brokerage is perfectly lawful. In such cases the forms of application usually bear the stamp of the bank or broker.

Commission cannot, however, be paid to a private individual, not being a broker, for procuring a subscription for shares unless it is permitted by the Articles and disclosed under s 97 like underwriting commission (*Andreae v Zinc Mines of Great Britain* [1918] 2 KB 454).

3.9 Financial Assistance to Subscribe or Purchase Shares

Only in certain circumstances may a company or its subsidiary give financial assistance, directly or indirectly, for the purpose of an acquisition or proposed acquisition of the company's shares or, such an acquisition having taken place and some liability having been incurred by anyone for the purpose of that acquisition, for the purpose of reducing or discharging that liability (ss 151 to 154). Financial assistance is widely defined and includes, for example, financial assistance by way of gift, loan, guarantee, security, indemnity (of certain types), release or waiver or any other financial assistance which reduces a company's net assets. A transaction under which a company receives less than market terms, ie a partial gift, is probably a gift for this purpose.

The main exceptions may be roughly summarised as follows:

(1) if the offending purpose is not the principal purpose of the assistance or the giving of the assistance for that purpose is but an incidental part of some larger purpose and in either case the assistance is given in good faith in the interests of the company (see *Brady v Brady* [1988] 2 WLR 1308);

(2) distribution of a company's assets by way of an otherwise lawful dividend;

(3) a distribution in the course of winding up the company;

(4) allotment of bonus shares;

(5) a redemption or purchase of a company's own shares made under ss 159 to 181 (see 4.11);

(6) where a company's ordinary business includes lending money, doing so in the ordinary course of that business;

(7) providing money in accordance with an employees' share scheme for the acquisition of fully paid shares in the company or enabling or facilitating transactions in the company's shares between, and involving the acquisition of beneficial ownership of those shares by, employees, former employees and their families;

(8) making loans to employees, other than directors, to enable the employees to acquire shares in the company for themselves;

(9) subject to certain conditions, the giving of assistance by a private company for the acquisition of shares in itself or, if it is also a private company, its holding company (s 153, as amended by s 196 of the Financial Services Act 1986, and s 155).

In the case of a public company, (6), (7) or (8) above applies only if the company has net assets which are not reduced by the giving of the assistance or, to the extent that those assets are thereby reduced, if the assistance is provided out of distributable profits (s 154).

The conditions mentioned in (9) above may in the case of a company assisting the purchase of its own shares be likewise roughly summarised as follows (further provisions applying where a company assists the purchase of shares in its holding company):

- (a) the company must have net assets which are not thereby reduced, or if they are reduced, the assistance must be provided out of distributable profits;
- (b) the giving of the assistance must be approved by special resolution in general meeting unless the company is a wholly owned subsidiary;
- (c) the directors must before the assistance is given make a statutory declaration giving certain particulars of the proposals and their opinion on certain points concerning the company's future ability to pay its debts (Form 155(6)(a)),
- (d) there must be annexed to this statutory declaration a report by the company's auditors stating that they have enquired into the company's state of affairs and are not aware of anything to indicate that the directors' opinion mentioned above is unreasonable;
- (e) there are detailed requirements on the timing of the various steps involved, making documents available for inspection by members and filing documents with the Registrar (ss 156 to 158).

There are certain rights for members of the company to apply to the court to cancel the resolution approving the assistance.

3.10 Issue of Shares at a Discount

Shares may not be allotted at a discount (s 100). If they are, the allottee is, and a later holder may be, liable to the company for the discount and interest thereon. The company and any officer in default is liable to criminal penalties (s 114).

3.11 Issue of Shares at a Premium

There is a basic rule that if shares are issued at a premium (ie for more than their nominal value), the premium must be transferred to a 'share premium account', which must be shown separately in the balance sheet (s 130).

This share premium account is similar to the share capital inasmuch as it is not available for paying dividends and may not generally be reduced except in the manner in which share capital is reduced (see 4.12.2). It may, however, be applied in paying up unissued shares to be issued to members of the company as fully paid bonus shares; in writing off preliminary expenses or the expenses of, or commission paid on, any issue of shares or debentures; or in providing any premium payable on redemption of debentures.

However, there are exceptions to this basic rule where, broadly:

(1) a company secures a 90 per cent equity holding in another company by an arrangement whereby it issues equity shares in consideration of the issue or transfer to it of equity shares in that other company (s 131) (this is called merger relief and where it applies certain information must be given in a note to the company's accounts as required by Part VI of Schedule 4 or, if applicable, Part IV of Schedule 9);

(2) a wholly owned subsidiary allots shares to its holding company or another wholly owned subsidiary in consideration of the transfer to it of assets other than cash (which may be shares in a third company) (s 132); or

(3) a wholly owned subsidiary allotted shares to its holding company or another wholly owned subsidiary in consideration of the transfer to it of shares in another subsidiary, whether wholly owned or not (but not of other assets) (s 132(6) and (7) and Companies Act 1981 s 38); or

(4) a company issued shares, the consideration for which was the issue or transfer to it of shares in another company, that other company was or thereby became its subsidiary and the premium or part of it was not transferred to share premium account (Companies Consolidation (Consequential Provisions) Act 1985 s 12).

Case (1) cannot apply where case (2) or (3) applies.

3.12 Control of Borrowing etc

In 1989 the requirement for companies to apply to the Bank of England for timing consent for public issues of sterling securities was abolished (formerly a requirement of the Control of Borrowing Order 1958 (as amended) SI 58 No 1208). Following this abolition the British Merchant Banking and Securities Houses Association and the Stock Exchange agreed in consultation with the Bank of England to exchange information on an informal basis about new sterling issues for amounts in excess of £20 million.

The advisers to a public sterling issue will thus, in compliance with guidelines published on 11 September 1989, notify the Bank of England (initially by telephone with subsequent written confirmation) as soon as possible in advance of a proposed sterling issue, of details of the issuer, the amount of the issue and the proposed impact date. Although the Bank of England has no right to prohibit an issue going ahead, it will advise the relevant parties if there is likely to be a clash of sterling issues on a proposed impact date. If the advisers to any later competing issue decide none the less to proceed, the advisers of the earlier notified issue will be told, so that they may be given the opportunity to elect to change their impact date.

Whilst these guidelines are not directly applicable to companies (but rather their merchant banks and brokers) companies should be aware of them in scheduling any substantial issue of sterling securities.

Chapter 4

Shares and Shareholders

4.1 Classes of Shares

Unless the Memorandum or Articles forbid it, the company's shares may be divided into different classes, eg into preference, ordinary and deferred shares (reg 2). The rights of the holders of shares of different classes are normally defined in the Articles.

4.1.1 Preference shares

Every company may issue preference shares, unless the Memorandum or Articles provide to the contrary (*Andrews v Gas Meter Co* [1897] 1 Ch 361).

Where shares are given preferential rights, these usually include a right to receive out of the profits of the company a certain fixed dividend, which must be paid before any dividend at all can be paid to the holders of ordinary or deferred shares. If the Memorandum or Articles do not provide otherwise, a preference dividend is assumed to be cumulative, ie any part of it not paid in any year is carried forward to the next year and must be paid to the holders of the preference shares before any dividend is paid to the other shareholders (or carried forward as arrears again). Usually the Articles will expressly provide whether preference shares are cumulative or non-cumulative.

In some cases preference shares carry, in addition to the fixed preferential dividend, a right to participate with the ordinary shares in profits available for dividend after the fixed preference dividend has been paid. Such shares are known as participating preference shares.

Preference shares are usually given, in addition to the right to a preference dividend, a preferential right to repayment of paid-up capital if the company is being wound up, ie the right to have capital repaid before any repayment can be made to holders of ordinary shares; but no such right is enjoyed unless it is given by the Memorandum or Articles. Where such a preferential right to repayment of capital is given, it applies on a reduction of capital as on a liquidation. In *Scottish Insurance Corporation Ltd v Wilsons and Clyde Coal Co Ltd* [1949] AC 462 and in *Prudential Assurance Co Ltd v Chatterley-Whitfield Collieries Ltd* [1949] AC 512 the court approved as 'fair and equitable' reductions of capital by which preference shares were paid off first even though some holders of preference shares opposed this.

Whether arrears of cumulative preference dividends which have never been declared are payable in a winding-up depends on the true construction of the Memorandum and Articles (see *Re Roberts and Cooper Ltd* [1929] 2 Ch 383; *Re Walter Symons Ltd* [1934] Ch 308; and *Re Wood, Skinner & Co Ltd* [1944] Ch 323).

4.1.2 Deferred shares

Deferred shares are usually given the right to an undetermined dividend out of profit available after a certain maximum dividend has been paid to the holders of ordinary shares. The rights attaching to them are determined by the Memorandum or Articles.

4.1.3 Redeemable shares

Shares of any type may be redeemable. Since the Companies Act 1981 shares need not be preference shares to be redeemable. Section 159A (which has not yet come into force), unless amended prior to coming into force, will provide that certain of the rights must be specified in the Articles. As currently drafted these include the dates on, by which or between which the shares are to be or may be redeemed (unless such dates are to be fixed by the directors, in which case the Articles must state that fact and the directors' determination must be made before issue; the amount payable on redemption or its manner of calculation; and any other terms and conditions of redemption.

4.1.4 Classes of members of company without share capital

Any company which does not have a share capital must file at the Companies Registry within one month particulars of the following, unless they appear in an amendment of its Memorandum or Articles or in a resolution or agreement which must be filed under s 380:

(1) the rights of any class of members which it creates (Form 129(1) (s 129(1));
(2) the variation of the rights of any class of members (Form 129(2) (s 129(2));
(3) the assignment of a name or other designation, or new name or other designation, to any class of members (Form 129(3) (s 129(3)).

For amendment of the rights attaching to any class of shares, see 4.13.

4.2 Register of Members

Procedures are expected to be introduced by the Stock Exchange in 1993 for the creation and transfer of uncertificated securities of listed companies. The practical and legal matters set out below will be affected by these procedures. The legal framework for this new regime is outlined in 5.3, below.

4.2.1 Maintenance of register

Every company must keep a register of members (s 352) and enter in it:
(1) the names and addresses of the members, and, where applicable, the amount, distinguishing numbers and class of the shares held by each member and the amount paid or agreed to be considered as paid thereon;
(2) the date at which each person was entered in the register;
(3) the date at which any person ceased to be a member.

Additional columns are also usually provided for any other particulars it is found convenient to record.

Where the company has converted any shares into stock and given notice of the conversion to the Registrar, the register must show the amount of stock instead of the amount of the shares.

Where there are more than 50 members, if the register itself is not in such a form as to constitute an index, an index to the names of members in the register must be kept (s 354), and within 14 days of any alteration in the register the company must make any necessary alteration in the index. The index must be kept at the place at which the register is kept.

The register of members is prima facie evidence of any matter required or authorised by the Act to be inserted therein (s 361).

If the name of any person is omitted from the register or has been entered in it when it ought not to have been, or if there has been unnecessary delay in recording that any person has ceased to be a member, the person aggrieved, any member of the company or the company itself may apply to the court for rectification of the register (s 359).

4.2.2 Form of register

The register and its index may be kept either by making entries in bound books or by recording the matters in question in any other manner (s 722(1)). Loose-leaf or card index systems may, therefore, be employed; and by s 723 any such register or record (including a register of debenture holders) may be kept otherwise than in legible form (eg on computer) provided that it is capable of being reproduced in legible form, and subject to compliance with the Companies (Registers and Other Records) Regulations 1985 (SI 1985 No 724). Where entries are not made in bound books, adequate precautions must be taken to guard against falsification, and, if such precautions are not taken, directors and officers in default are liable to be fined (s 722(2)).

4.2.3 Place at which register must be kept

The register of members must be kept at the registered office or at any office at which the work of making it up is done, provided that it is not outside the country, ie England and Wales or Scotland, in which the company is registered (s 353(1)). Notice of the place at which the register is kept or of any change therein (Form 353) must be sent to the Registrar of Companies, unless it has been kept at the company's registered office (a) at all times since the company came into existence, or (b) in the case of a register in existence on 1 July 1948, at all times since then (s 353(3)). A duplicate of any overseas branch register (see 4.2.6) must be kept at the same place as the register of members (Sched 14, Part II, para 4).

4.2.4 Inspection of register

The register and any index must be open to inspection during prescribed hours (currently at least two hours in each business day) by any member of the company or the general public (s 356). Members may inspect free of charge, but any other person may be charged a fee not exceeding such amount as may be prescribed from time to time (currently £2.50).

In addition, any person may require a copy of any part of the register to be supplied on payment of such amount as may be prescribed from time to time (currently £2.50 for the first 100 entries, £20 for the next 1,000 and £15 for each 1,000 thereafter), or such less sum as the company prescribes. A person who inspects the register has no right to take extracts from, or make copies of, the register (*Re Balaghat Gold Mining Co* [1901] 2 KB 665).

Any copy so required must be supplied within the ten days commencing on the day after that on which the request is received by the company.

Where a company arranges for some other person to make up its register of members, and the register is kept at the office of such person at which the work is done, such person is liable, as if he were an officer of the company, if any person entitled thereto is refused inspection or copies of the register (s 357).

4.2.5 Closing the register

On advertising its intention in a newspaper circulating in the district in which the registered office is situated, a company may close the register for a period or periods not exceeding 30 days in each year (s 358). This power is sometimes exercised for a period preceding the annual general meeting to avoid the need to register transfers until after the declaration of a dividend.

4.2.6 Overseas branch register

A company which is empowered to and does carry on business in any territory listed in Part I of Sched 14 to the Act (basically the Commonwealth but excluding the Channel Islands and the Isle of Man and including Northern Ireland, the Republic of Ireland and South Africa) may keep there a branch register of members resident there, called an overseas branch register (previously a 'dominion register') (s 362). Notice of the situation of the office where such a register is opened, and of any change in its situation and of its discontinuance, must be given to the Registrar on the prescribed form within 14 days (Sched 14, Part II, para 1) (Form 362).

A duplicate of the overseas branch register must be kept at the same place as the principal register of members and a copy of every entry made in the overseas branch register must be transmitted to the company's registered office as soon as possible and entered in the duplicate register (Sched 14, Part II, para 4).

Notice of intention to close an overseas branch register temporarily must be advertised in a newspaper circulating in the district in which the register is kept (Sched 14, Part II, para 2).

4.3 Disclosure of Interests in Shares

4.3.1 Notification of substantial interests

Sections 198 to 210 contain complicated provisions relating to the disclosure to a public company of notifiable interests in its relevant share capital. Relevant share capital means issued share capital carrying rights to vote in all circumstances at general meetings. A notifiable interest is an interest in three per cent or more of any class of the company's relevant share capital. The figure of three per cent may be altered by statutory instrument.

Where a person:

(1) to his knowledge acquires an interest in shares comprised in relevant share capital or ceases to be interested in such shares; or

(2) becomes aware that he has acquired an interest in such shares or has ceased to be interested in such shares;

and:

  (i) he has a notifiable interest after but not before; or

  (ii) vice versa; or

  (iii) he has a notifiable interest before and after but the percentage levels (rounded down to a whole number) are at least one per cent different;

certain disclosure obligations arise. These also arise where otherwise than in the above circumstances a person:

(a) is aware at the time it occurs of any change of circumstances affecting any facts relevant to the application of the above rules in relation to an existing interest of his in shares of any description; or

(b) otherwise becomes aware of any such facts.

Case (a) above would occur, for example, where shares which previously had restricted voting rights were given voting rights in all circumstances and thus became relevant share capital.

A person is deemed to be interested in shares if his spouse or infant child or a body corporate which is under his effective control or in which he can exercise one-third or more of the voting power is interested in them. There are a number of further rules for determining whether a person has an interest in shares. For example, one is taken to have an interest in shares if one has entered into a contract to buy them or is entitled to exercise or control the exercise of any right conferred by the shares, but an interest as a bare trustee (or nominee) or an interest in reversion or remainder is disregarded.

By ss 204 and 205 if two or more persons make an agreement (which may include arrangements not binding in law) which restricts their use, retention or disposal of shares they may acquire in a company (the target company) and any of them acquires an interest in the target company's shares in pursuance of the agreement, each party to the agreement, commonly known as a 'concert party', is deemed to be interested in all shares in which any other party is interested. Each member of the concert party must notify all other members of his interests in the target company so that they can for the purposes of their disclosure obligations take account of the shares in which they are deemed to be interested by virtue of the concert party (s 206).

A person's duties where the disclosure obligations of ss 198 to 210 apply may be summarised as follows:

(1) notify the class of relevant share capital concerned and either the number of shares in which he is interested or the fact that he no longer has a notifiable interest;

(2) include in such notification (unless it states that he no longer has a notifiable interest) particulars of the registered holders of the shares concerned and the number of shares held by each of them, so far as he knows such particulars;

(3) notify those particulars on learning them later;

(4) notify any change in those particulars;

(5) if a party to a s 204 agreement, state certain further matters in his notification, eg the names and addresses of the other parties;

(6) if his notification is because he or another has ceased to be a party to a s 204 agreement, state this in the notification and, in the latter case, identify that other.

All such notifications must be in writing and state the name and address of the person giving them. If he is a director, the obligation being fulfilled must be stated. Generally, these notification obligations must be performed within two days following the day on which they arise.

A person who authorises another ('the agent') to acquire or

dispose of, on his behalf, interests in shares in the relevant share capital of a public company (eg a person who delegates the management of investments to a stockbroker or bank) must secure that the agent notifies him immediately of acquisitions or disposals which will or may give rise to an obligation to make a notification (s 210(1)).

4.3.2 Register of substantial interests

Every public company must keep a register for the purposes of the above disclosure requirements and within three days inscribe in it all information received in fulfilment of those requirements (s 211). The register must be kept at the same place as the register of directors' interests (see 8.9.1), must unless it constitutes such an index in itself have an index of names therein and (save insofar as it contains information with respect to certain overseas interests) be open to inspection by any member of the company or the general public in the same way as the register of members (see 4.2.4).

4.3.3 Investigation of interests

A public company may by written notice require anyone (including foreign persons and corporations — *Re F H Holdings plc* [1985] BCLC 293) whom it knows or has reasonable cause to believe to be or to have been within the previous three years interested in shares in its relevant share capital to confirm that fact or indicate whether it is or is not so and to give certain further information as to his interest in such shares which can include particulars of other persons so interested (s 212). The information must be provided within a reasonable time, which will depend on the nature of the information requested and from whom. In situations of particular urgency the recipient of a s 212 notice could only in exceptional circumstances require more than two days; in less urgent situations no more than five (*Lonrho v Edelman* [1989] 5 BCC 68). Information acquired by a company by this procedure must be entered in a separate part of the register of substantial interests (s 213) (and see Appendix 5 for a specimen notice).

A company can be required to exercise its power under s 212 on the requisition of members holding at least ten per cent of such of its paid up share capital as carries the right of voting at general meetings (s 214). The company must make a report of the information obtained in an investigation resulting from such a requisition (s 215): if the investigation takes more than three months an interim report must be made every three months. Such reports must be kept at the registered office and be open to inspection in the same way as the register of members.

Where a person fails to comply with a requisition for information made by a company under s 212, the company can apply to the court for an order under Part XV of the Act placing restrictions on the shares. Such restrictions will prevent transfer of the shares or the exercise of voting rights or payment of dividends in respect of them (see *Re F H Lloyd Holdings plc* [1985] BCLC 293 and *Re Geers Gross Plc* [1987] 1 WLR 887; [1987] 1 WLR 1649, CA). If the company's Articles permit, voting rights can also be suspended in such circumstances without the need to apply to the court.

4.4 Numbering of Shares

Prima facie every share must have a distinguishing number so that it is possible to ascertain which shares each member holds; but if all the issued shares in the company or all the issued shares of a particular class are fully paid up and rank pari passu for all purposes, they need not (s 182(2)). If, after the distinctive numbering of shares of a class has been dispensed with, further shares of that class are created not ranking pari passu for all purposes then, strictly speaking, the original shares of the class should be renumbered unless the new shares are distinguished as a separate class until they are all issued and fully paid and rank pari passu with the original shares. Where, however, newly created shares are not pari passu only because they do not rank for a dividend which is declared shortly afterwards on the original shares of the class, the point is often ignored in practice.

4.5 Share Certificates

Again, the proposed TAURUS regulations (see 5.3 below) will affect the application of the matters described below to listed companies.

4.5.1 Issue of certificates

Section 185 requires every company within two months of an allotment or of receipt of a transfer to complete and have ready for delivery share certificates, unless the conditions of issue otherwise provide. Where a broker's transfer is used in conjunction with a stock transfer (see 5.1.5), the two months begin to run from receipt of the later of the two transfers to be lodged (Stock Transfer Act 1963, s 2(3)(*b*)). A company need not, however, issue certificates for shares or debentures allotted or transferred to Sepon Limited, The Stock Exchange nominee used for the 'Talisman' computerised settlement system (s 185 and the Stock Exchange (Designation of Nominees) Order 1985 (SI 1985 No 806)). Under s 194 of the Financial Services Act 1986 this exception also applies to shares or debentures allotted or transferred to a recognised clearing house or a nominee of a recognised clearing house or of a recognised investment exchange.

Certificates are issued in accordance with the Articles. Unless power is taken to affix mechanical signatures or to dispense with signatures or advantage is taken of the provision outlined below relating to use of a securities seal, they are usually signed by the secretary and one or more directors. Share certificates can also be sealed by the company, which will give prima facie evidence of the title of the member to the shares (s 186). Certificates for securities may also be sealed with a facsimile of the common seal with the addition on its face of the word 'Securities', called a securities seal, (s 40) and in the case of a company formed before 12 February 1979 such a seal may be used and, if it is, no signatures are required, notwithstanding anything in the Articles (Companies Consolidation (Consequential Provisions) Act 1985, s 11). The provisions of s 186 (evidence of title) extend to share certificates sealed with a securities seal.

Apart from the statutory obligation, The Stock Exchange requires · companies whose securities are listed to issue certificates within one month of the expiration of any right of renunciation and within 14 days of the lodgment of a transfer.

The Stock Exchange forbids a listed company to charge for the issue of a share certificate and other companies rarely make such a charge.

Share certificates for different classes of shares should be easily distinguishable, preferably by colour; and where further shares are issued of an existing class, but not ranking for the next dividend, it is advisable to defer the issue of certificates until after payment of the next dividend (if possible within the above time limits) or mark the certificates for the later shares appropriately. Listed companies must comply with certain rules laid down in the Yellow

Book regarding the size of and details to be stated on share certificates.

4.5.2 Lost certificates

The Articles usually authorise directors to issue new certificates in place of those which have been lost, defaced or destroyed, but the power should be exercised with caution, as the company may incur liability to any person who suffers loss through such an issue. Before issuing a new certificate, adequate protection should be obtained, the applicant being required to enter into an agreement to indemnify the company for any consequential loss with one or more sureties to the indemnity (see Appendix 5). In the case of listed securities no fee may be charged (other than exceptional out of pocket expenses).

4.5.3 Effect of certificate

The need for care in issuing share certificates is emphasised by the effect which the certificate may have on the company.

Every sealed certificate issued by the company is, in the first place, prima facie evidence of the title of the person named therein to the shares concerned (s 186) and the company may be estopped from denying that the person named in a properly issued certificate is entitled to the shares (*Re Bahia, etc Railway Co* (1868) LR 3 QB 584).

In addition, the company may be estopped as against a holder who acts on the faith of the certificate from denying that the amount specified as paid up in the certificate has been duly paid (*Bloomenthal v Ford* [1897] AC 156).

But the company may not be bound by a certificate issued without the authority of the board of directors (*South London Greyhound Racecourses Ltd v Wake* [1931] 1 Ch 496).

4.6 Share Warrants

4.6.1 Issue of warrants

If the Articles permit, share warrants may be issued under the company's seal to the holders of fully paid shares (s 188). They must, if they relate to sterling denominated securities, be stamped with duty of an amount equal to three times the current rate of duty (see 5.1.9) payable on a transfer of the shares or stock represented thereby at their market value (Finance Act 1963, s 59 (as amended)).

Warrants are made out to bearer and are negotiable instruments, transferable by delivery.

The conditions upon which such warrants are issued are laid down by the Articles which authorise the issue, and it is usual to supply a printed copy of these conditions to warrant holders on application or with the warrant. In the case of listed securities, The Stock Exchange requires the company to issue certificates in exchange for warrants (and vice versa if permitted) within 14 days of the deposit of the warrants (or certificates) and to certify transfers against the deposit of warrants on the day of deposit or if that is not a business day on the first following business day. The Stock Exchange also requires that no new share warrant is issued to replace one which has been lost unless the company is satisfied beyond reasonable doubt that the original has been destroyed.

Subject to the Articles, the bearer of a share warrant is entitled to have his name entered on the register of members on surrendering the warrant for cancellation (s 355(2)). The company is held responsible for any loss incurred by any person if the name of a bearer of a share warrant is entered in the register without the warrant being surrendered and cancelled (s 355(3)).

4.6.2 Status of warrant holders

The holders of share warrants are not members of the company, but the Articles may provide that they may be deemed to be for all or only some purposes (s 355(5)). The Articles cannot, however, provide that shares held by warrant shall count towards a director's qualification (s 291(2)). If a holder is authorised by the Articles to attend and vote at meetings, it is usually necessary for the warrant holder to deposit his warrant with the company three days before the meeting.

4.7 Notice of Trusts

Section 360 forbids the entry on the register of members of any trust affecting the shares, whether express, implied or constructive. As a consequence the company is relieved from all responsibility to persons, other than the registered holders, who enjoy equitable claims over its shares. However, if notice is given to the company of any lien, charge or other claim over its shares, it may be helpful to inform the person giving the notice at once that the claim cannot be recognised.

Thus if A, the registered holder of shares, holds such shares as trustee in trust for B the trust is no concern of the company. A is the person capable of signing a form of transfer and liable for any sums due on the shares. But the claims of persons other than the registered holder must be recognised where a stop notice (formerly a notice in lieu of distringas) is issued under Order 50, r 11, of the Rules of the Supreme Court.

Where such a notice is received and the registered holder subsequently attempts to transfer the shares concerned, notice of the intended transfer must be given to the person on whose application the notice has been issued, and no transfer must be registered within 14 days of this latter notice. If, however, at the end of these 14 days no order of the court restraining the transfer is issued, the transfer should be registered in the ordinary manner.

The rule that a company cannot take notice of a trust does not, however, enable the company to obtain priority over equitable interests of which it has received notice (*Bradford Banking Co v Briggs* (1886) 12 App Cas 29).

The receipt of information for the purpose of completing the register of directors' holdings or the register of substantial interests in voting shares of public companies does not constitute notice of a trust (Sched 13, para 24 and s 211(4)). The same applies to information obtained by a public company in any investigation of interests in its voting shares under s 212 (s 213(3)) (see 4.3.3).

4.8 Members

4.8.1 Companies

A limited company cannot acquire its own shares for valuable consideration except:

(1) by a redemption or purchase in accordance with Chapter VII of Part V of the Act (see 4.11);
(2) in a reduction of capital approved by the court (see 4.12.2);
(3) in certain other cases involving an application to the court (see 4.12.2); and
(4) by forfeiture of shares, or their surrender in lieu of forfeiture, for failure to pay sums due on them (s 143).

Certain consequences are prescribed by ss 144 and 149 where shares in a company are acquired by the company itself or its nominee.

As a general rule, a body corporate cannot be a member of a company which is its holding company and any allotment or transfer of a company's shares to its subsidiary is void (s 23). This general rule is subject, however, to the following exceptions:

(1) a subsidiary may acquire shares of its holding company in the capacity of a personal representative or trustee, provided that it is not beneficially interested. (The proviso does not apply where the beneficial interest is only by way of security for the purposes of a transaction entered into by the company in the ordinary course of a business which includes the lending of money, and Sched 2 provides that residual interests under pension and employees' share schemes and certain rights to reimbursement or indemnity are disregarded in determining whether a subsidiary is beneficially interested.)

(2) a subsidiary which is a market maker is outside the prohibition.

(3) a subsidiary which became a member of its holding company without offending against s 23, but which after 1 November 1990 fell within its prohibitions, may continue to be a member but may not vote at meetings of the holding company or at meetings of any class of members in respect of any shares held or subsequently acquired on a capitalisation issue.

A nominee of a body corporate is subject to a similar restriction against being a member of the body corporate's holding company (s 23(7)).

Apart from the above restrictions, any company may, subject to its Memorandum and Articles, hold shares in another company.

A corporation which holds shares in a company may authorise any person it thinks fit to act as its representative at meetings (s 375). The authorisation should be given by resolution of the directors or other governing body; and the person so authorised should prove (although cannot be compelled to prove) his authority by producing a certified copy of the resolution. See Appendix 5 for forms of authorisation. This person is not a proxy. He has the same powers of voting, etc, as the corporation would be able to exercise were it an individual (s 375). The company cannot, therefore, insist that the representative's authorisation be lodged at the registered office before the meeting.

4.8.2 Partnerships

Since an English partnership has no corporate existence, the company may refuse to register a transfer into the name of such a partnership (*Re Vagliano Anthracite Collieries Ltd* (1910) 79 LJ Ch 769). The transfer should be executed in favour of all the partners (or up to four of them as trustees for all the partners) who should be registered as joint holders of the shares.

4.8.3 Minors

Subject to the provisions of the Articles a minor may become a member of a company. The membership contract is voidable at the instance of the minor up to or within a reasonable period after attaining the age of 18 and any sums paid to the company can then be recovered. Until repudiation, a minor has full powers of membership. If partly paid shares are transferred to a minor the transferor will remain liable for all future calls on such shares while they are held by the minor.

4.8.4 Joint holders

In the absence of other provisions in the Articles, where one of a number of joint holders of shares dies, the survivors acquire all the rights of the deceased holder, but a death certificate or grant should be required as evidence of the death.

Articles usually provide that where shares are held by persons jointly notices of meetings need to be sent only to the holder who is named first on the register, that dividends shall be sent to that person and that a receipt signed by any one of the joint holders shall bind the others. For this reason joint shareholders are entitled to require the company to register some of the shares with the name of one holder first and others with the name of another first (*Burns v Siemens Bros Dynamo Works (No 2)* [1919] 1 Ch 225).

A transfer of shares held jointly must be executed by all the registered holders but on the death of one, execution by the survivors is valid without the assent of the deceased holder's personal representative since the shares were held jointly and not, at any rate so far as the company is concerned, as 'tenants in common'.

4.8.5 Bankrupt members

If a member becomes bankrupt his shares vest in his trustee who is entitled to execute transfers. If the trustee has been appointed by the court, his title is proved by production of the original court order appointing him or an office copy of the order. If he has been appointed by a creditors' meeting, his title is proved by the production of the original certificate of appointment issued by the chairman of the meeting or a certified copy. If he has been appointed by the Secretary of State, the appropriate document is the original certificate of appointment or a certified copy (Insolvency Act 1986, ss 292–7 and the Insolvency Rules 1986 (SI 1986 No 1925), as amended, rules 6.120–4). Alternatively, if the appointment is by the court or the Secretary of State and is advertised in the *London Gazette*, a copy of the relevant issue of the *Gazette* may be accepted.

If it is discovered that a shareholder is an undischarged bankrupt, dividends should not be paid to him. The existence of the dividend should be reported to the Official Receiver or the Department of Trade.

The trustee of a bankrupt shareholder has a power of disclaimer where the shares are of an onerous nature, eg where calls are likely to be made. The exercise of this power, however, entitles the company to prove in the bankruptcy for any damages suffered through the disclaimer.

Proof may always be made for debts, calls actually due at the date of the commencement of the bankruptcy and the estimated present value of future calls; but the trustee in bankruptcy may set off against a call any debt due from the company.

Subject to compliance with the Articles, particulars of the bankruptcy and the name of the trustee should be entered in the register (reg 30). While the bankrupt's name remains on the register, unless the Articles provide otherwise, he is entitled to vote or tender a proxy at meetings (*Morgan v Gray* [1953] Ch 83), although his vote must be cast as his trustee directs. Until the trustee obtains registration of the shares in his own name, he cannot petition for compulsory winding-up (*Re HL Bolton Engineering Co Ltd* [1956] Ch 577, but see *Re Bayswater Trading Co* [1970] 1 All ER 608).

4.8.6 Marriage of members

If a woman on marriage changes her surname (which is not obligatory) she may by producing her share certificate and marriage certificate have her name altered on the register and on her share certificate. If, however, she omits to do this she may on transferring the shares execute the transfer in her former name. But if her former name remains on the register dividend warrants will be made out in that name.

4.9 Calls on Shares

4.9.1 General

Where the conditions of issue provide that moneys payable for shares are to be paid by fixed instalments on fixed dates, such instalments are not calls since no call is made by the company.

Where there are partly paid shares, it may be necessary to call on the holders from time to time to pay the whole or a portion of the amount unpaid on their shares. Although partly paid shares are now rare, in such a case the provisions in the Articles must be observed, and usually the board will need to pass a resolution authorising the call to be made, though sometimes a resolution of the company in general meeting is required. Whichever form of resolution is employed, the sum to be called up and the date of payment should be specified. Unless the Articles or terms of issue provide to the contrary, a call should not be made on certain members of a class to the exclusion of others (see reg 17).

The amount which may be called up from time to time may be limited by the Articles or by the terms of issue.

Notice of the call should be given to shareholders and care must be taken to give the notice specified in the Articles and to state the time and place for making payment, as failure to do this may render the call unenforceable (*Re Cawley & Co* (1889) 42 Ch D 209 at p 236 per Lord Esher MR).

The Articles sometimes provide for interest on calls not paid by the appointed day (reg 15).

The Articles may allow the directors, at their discretion, to accept in advance of calls amounts unpaid on shares (s 119(*b*)), and to pay interest on such amounts. Such interest must be paid from distributable profits (s 263). Dividends must not be payable on amounts paid in advance of calls if a Stock Exchange listing is desired, and amounts so paid cannot subsequently be refunded to the shareholder except on a winding-up (*Re Wakefield Rolling Stock Co* [1892] 3 Ch 165). Where some consideration other than cash is accepted in settlement of a call, the court may subsequently challenge the validity of the consideration (*Re White Star Line Ltd* [1938] Ch 458).

4.9.2 Non-payment of calls

The effect of non-payment of a call will depend on the Articles. In any case action for the amount may be taken against the holder, or his personal representative if he is dead, but additional rights may be exercised if the Articles permit. Thus, Articles usually empower the directors to refuse a transfer of shares on which calls remain unpaid; or to forfeit the shares; or to prohibit the holder from attending or voting at meetings.

Unpaid calls are debts in the nature of specialty debts (s 14(2)) which are not statute-barred until after 12 years.

In proceedings against shareholders for unpaid calls, difficulty may arise in the following cases:

(1) *Minors* may be able to repudiate all liability during minority or within a reasonable time of attaining full age.

(2) *Mentally disordered persons* may repudiate liability if it can be shown that they took the shares while of unsound mind and that the company was aware of the insanity at the time.

(3) *Bankrupts* cannot be sued, but a proof for unpaid calls may be made in the bankruptcy.

4.9.3 Forfeiture

Articles invariably provide that, in the event of non-payment of a call, any share in respect of which the call is unpaid may be forfeited by resolution of the directors (see regs 18 to 22). Forfeiture cannot usually be carried out until the member has been warned of the consequences of the call remaining unpaid and the provisions of the Articles must be strictly observed.

In such cases it is usual for the board to instruct the secretary to write to the holder of the shares concerned, before a resolution for forfeiture is passed, warning him that if the call is not paid by a certain date the shares will be liable to forfeiture. If no satisfactory reply to this letter is received, the board may resolve that the shares be forfeited and a letter will be sent notifying the holder of the forfeiture. The following form of letter warning a holder of forfeiture may be employed:

Dear Sir,

I am directed by the Board to remind you that the call on shares held by you in this company made on the ..... day of .... 19..., and amounting to ....., has not yet been received.

The Board hereby require you to pay this call in accordance with Article ..... of the Articles of Association on or before ...., 19.....together with interest at the rate of ..... per cent per annum from the .... day of ..... 19.... (the day on which the call became due) until the date of payment.

I hereby give you notice that in the event of non-payment within the time specified, the shares in respect of which the above call is made will be liable to forfeiture in accordance with Article .... of the Articles of Association, together with all dividends declared in respect of such shares. [In addition, you will remain liable to pay any sums due in respect of such shares notwithstanding the forfeiture.]

By order of the Board,

.... *Secretary*

Forfeited shares may be cancelled, sold or re-allotted, but the Articles normally provide that the former holder remains liable for the unpaid calls until the amount has been paid. In the case of a resale, the purchaser also becomes liable for the amount of the call outstanding, and cannot vote until the liability has been extinguished, but it is advisable to call upon him specifically for the sum due.

Articles sometimes empower directors to accept a surrender of shares, but it appears that this power can be exercised only where the shares surrendered are subject to forfeiture (or perhaps where a surrender of fully paid shares is accepted in exchange for shares of the same nominal value), for an unlawful reduction of capital might otherwise result (*Bellerby v Rowland & Marwood's Steamship Co Ltd* [1902] 2 Ch 14).

The purchaser of forfeited or surrendered shares may be credited with the amount paid up at the time of the forfeiture, but the shares cannot be credited as fully paid if the sum paid on reissue is less than the amount unpaid at the time of the forfeiture, for this would amount to the issue of shares at a discount.

To safeguard the purchasers of forfeited shares, Articles frequently provide that a statutory declaration by an officer of the company as to the propriety of the forfeiture shall, together with the receipt for the purchase consideration, constitute the purchaser's title and be deemed conclusive evidence of the facts therein stated as against all persons claiming to be entitled to the shares. This declaration should be supplied if required. As, however, under s 183, an instrument of transfer must be deposited with the company, the alternative method by which the board authorises one of its number to execute a transfer to the purchaser is to be preferred.

If shares in a public company are forfeited or surrendered in lieu of forfeiture, the company:

(1) must, if they are not previously disposed of, cancel them within three years, reducing the company's allotted share capital accordingly, and if such reduction brings its allotted share capital below the minimum for a public company re-register as a private one (s 146(1) and (2));

(2) must not vote in respect of those shares (s 146(1) and (4)); and

(3) must, if it shows those shares as an asset in its balance sheet, transfer an amount equal to their value out of profits available for dividend to a non-distributable reserve fund (s 148(4)).

4.10 Lien

In addition to the right of forfeiture and accompanying power of sale, a private company often has under its Articles a right of lien over the shares of its members in respect of any debts due from them to the company, which is enforceable by sale of the shares (see regs 8 to 11, which however confine the lien to moneys payable at a fixed date or called in respect of the shares). The right often differs from the right of forfeiture in that any surplus proceeds of sale, after the payment of the debt and expenses, must be refunded to the shareholder, but the methods employed in exercising the right are usually similar. The Articles *must* be observed carefully in every case. For example, the right of lien may not apply if the moneys are due otherwise than in respect of the shares concerned or are due from only one of two or more joint holders.

A public company may similarly be given by its Articles a lien over members' shares but, unless its ordinary business includes lending money or certain similar activities and the lien arises in the ordinary course of its business, only for amounts payable on those shares (s 150).

A right of lien is usually extended to dividends due on the shares concerned.

4.11 Redemption or Purchase by a Company of Own Shares

4.11.1 General

This is governed in the case of limited companies having a share capital by s 143 (see 4.8.1) and ss 159 to 181 (Chapter VII of Part V of the Act). The law restricts such a company's ability to issue redeemable shares or buy its own shares to prevent funds passing out of the company to shareholders to the detriment of those who deal with it, since if the company is unable to meet its obligations they will, because it is a limited company, have no recourse to the shareholders. An unlimited company may, subject to its Memorandum and Articles, freely issue redeemable shares or buy its own shares, but the rest of this heading is concerned with limited companies.

Section 159 enables a company to issue redeemable shares, if authorised by its Articles, including shares redeemable at the option of the company or the holder. A company must always have some irredeemable shares in issue: otherwise it might be left without any members or issued shares. Redeemable shares may not be redeemed unless they are fully paid: thus redemption cannot relieve a holder of partly paid shares of his uncalled liability. There must be payment on redemption. The terms and manner of redemption must be specified in the Articles: at present this requirement is expressed in general terms, but when s 159A comes into force further details will need to be specified (see 4.1.3 above). A share which is redeemed is thereby cancelled and the amount of the company's issued share capital is thereby reduced accordingly: there is no consequent reduction in the company's authorised share capital. If a company is about to redeem shares it can issue further shares up to the same nominal amount as if those to be redeemed had never been issued: in other words, it can temporarily have the same amount of its authorised share capital issued twice.

Appendix 2 contains a diagram to illustrate the rules in s 160 relating to the accounts (distributable profits or the proceeds of a fresh issue) from which the moneys payable on redemption can be drawn but see also 4.11.2 for private companies applying capital for the purpose.

Section 162 enables a company, if authorised by its Articles, to purchase its own shares, including redeemable shares, and applies the rules summarised above as if the purchase were a redemption save that the terms and manner of purchase need not be specified in the Articles. The procedure is outlined below at 4.11.3. In the remainder of this section 4.11 references to redemption include purchase by a company of its own shares.

To maintain a company's capital for the protection of those dealing with it, s 170 requires, when a redemption takes place, certain transfers to a capital redemption reserve: distribution of this is restricted in the same way as distribution of a company's share capital save that the capital redemption reserve may be used to pay up a fully paid bonus issue.

4.11.2 Private companies

Section 171 enables private companies to redeem shares from capital (ie otherwise than from distributable profits or the proceeds of a fresh issue). Complex rules ensure that so far as possible distributable profits are, however, used first and that the undistributable accounts and reserves are maintained at the highest possible figure. For the protection of shareholders and those dealing with a company a procedure with tight time limits (for which reference should be made to the legislation) is prescribed for redemptions (or purchases) out of capital as summarised below (such procedure being in the case of purchases additional to the procedure set out below at 4.11.3):

(1) the directors make a statutory declaration in Form 173 relating to the company's ability to pay its debts immediately after the payment out of capital and carry on business as a going concern (paying its debts as they fall due) during the ensuing year. To this declaration there must be annexed a report by the company's auditors stating, inter alia, that they have inquired into the company's state of affairs, that the permissible capital payment as stated in the directors' declaration is in their view properly determined and that they are not aware of anything to indicate that the opinion expressed by the directors in the declaration is unreasonable;

(2) next follows a special resolution approving the proposed payment out of capital;

(3) copies of the statutory declaration and of the auditors' report must be filed at the Companies Registry;

(4) notice of the proposed payment out of capital, stating certain matters, must (i) be published in the *London Gazette* if the company is registered in England and Wales or in the *Edinburgh Gazette* if the company is registered in Scotland

and (ii) be published in a national newspaper or given to individual creditors;

(5) the statutory declaration and auditors' report must be open to inspection;

(6) within five weeks of the special resolution a creditor or non-consenting member can apply to the court for cancellation of the resolution approving payment out of capital;

(7) finally, the payment out of capital can be made from five to seven weeks after the special resolution (ss 173 to 176).

If a company is wound up within a year after a payment out of capital any deficiency in the winding-up can be recovered from the recipients of the payment and, unless he shows that he had reasonable grounds for the opinion expressed in the statutory declaration, any director who signed it (Insolvency Act 1986, s 76).

4.11.3 Procedure on purchase of own shares

If the purchase is a 'market purchase' (basically one on The Stock Exchange or its Unlisted Securities Market) it must be authorised by a resolution in general meeting, which may be an ordinary resolution. The authority may be general or limited, conditional or unconditional. It must specify the maximum number of shares which may be acquired, the maximum and minimum prices (which may be expressed by formulae) and an expiry date for the authority not more than 18 months ahead. The shares to which the authority relates can be voted on the resolution (s 166).

An 'off-market purchase' (one which is not a market purchase) must, however, be authorised by a *special* resolution which must authorise the *terms of the contract of purchase*, not merely purchases. Again, the authority must have an expiry date not more than 18 months ahead. The shares to which the authority relates may *not* be voted on the special resolution. The proposed purchase contract or a memorandum of it if it is not in writing must be available for inspection by members at the meeting and at the registered office for at least 15 days before the meeting (s 164).

A resolution to authorise market purchases or the terms of off-market purchases must be filed at the Companies Registry (ss 166(7) and 380(1) and (4)(*a*) and (*h*)).

A return of purchases must be made to the Companies Registry (Form 169) (s 169(1), (2) and (3)): public companies have to give extra details relating to prices paid and listed companies must notify the Stock Exchange.

Copies of purchase contracts or memoranda of them if they are not written must be kept at the registered office for ten years and be open to inspection by any member and, if the company is a public one, anyone else (s 169(4) and (5)).

There are provisions relating to contingent purchase contracts, the assignment or release by a company of a right to buy its own shares and payments apart from the purchase price (ss 165, 167 and 168).

4.12 Alteration of Share Capital

4.12.1 Increase of capital

If the *issued capital* is less than the *authorised* or *nominal capital*, the issued capital may be increased by the issue of additional shares without any increase in the authorised capital. The procedure in such a case is governed by the Articles, and the exercise of any discretion to issue unissued shares vested in the directors by the Articles is subject to the provisions of ss 80 and 89 (see 3.1).

An increase in the *authorised capital* may be effected by the company by ordinary resolution in general meeting *if the Articles permit* (s 121). The procedure to be employed as regulated by the Articles must be closely followed (see regs 32 and 33 of Table A). If the Articles do not give power to increase the capital, the power may be taken by special resolution, and it appears that by the same resolution the company may exercise the power so obtained (*Campbell's Case* (1874) 9 Ch App 1).

In any event, care must be taken in wording the notice of the meeting, which should state the nature of the resolution required by the Articles and the amount of the increase proposed.

It is not necessary to notify creditors of the alteration, or to obtain the consent of the court, but a notice of increase (Form 123) must be filed with the Registrar together with a copy of the resolution authorising the increase (s 123). Particulars of class rights must be given in the notice. A copy of such resolution must be filed even if the resolution is ordinary (s 123(3)).

4.12.2 Reduction of capital

Section 121(2)(*e*) provides that, if the Articles permit, unissued shares may be cancelled. This will diminish the amount of the *nominal capital*. The consent of the court is not required, but notice

(Form 122) must be given to the Registrar within one month of the resolution (s 122).

A reduction of capital in any other form must be carried out in conformity with the provisions of s 135 which requires:

(1) power to reduce in the Articles;
(2) a special resolution; and
(3) confirmation by the court.

If no power is given by the Articles, it may be taken by special resolution, but a second resolution must be employed to exercise the power. The second resolution may be passed at the same meeting as the first resolution.

After the passing of the necessary resolution, in order to make the reduction of capital effective, it has to be confirmed by the High Court. Proceedings for this purpose are instituted by petition supported by affidavit evidence, such proceedings being governed by the provisions of Order 102 of the Rules of the Supreme Court.

In all proceedings before the court, the company has to be legally represented. It will therefore be necessary for the company's solicitors, who doubtless will already have been consulted in connection with the preparation of the resolution, to be instructed to make the application to the court for this confirmation. The petition and affidavits in support are all documents of a special nature and will be drafted by the solicitors.

The court has to be satisfied that the meeting at which the resolution was passed, and any other meetings which may be necessary in order to obtain the approval of separate classes of shareholders (unless the company can prove that the reduction of capital is fair and reasonable—see *Re Holders Investment Trust Ltd* [1971] 1 WLR 583) have all been properly convened and requires this to be strictly proved. This requirement is met by affidavit evidence from the Secretary or the Registrar of the company to establish that a notice of the meeting was sent or delivered to all members entitled pursuant to the provisions of the Articles of Association to receive notice of the particular meeting or meetings. It is therefore essential that a note is kept of the date, time and place of posting or delivery of the notice or notices.

If the reduction involves either a diminution of liability in respect of unpaid share capital or the payment to any shareholder of paid-up capital, the main concern of the court is to see that the creditors of the company will not be prejudiced and, unless the court is satisfied that this is so, it has power under the provisions of s 136(4) to direct an inquiry as to creditors. Such an inquiry involves the preparation of a list of creditors at a date fixed by the court, advertising in the press a notice to creditors of the application and where the list of creditors may be inspected, circularising the known creditors with forms of consent to the reduction, and making provision for the debts of those creditors who do not consent.

If there are special circumstances, the court may rule that the provisions of s 136(2) shall not apply to any class or classes of creditors, in which case the consent of the creditors of that class is not required. The company's solicitors will advise as to what the court regards as a special circumstance; the mere fact that the company is solvent will not be sufficient but in practice an inquiry is almost invariably dispensed with on the basis that, for example, the company demonstrates to the satisfaction of the court that it has adequate cash resources or trustee securities to satisfy the court that creditors are protected or that it can provide an appropriate bank guarantee for this purpose.

When the order of the court has been drawn up and completed, the next and final step to make the reduction effective is to deliver a copy thereof to the Registrar (s 138(1)). This section also requires that, in addition to delivering a copy of the order, a copy of a minute approved by the court, showing the amount of the reduced share capital, its division into shares and the amount deemed to be paid up on each share, be delivered to the Registrar. In practice this minute is scheduled to the order and the Registrar regards the delivery to him of a copy of the order as a full compliance with the section. A certificate of registration is issued by him and constitutes evidence of the share capital as stated therein and that the requirements of the Act have been complied with (s 138(4)).

Notice of the delivery of the order and minute to the Registrar has to be advertised in a newspaper directed by the court usually within 21 days of delivery.

Where an order confirming a reduction of capital is made, the court has power to include a direction in the order that the words 'and reduced' be added to the company's name for a certain period and to direct that the reasons for the reduction be published together with any other information in regard thereto which the court may think expedient (s 137(2)). These powers are, however, seldom exercised today, but if the first of these directions is given, then the words 'and reduced' are deemed to be part of the company's name and must therefore be added where it appears on all nameplates, the seal, and all the documents mentioned in s 349(1).

The minute when registered becomes part of the Memorandum and takes the place of the corresponding part thereof. It must be embodied in every copy of the Memorandum subsequently issued (s 138(5)).

On a reduction of capital, a shareholder shall not be liable for any call or contribution exceeding in amount the difference between the amount of his shares as fixed by the minute and the amount paid or deemed to be paid thereon. But if any creditor entitled to object to the reduction is omitted from the list of creditors and the company cannot pay his debt, a shareholder may be called upon to pay the sum for which he would have been liable had the reduction not taken place (s 140).

The court may provide for the reduction of the company's capital when it makes an order for the purchase by the company of the shares of any member under s 5(5) or s 459 or exercises similar powers under s 54 and s 157 or s 177.

As to the redemption or purchase by a company of its own shares, see 4.11.

4.12.3 Consolidation and sub-division of shares

If authorised by its Articles, a company may by resolution either:

(1) consolidate its shares into shares of a larger amount; or
(2) sub-divide its shares into shares of a smaller amount (s 121).

In the case of a sub-division, the proportion between the amounts paid and unpaid on the reduced shares must be the same as it was on the old shares. Thus, £1 shares, 80p paid, cannot be divided into two 50p shares, one 50p paid and the other only 30p paid.

Notice must be given to the Registrar, on Form 122, within one month of the resolution authorising the alteration (s 122(1)). The type of resolution to be passed may vary with the Articles of different companies.

4.12.4 Conversion of shares into stock

If the Articles allow, a company may by resolution convert its fully paid shares into stock or reconvert stock into shares. Notice of such a conversion must be given to the Registrar within one month of the resolution on Form 122, as above (s 122(1)). The names of stockholders must be shown as such in the register of members and the annual return.

4.13 Alterations Affecting Shareholders' Rights

4.13.1 Variation of class rights

Where the company's share capital is divided into shares of different classes, great care must be taken where any variation of the Memorandum or Articles involves a variation or abrogation of the rights attaching to any class of shares eg an alteration in dividend entitlement or voting rights.

The formalities which must be complied with depend primarily upon whether the rights are attached by the Memorandum or otherwise (eg by an ordinary resolution increasing the company's capital by the creation of a new class of share) and whether the Memorandum or the Articles contain provisions for the variation of those rights:

(i) Rights otherwise than in Memorandum; provision for variation in Articles The Articles of most companies incorporated prior to 1 July 1985 include either reg 4 of the previous Table A (ie that in force prior to the implementation of the Companies (Tables A-F) Regulations 1985) or some clause similar to it. Reg 4 provided that class rights may not be varied except with the consent in writing of the holders of three-fourths of the issued shares of the class concerned, or with the sanction of an extraordinary resolution passed at a separate meeting of the holders of the shares of the class (unless, in the case of companies registered before 22 December 1980, the terms of issue otherwise provided). Table A no longer contains such a regulation presumably because sufficient protection is now provided by s 125(2) of the Act (see below). (As to extraordinary resolutions, see 6.6.2.)

Any variation must be effected in accordance with the relevant provision(s) of the Articles (s 125(2)) and subject to the following statutory provisions (so far as applicable):

(1) Section 127 which provides that the holders of not less in the aggregate than 15 per cent of the issued shares of the class purported to be varied, being persons who did not consent to or vote in favour of the variation, may apply to the court to have the variation cancelled on grounds that it would unfairly prejudice the claim of shareholders represented by the applicant(s). Where such an application is made, the variation shall have no effect unless and until it is confirmed by the court. Such an application to the court

must be made within 21 days after the date on which the consent to the variation was given or the resolution appeasing the variation was passed, as the case may be. Within 15 days after any order is made by the court, an office copy of the order must be delivered to the Registrar of Companies.

(2) Section 125(3), which provides that where the rights are to be varied in connection with the giving, variation, revocation or renewal of an authority under s 80 (see 3.1) or with a reduction of capital under s 135, the holders of three-quarters in nominal value of the issued shares of the class must consent in writing or an extraordinary resolution must be passed at a separate general meeting of the holders to sanction the variation (even if the requirements of the Articles are less stringent) and any other requirements under the company's Memorandum or Articles must be complied with.

(ii)   Rights otherwise than in Memorandum; no provision for variation in Articles   Section 125(2) provides that the rights may be varied if, but only if, the holders of three-quarters in nominal value of the issued shares of the class consent in writing or an extraordinary resolution passed at a separate general meeting of the holders of the class sanctions the variation and any other requirement (however imposed) is complied with.

The rights of dissenting shareholders under s 127 (see (*i*) above) also apply (by s 127(1)(*b*)) to variations of rights in these circumstances.

(iii) Rights   in   Memorandum;   provision   for   variation   in Memorandum   The procedure in the Memorandum must be followed and will be subject to ss 127 and s 125(3) (see (*i*) above)

(iv) Rights   in   Memorandum;   provision   for   variation   in Articles   Where the rights are to be varied in connection with the giving, variation, revocation or renewal of an authority under s 80 (see 3.1), or with a reduction in capital under s 135, s 125(3) again applies (see (i) above).

In any other case, if the provision for variation was included in the Articles at the time of incorporation the procedure set out in the relevant provision in the Articles should be followed (s 125(4)); but if the provision for variation was included in the Articles subsequent to incorporation, proceedings must be taken under s 425 to effect the variation (see 4.14).

(v) Rights in Memorandum; no provision for variation in Memorandum or Articles The rights may be varied with the agreement of all the members of the company (s 125(5)) or by a scheme of arrangement under s 425 (see 4.14).

4.13.2 Meetings of holders of shares of a class

Section 125 also contains provisions for regulating the convening of and proceedings at class meetings, whether held in compliance with the section or otherwise. The provisions relating to general meetings of the company under ss 369, 370 and 376 and under its Articles are to apply, save that the quorum for a class meeting is two persons at least holding or representing by proxy not less than one-third of the issued shares of the class, but at an adjourned meeting any one holder will form a quorum. Any one such holder present in person or by proxy may demand a poll.

4.13.3 Registration of class rights

Section 128 requires that where:

(1) shares are allotted with class rights which are not stated in the Memorandum or Articles or in any resolution or agreement which has to be filed pursuant to s 380; or
(2) class rights are varied or abrogated otherwise than by alteration of the Memorandum or Articles or by such resolution or agreement as aforesaid; or
(3) a new name or designation is assigned to a class of shares in the manner described in (2) above;

a statement in the appropriate prescribed form (Form 128(1), 128(3) . or 128(4)) must be delivered to the Registrar of Companies within one month.

The mere fact that some shares, otherwise identical with others, rank differently for dividend during the first 12 months after allotment does not involve their being treated for these purposes as a separate class.

Contravention involves the company and every officer who is in default in liability to a fine and for an additional default fine on continued contravention.

4.14 Scheme of Arrangement under s 425 between a Company and its Shareholders

Section 425 provides extremely useful machinery for making what it calls a compromise or arrangement between inter alia the company and its members or any class of them, and may be used in any case in which it is desired to vary the rights of any class of shareholder and no other means of variation is available or desired to be followed.

The proposals for the compromise or arrangement when formulated are embodied in a document generally known as a scheme of arrangement with a view to placing it before the persons affected for approval. This document is usually prepared by the company's solicitors.

Section 425 permits the court to order a meeting of the creditors or members affected by the compromise or arrangement and accordingly, following the formulation of the scheme, the next step is to apply to the court for an order directing the convening of a meeting of the class of creditors or members affected.

With every notice summoning such a meeting, there must be sent a statement explaining the effect of the proposed compromise or arrangement, and in particular stating any material interests of the directors of the company, whether as directors or as members or as creditors of the company or otherwise, and the effect thereon of the compromise or arrangement, in so far as it is different from the effect on the like interests of other persons; and in every notice summoning the meeting which is given by advertisement must be included either such a statement or a notification of the place at which and the manner in which creditors or members entitled to attend the meeting may obtain copies of the statement (s 426). In the latter case, every such creditor or member must be furnished with a copy of the statement free of charge on application therefor. It is the duty of directors to give notice to the company of such matters relating to themselves as may be necessary to enable the company to prepare the statement.

At the meeting so summoned, the scheme must be approved by a simple majority in number, such majority representing three-fourths in value of the creditors or class of creditors, or members or class of members, as the case may be, present and voting either in person or by proxy at the meeting (s 425(2)).

A petition asking the court to sanction the scheme is then presented and the result of the voting at the meeting is reported to the court. On the hearing of the petition by the judge, opponents of the scheme can attend and make their submissions to the court.

If the scheme is sanctioned by the court, to make it effective and binding on the creditors or members concerned and on the company, an office copy of the order made by the court must be delivered to the Registrar; and every copy of the Memorandum of Association of the company issued after the order has been made must have a copy of the order annexed thereto (s 425(3)).

The above procedure may be employed also where a company is being wound up, in which event the compromise or arrangement will be binding also on the liquidator and the contributories.

4.15 Compulsory Acquisition of the Shares of a Minority after a Takeover Offer

Part XIIIA of the Act (ss 428 to 430F), as substituted by the Financial Services Act 1986, relates to the position of minority shareholders after a takeover offer, ie an offer to acquire on the same terms all the shares in a company other than ones already held by the offeror. The provisions also apply to an offer in respect of the shares of any class or classes. A takeover offer may relate not just to shares which are already allotted but also to shares which are to be allotted subsequently before a particular date (eg, shares which are allotted as a result of the takeover on the exercise of options) (s 428).

If the offeror acquires (or contracts to acquire) by virtue of acceptances of the offer 90 per cent or more of the shares to which the offer relates within four months of the offer, he can, within two months after he attains 90 per cent, give a notice to the holders of the remaining shares: he is then entitled and bound to acquire the remaining shares on the same terms unless the court orders otherwise (ss 429 and 430C).

For the above purposes, shares which are at the date of the offer the subject of undertakings to accept the offer are counted as shares subject to the offer rather than as shares already held by the offeror (s 428(5)). The revision of an offer (ie, an increase in the consideration offered) is not treated as the making of a fresh offer (s 428(7)). An offer is treated as on the same terms notwithstanding certain variations arising from foreign law provided that the offer to all shareholders is of substantially equivalent value (s 428(4)).

The notice referred to above must be given in the prescribed manner and a copy of it must be sent to the company with a statutory declaration by a director of the offeror in the prescribed form stating that the conditions for the giving of the notice are satisfied (s 429(4) and (5)).

Six weeks after the date of the notice the offeror pays or transfers to the company the consideration for the remaining shares with a transfer of these shares executed on behalf of the holders by a person appointed by the offeror. The company must then register the offeror as the holder of the shares and hold the consideration on trust for the shareholders concerned. (Special rules apply where the offer includes alternative consideration eg shares in the offeror or cash.) Cash consideration and any dividends received in respect of share consideration must be paid into a separate interest-bearing bank account. If after reasonable enquiries have been made the persons entitled cannot be found and 12 years have passed, the consideration and any accrued income must be converted into cash and paid into court (s 430).

Conversely, if by acceptances of a takeover offer the offeror acquires shares which, with or without any others which he has acquired, amount to 90 per cent of the shares in the company, the holders of the remaining shares may require the offeror to acquire them on the same terms (s 430A). The offeror must give the remaining shareholders notice of this right.

Special rules apply where a takeover is made by two or more parties jointly (s 430D). An offer is treated as made to all shareholders notwithstanding that shares already held by associates of the offeror are excluded from it. An associate means:

(1) a nominee of the offeror;
(2) a holding company, subsidiary or fellow subsidiary of the offeror or a nominee of the same;
(3) bodies corporate which act in accordance with the offeror's directions or in which the offeror controls one-third or more of the voting power;
(4) a member of a 'concert party' (see 4.3.1) which includes the offeror or a nominee of the same (s 430E).

The above rules relating to compulsory transfer following a takeover also apply to securities which are convertible into or entitle the holder to subscribe for shares (eg, convertible loan stock or warrants to subscribe shares) (s 430F).

4.16 Protection of Minority Shareholders

4.16.1 Unfair prejudice

Where any member of a company (including for this purpose the personal representative(s) of a deceased member) considers that the affairs of the company are being or have been conducted in a manner unfairly prejudicial to the interests of the members of the company generally, or to the interests of some part of the members (including at least himself), or that any actual or proposed act or omission of the company (including an act or omission on its behalf) is or would be so prejudicial, he can petition the court for an order under s 459. The petitioner must satisfy the court that the company's affairs are being conducted at the time of the petition in a manner unfairly prejudicial to him *in his capacity as a member* ie as a shareholder and not, for example, as a director. Prior to the 1989 Act a petition under s 459 would have been unsuccessful if the conduct in question prejudiced *all* and not just some members of a company (eg *Re Broadhurst* [1990] BCLC 384). The 1989 Act amended this defect in s 459 by making it clear that prejudicial conduct (such as failing to call meetings of shareholders *generally*) could found an action under s 459. For other recently decided cases on the interpretation of s 459 see, for example *Re a Company (No 008699 of 1985)* [1986] PCC 296, *Re a Company (No 001761 of 1986)* [1987] BCLC 741, *Re Elingdata* [1991] BCLC 959 and *Re Nuneaton Borough Association Football Club (No 2)* [1991] BCC 44.

The Secretary of State may present a petition in the circumstances provided in s 460(1).

If the petitioner satisfies the court that the affairs of the company are being conducted as aforesaid it may make such order as it thinks fit, including (inter alia) an order regulating the conduct of the company's affairs in future, or requiring it to do or refrain from doing a particular act, or authorising proceedings to be brought in its name, or requiring the members of the company, or the company, to purchase the shares of the prejudiced members. If the company is ordered to purchase such shares, a reduction of capital may be ordered.

4.16.2 Appointment of inspectors by the Department of Trade

Under s 431, the members of a company may apply to the Department of Trade to investigate the company's affairs. Such an application must be made by 200 members or by members holding not less than one-tenth of the issued shares or (where the company has no share capital) on the application of one-fifth of the members. Such application can also be made by the company itself (s 431(2)(c)). Supporting evidence must be provided and security for costs may be required.

Secretaries should note that it is their duty to assist the Department of Trade representatives in making such investigations and to produce for them all books or documents in their custody or power. Past as well as present officers of the company may be called upon to assist in the investigation (s 434(2)).

The Department of Trade may itself appoint an inspector if there are circumstances suggesting that:

(1) the affairs of the company are being or have been conducted with intent to defraud creditors or for some other fraudulent or unlawful purpose or in a manner unfairly prejudicial to some part of the members or that any actual or proposed act or omission would be so prejudicial or that the company was formed for some fraudulent or unlawful purpose; or

(2) persons concerned with the formation of the company or the management of its affairs have been guilty of fraud, misfeasance or other misconduct towards the company or its members; or

(3) the members of the company have not been given all the information with respect to its affairs which they might reasonably expect (s 432(2)).

The above provisions apply, with certain exceptions listed in s 453(2), to bodies corporate incorporated outside Great Britain which are carrying on, or have at any time carried on, business in Great Britain (s 453(1)).

Under s 442 the Department of Trade may appoint inspectors of its own volition if it appears necessary in the public interest to investigate and report on the membership of a company or otherwise with a view to determining the true persons who are or have been financially interested in the success or failure of the company or able to control or influence its policy.

In the event of an appointment being made under this section, the Department of Trade may, in certain circumstances, direct inter alia that transfers of certain shares shall be void, that no voting rights shall be exercisable in respect of such shares, that no further shares shall be issued in right of those shares or in pursuance of any offer made to the holder thereof, and that no dividends shall be paid in respect of such shares.

The Department may also appoint inspectors if it appears that there are circumstances suggesting contravention of s 323 (see 8.9.2), s 324 (see 8.9.1), or s 328(3) (s 446).

Section 447 contains powers for the Department of Trade to require production of a company's books and papers, thus facilitating the work of the Department in relation to its powers to appoint inspectors.

4.17 Dividends

4.17.1 Profits available for dividends

Part VIII of the Act governs the amount of profits available for distribution, eg as dividend. In addition, dividends may not be paid out of share capital, share premium account (s 130) or capital redemption reserve (s 170) (see 4.11.1) and any provision of the Memorandum or Articles must be observed.

The rules of Part VIII of the Act are complex. The following are the most basic rules and there are exceptions even to these.

(1) A company's profits available for distribution are its accumulated, realised profits, so far as not previously utilised by distribution or capitalisation, less its accumulated, realised losses, so far as not previously written off in a reduction or reorganisation of capital (s 263).

(2) Realised profits mean such profits as fall to be treated as realised profits in accordance with generally accepted accounting principles (s 742(6) and Sched 4, para 91). (Thus for example, an unrealised profit on a fixed asset cannot be distributed.)

(3) A public company may pay a dividend only if:

(a) the amount of its net assets equals or exceeds the aggregate of its called-up share capital and its undistributable reserves; and

(b) payment of the dividend will not reduce those assets to less than that aggregate (s 264).

There are elaborate rules for determining by what figures taken from what accounts these questions are determined (ss 270 to 274).

A company is not bound to distribute its profits among its members in the form of dividends unless the Articles so provide, and profits are frequently used for other purposes. Thus, the directors may set aside as a reserve the whole or a portion of the profits, to make provision for future contingencies or to expand the business; and this may be done unless the Articles forbid. Such a reserve does not lose its nature as profit and may subsequently be used to pay dividends.

4.17.2 Basis of payment

Where the Articles are silent, and the relevant regulation of Table A (eg reg 104) is excluded, dividends must be divided among shareholders in proportion to the nominal value of their shares. That is however rare: usually in accordance with Table A or an express provision in the Articles they will be divisible in proportion to the amount paid up on the shares. If the Articles provide that payment is to be made 'according to the value of the shares', the nominal value should be taken as the basis of calculation (*Oakbank Oil Co v Crum* (1882) 8 App Cas 65). In addition, the respective rights of the various classes of shares, as fixed by the Memorandum or Articles, must be considered, eg the rights of the holders of preference shares. In the absence of provision to the contrary in the Memorandum or Articles, preference shares are presumed to be cumulative.

4.17.3 Declaration of dividends

The Articles usually empower the directors to declare an interim dividend but this will not become a debt due to the members until the date of payment and accordingly the declaration can be revoked at any time prior to that date.

A final dividend is normally recommended by the directors but is subject to the approval of the company in general meeting. Following the resolution of the board which recommends the dividend, warrants should be prepared by the secretary in readiness for despatch as soon as the general meeting has given its approval, unless, of course, the general meeting is likely to vary the amount declared by the board or the dividend is payable at a future date.

Variation by the company in general meeting is, however, extremely unusual, and, where Table A applies, by reg 102 the company has no power to *increase* a dividend recommended by the directors.

Reference should be made to regs 102 to 108 or the corresponding Articles.

4.17.4 Dividend warrants

Dividends do not have income tax deducted but instead carry a tax credit for the recipient. A voucher or statement (see Appendix 5) should accompany the dividend warrant (or cheque) and should state the actual dividend payment and the amount of tax credit; it should also certify that an amount of advance corporation tax equal to the tax credit will be paid to the Collector of Taxes.

With the aid of a dividend list, the correctness of the warrants may be checked before despatch and a record maintained of payments made and dividends unclaimed.

A form similar to that referred to above will be employed in the case of an interim dividend.

In the case of joint holders, the warrant is usually made payable to the first named alone, provided the Articles state that any one of such holders can give an effectual receipt (see reg 106).

4.17.5 Lost dividend warrants

If a dividend warrant is lost in transit or by the shareholder to whom it is addressed, a new warrant may be issued after it has been ascertained that the warrant has not been paid by the bank, the bank has been instructed to stop payment of the lost warrant and the shareholder has provided the company with an indemnity.

4.17.6 Dividend mandate forms

Where a shareholder desires payment of a dividend to be made to a bank or some person other than himself a dividend mandate form (see p 309) should be lodged with the company. In the case of a joint holding, such a request must be signed by all the holders.

4.18 Bonus Shares

If the Articles permit, profits may be distributed among the existing members in the form of bonus shares in the proportions in which they would share dividends, profits equivalent to the paid-up value of the shares being capitalised. Such an issue will often involve an increase of the authorised capital. A return of allotments must be made upon the issue (Form 88(2)) and, unless a mere writing up in the nominal value of their shares is involved, allotment letters or share certificates should be sent to the members who are entitled to the new shares.

Part VI of the Income and Corporation Taxes Act 1988 should be considered in relation to bonus issues of share capital.

As to the use of share premium account or capital redemption reserve for paying up bonus shares, see 3.11 and 4.11.1.

4.19 Financial Services Act 1986, Part I

4.19.1 General

Part I of the Financial Services Act 1986 (in this section 'the FSA') regulates investment business. The FSA has a substantial impact on persons engaged in the financial services industry, but can also affect those who are outside that industry. The following summarises Part I but only very briefly; it may however help the company secretary to know when he should investigate further whether a particular aspect of a company's affairs or a particular proposed transaction may be affected by the FSA. He will often need to obtain professional advice on these questions.

Many of the regulatory functions under the FSA have been delegated by the Secretary of State to The Securities and Investments Board Limited (SIB).

4.19.2 'Investments'

No-one may carry on investment business in the United Kingdom unless authorised or exempted (FSA, s 3). Before examining what constitutes investment business, one must understand the meaning of 'investments' in the Act. These comprise the following (set out in Part I of Schedule 1 to the FSA):

(1) shares and stock in the share capital of a company;

(2) debentures, debenture stock, loan stock, bonds etc;

(3) securities issued by a government or local or public authority;

(4) warrants or other instruments entitling the holder to subscribe for investments within (1), (2) or (3) above;

(5) certificates or other instruments which confer rights in respect of an investment within (1), (2), (3) or (4) above (eg, depositary receipts);

(6) units in collective investment schemes such as unit trusts;

(7) options over other investments, currency or precious metals;

(8) futures including commodity futures and currency futures

(contracts made for commercial rather then investment purposes are not included, but contracts made or traded on, eg, LIFFE are always regarded as being for investment purposes);

(9) contracts for differences (which can include, for example, some arrangements by employers to protect their employees from loss when moving house because of a change in job location);

(10) life assurance and pensions policies and annuity contracts;

(11) rights to and interests in any of the foregoing.

4.19.3 Investment business

'Investment business' means the business of engaging in one or more of the activities specified in Part II of Schedule 1 (FSA, s 1(2)). These activities are:

(12) buying, selling, subscribing for or underwriting investments or offering or agreeing to do so, either as principal or as agent;

(13) arranging deals in investments (which includes making arrangements with a view to such deals);

(14) managing, or offering or agreeing to manage, assets belonging to others which do or can consist of or comprise investments;

(15) giving, or offering or agreeing to give, investment advice;

(16) establishing, operating or winding up collective investment schemes. (The definition of such schemes in the Act is complex: it includes unit trusts but can also include many other pooling arrangements.)

4.19.4 Exclusions

Various exclusions to paras 12 to 16 above are set out in Parts III and IV of Schedule 1. They are too complicated to explain in detail here and are subject to alteration by statutory instrument. Because of their complicated nature the exclusions may not, on close examination, exclude transactions which a company might expect them to: where this is so, authorisation will be needed. The exclusions are in the following areas:

(1) dealings as principal;

(2) activities between members of a group of companies or persons involved in a joint enterprise;

(3) activities for the purposes of or in connection with a sale of goods or supply of services when the supplier's main

business is such sale or supply and not investment business activities;

(4) employees' share schemes;

(5) sale of a body corporate (other than an open-ended investment company);

(6) trustees and personal representatives;

(7) advice or arrangements in the course of a profession or non-investment business;

(8) newspapers;

(9) advice in sound, television or cable programmes.

There is also an exclusion for dealings by a person whose main business is not investment business and to whom SIB gives a permission (FSA, Sched 1, para 23): this may be of help to a company outside the financial services sector which finds itself unexpectedly caught by the legislation.

4.19.5 The need for authorisation

If a company has any involvement with investments (as defined) and engages in any of the activities set out in paras 12 to 16 above but such activities are not within any of the exclusions, then it is next necessary to consider whether the activities constitute the carrying on of a business. The answer to this question will sometimes be clear but in many cases it can be a difficult matter of judgment attended by the need to have regard to case law on analogous legislation (there is as yet no case law on the FSA). If the activities do constitute the carrying on of a business and no exemption is available, authorisation is required. The Act classifies as exempted persons the Bank of England, various exchanges and clearing houses, Lloyd's and underwriting agents at Lloyd's, listed money market institutions, certain tied agents (other than employees) of insurance offices and of unit trust managers and the holders of certain official positions. There is power to grant further exemptions by statutory instrument and such exemptions have been given to various public, international or official bodies.

Employees do not generally need to become authorised. They may carry on their employer's activities but their doing so does not constitute the carrying on of business by them: the business is their employer's. Exceptionally, a person who engages in the activity of managing the investments of an occupational pension scheme may need to become authorised even if he does not carry on business, eg, because he is an employee (FSA, s 191).

4.19.6 Carrying on investment business without authorisation

First, a person who carries on investment business without being authorised or exempted commits a criminal offence, subject to a defence of having taken all reasonable precautions and exercised all due diligence to avoid doing so (FSA, s 4).

Secondly, any agreement entered into by him which involves his carrying on investment business is unenforceable by him and money paid or property transferred to him can be recovered by the other party, unless the court in certain circumstances orders otherwise (FSA, s 5).

4.19.7 Obtaining authorisation

Under the FSA the following are authorised persons:
(1) Members of recognised self-regulating organisations (SROs). At present there are four SROs, the Financial Intermediaries, Managers and Brokers Regulatory Association (FIMBRA), the Investment Management Regulatory Organisation (IMRO), The Securities and Futures Authority (SFA) (which includes The Stock Exchange), the Life Assurance and Unit Trust Regulatory Organisation (LAUTRO).
(2) Members of recognised professional bodies (RPBs), such as the Law Society and the three Institutes of Chartered Accountants, if they are certified by their body for the purposes of investment business.
(3) Certain insurance offices, friendly societies and operators and trustees of certain overseas collective investment schemes.
(4) Persons directly authorised by SIB.
(5) Certain persons authorised in other Member States of the EEC.

4.19.8 Conduct of business by authorised persons

Chapter V of Part I of the FSA lays down various rules, or provides for SIB to make rules, as to the way in which authorised persons may conduct their businesses. The rules cover such topics as misleading statements and practices, conduct of business generally, financial resources, cancellation (or 'cooling off') periods following sales of investment products, insurance and compensation arrangements, the handling of clients' money, unsolicited calls, advertisements and the employment of prohibited persons. Since March 1990, there has been a three-tier system of regulation pursuant to Chapter 5. The first tier consists of ten rules of conduct published by SIB, which have direct application to almost all SRO members. The second tier rules are more detailed 'Core rules' which are again published by SIB, but take effect (with some modification) by incorporation in the rule books of SROs. The third and final tier comprises additional rules formulated by each SRO to accommodate the particular types of activity conducted by their members. It is not the scope of this book to explain the detailed operation of any of these rules.

Chapter 5

Transfer and Transmission of Shares

The duties described below will often be performed by a separate registrar rather than the secretary, but for simplicity it is assumed here that the secretary does them. The duties will be the same if they are undertaken by a separate registrar, who may be another employee of the company or an independent company or firm providing the services of a registrar.

Section 5.3 below describes the legal framework for the procedures which are expected to be introduced by the Stock Exchange in 1993 for the creation and transfer of uncertificated securities of listed companies. These procedures will radically alter the practical and legal steps for the transfer of shares of listed companies which have elected to participate in what will be known as TAURUS (Transfer and Automated Registration of Uncertificated Stock).

5.1 Transfer

5.1.1 General

A company's Articles may contain restrictions on transfers, for example pre-emption rights in favour of existing shareholders. Articles which prohibit the transfer of shares to an outsider if any member is willing to buy them imply a condition that shares should not be transferred to an outsider without reasonable steps having been taken to give members a chance to make an offer, and in such a case a transfer to an outsider made without the members' knowledge is invalid (*Tett v Phoenix Property & Investment Co Ltd* (1985) *Financial Times*, 10 December, CA). See also 5.1.7 and 5.1.8.

Notwithstanding anything to the contrary in the Articles, shares or debentures may be transferred only by an instrument in writing (s 183(1)), ie a verbal transfer is ineffective; but this rule does not extend to transmission by operation of law, eg on death or bankruptcy. An article providing for automatic transfer of shares on the death of a member is invalid (*Re Greene, decd, Greene v Greene* [1949] Ch 333).

With regard to the form of a transfer Articles usually state merely that transfers must be in the usual form or such other form as the directors approve (see reg 23) and that the directors may refuse to recognise a transfer relating to more than one class of share (see reg 24).

Prior to the Stock Transfer Act 1963 shares had to be transferred by a transfer executed by both transferor and transferee, each in the presence of a witness who also signed. (The transferee had to execute to signify that he agreed to become a member, as required by s 22(2).) Any additional requirements of the Articles (eg that the transfer be a deed) had to be observed: although this was rarely a requirement, transfers were usually by deed.

Fully paid registered securities of a company limited by shares are now almost always transferred by a stock transfer as permitted by the 1963 Act but the pre-1963 law continues to apply to transfers of other securities (eg partly paid shares or shares of an unlimited company, so that execution by the transferee is still necessary where transfer of the shares to him involves the possibility of liability for him). A transfer which could be effected by a stock transfer must however comply with the requirements of the 1963 Act as to execution and contents.

Where a stock transfer is not or cannot be used, material variation from the common form is necessary to justify refusal of registration (*Re Letheby & Christopher Ltd, Jones's Case* [1904] 1 Ch 815). Although both the transferor(s) and the transferee(s) must execute a transfer which is in a form other than a stock transfer, a person who is both a transferor and a transferee need execute only once.

The 1963 Act enables fully paid registered securities (including shares, stock, debentures, debenture stock, loan stock and bonds) of a company limited by shares to be transferred by a stock transfer as set out in Sched 1 to that Act or any other form which complies with the Act as to execution and contents.

The 1963 Act also provides that where a stock transfer has been executed for the purpose of a stock exchange transaction (ie a transaction on The Stock Exchange), particulars of the consideration and of the transferee may either be inserted in that stock transfer or, where a block of securities is being transferred to several transferees not in joint account, inserted in separate brokers' transfers (the 1963 Act s 1); however The Stock Exchange's Talisman system explained below has reduced the use of brokers' transfers.

The above provisions of the 1963 Act have effect notwithstanding anything to the contrary in any enactment or instrument (eg Articles of Association) relating to the transfer of the securities concerned, but nothing in s 1 affects any enactment or rule of law regulating the execution of documents by companies or other bodies corporate, or any Articles of Association regulating the execution of documents by any particular company or body corporate (1963 Act, s 2). Thus, transfers by companies and other bodies corporate can normally be executed either by the secretary and a director (or two directors) (s 36A(4)) or under their common seal but provision in a company's Articles to the effect, eg, that a transfer by that company must be executed in a particular manner must be observed.

As to the stamping of transfers, see 5.1.9. Articles can empower the directors to authorise a fee for the registration of a transfer but the practice of charging a fee has largely fallen into disuse. Listed companies are required to register transfers and other documents relating to or affecting title without payment of any fee.

After a transfer has been registered the old share certificate and the transfer form should be carefully filed and preserved unless (as is often the case) power is taken in the Articles to destroy them after a specified period (eg six years). The new share certificates must be ready for delivery within two months after the date on which the transfer is lodged with the company (time beginning to run where a transfer is by stock transfer and brokers transfer only when both have been lodged) unless the terms on which the shares were issued otherwise provide (s 185 and the 1963 Act s 2(3)(b)) or unless the transfer is to a recognised clearing house or a nominee of a recognised clearing house or of a recognised investment exchange (when no share certificate need be issued— see below under 'The Talisman system'). The Yellow Book however reduces this two month period to 14 days for listed companies and the general undertaking applicable to companies whose securities are traded on the Unlisted Securities Market does likewise for them.

5.1.2 Procedure on transfer in the simplest case

The simplest procedure for transfer occurs when in a non-market transaction (ie a transaction not made through The Stock Exchange) all the shares represented by one or more share certificates are transferred to one transferee. In such circumstances a stock transfer form is completed in full and the words in italics deleted. The form is then executed by the transferor and his agent (if any) places his stamp and the date in the box beside the transferor's signature. The form is then delivered, with the relative certificate(s), to the transferee who stamps it (see 5.1.9). The person lodging the stock transfer for registration, if different from the transferee, places his stamp in the appropriate box at the foot of the form before lodging it, accompanied by the relative certificate(s), with the company secretary for registration. If the transfer appears to be in order it is, if necessary, presented to the board of directors for authorisation or refusal of registration. If the transfer is registered, the old certificate(s) are cancelled, a new certificate sealed and issued to the transferee and entries and adjustments made in the register of transfers and register of members.

5.1.3 Certification of transfers

The more complicated procedure of certification of transfers is needed in non-market transactions where:

(1) although some of the shares represented by a certificate are transferred, others are retained, since the transferor will not be willing to part with possession of the certificate to the transferee, the transferee will if a sale is involved not be willing to part with the purchase price while the transferor retains possession of the certificate for all the shares and the company will not register the transfer unless the share certificate is delivered to it; or

(2) some of the shares represented by a certificate are transferred to one transferee and others to a second transferee, since neither transferee will be willing for the other to have possession of the certificate for all the shares and if a sale is involved neither will part with the purchase price for the shares he has bought while the transferor keeps the certificate.

In either case the secretary will be called on to certificate transfers, ie to sign certificates on transfers that the share certificates for the shares transferred have been deposited with him. The form of certificate is at the top right-hand corner of a stock transfer form. Transfers need not be stamped or dated, nor need the transferee's name be inserted, before certification.

A transfer is deemed to be certificated if it bears the words 'certificate lodged' or words to the like effect, and a certification is deemed to be made by a company if the person issuing the instrument is a person authorised to issue certificated instruments of transfer on the company's behalf, and the certification is signed by a person authorised to certificate transfers on the company's behalf or by any officer or servant either of the company or of a body corporate so authorised. Moreover, a certification is deemed to be signed by any person if it purports to be authenticated by his signature or initials (whether handwritten or not), unless it is shown that the signature or initials were placed there neither by himself nor by any person authorised to use the signature or initials for the purpose of certificating transfers on the company's behalf (s 184(3)).

The certification of a transfer by a company constitutes a representation by the company to any person acting on the faith of the certification that there have been produced to the company such documents as on the face of them show a prima facie title to the shares or debentures in the transferor named in the transfer; but they do not constitute any guarantee that the transferor has a title (s 184(1)).

A person who acts on the faith of a false certification by a company made negligently has the same right of action as if the certification had been made fraudulently (s 184(2)).

The fact that a transfer is certificated by the secretary does not imply that the directors will approve the transfer, but if the directors are unlikely to approve it, it is advisable that the secretary should inform the person lodging it. Certification by the secretary of a transfer of what purport to be fully paid shares will, however, estop the company from denying that the shares are fully paid (*Re Concessions Trust, McKay's Case* [1896] 2 Ch 757); but certification will not estop the company from challenging the title of the transferor (*Bishop v Balkis Consolidated Co Ltd* (1890) 25 QBD 512).

(*a*) *Where the transferor is transferring to one person part only of the shares represented by a certificate*   A stock transfer form is completed in full and the words in italics deleted. The form is then executed by the transferor and his agent (if any) places his stamp and the date in the box beside the transferor's signature before lodging the form and the share certificate with the company for certification of the transfer.

The share certificate is retained by the company, a non-returnable balance ticket is issued to the transferor entitling him to apply for a new certificate for the shares which are not transferred, and the stock transfer form is certified and returned to the transferor. The form is then delivered to the transferee who stamps it (see 5.1.9). The person lodging the stock transfer for registration, if different from the transferee, places his stamp in the appropriate box at the foot of the form before lodging the form for registration. The procedure thenceforward is the same as if all the shares represented by the share certificate had been transferred, except that on registration two new certificates will be issued, one to the transferee for the shares transferred, and the other to the transferor for those retained.

(b) *Where the transferor is transferring some or all of the shares represented by a certificate to more than one transferee* The procedure is practically the same as in (a) above. Separate stock transfer forms will be executed for each transferee, and each form must be certified, a non-returnable balance ticket being issued to the transferor if he is retaining some shares.

5.1.4 The Talisman system

This computerised system (taking its name from Transfer Accounting Lodgment for Investors, Stock Management for jobbers) now deals with nearly all transactions effected on The Stock Exchange in UK, Irish, South African and Australian registered company securities.

Under Talisman a special type of stock transfer form, called a 'Talisman Sold Transfer', transferring the securities to Sepon Limited, is completed. (Sepon Limited is a company owned by The Stock Exchange, the word Sepon denoting Stock Exchange Pool Nominees, and is below referred to simply as Sepon. It is designated by the Stock Exchange (Designation of Nominees) Order 1985 (SI 1985 No 806) as a nominee of the Stock Exchange for certain purposes relating to the issue of certificates.) Member Firms of The Stock Exchange trade either as agents for their clients or as principals acting on their own behalf. On a sale by a Member Firm, the certificate for the securities concerned and a Talisman Sold Transfer are sent to the company for registration. This transfers the securities into the name of Sepon. The initial sale and any subsequent sales between Stock Exchange Member Firms are settled by transferring the beneficial ownership of the securities by computerised book entry transfers within the Talisman system. However, the securities will in due course be allocated (or 'apportioned') to a bargain where the purchaser is a client of a

Member Firm; a 'Talisman Bought Transfer' from Sepon to that client is then prepared and lodged with the company for registration in the normal way. Throughout the time while the securities are registered in Sepon's name Sepon holds them as nominee for the person entitled at the time. This central pooling system saves much certification work formerly undertaken by The Stock Exchange for companies. The Talisman system also sets off the payments due to or from each Member Firm in consequence of bargains on The Stock Exchange settled through it.

A company need not issue a certificate for securities transferred to Sepon which is a 'nominee of a recognised investment exchange' (s 185) but only in favour of the ultimate purchaser.

No stamp duty is payable on a Talisman Sold Transfer (Finance Act 1976, s 127(1) and Stock Exchange (Designation of Nominees) (Stamp Duty) Order 1979 (SI 1979 No 370)). Stamp duty on Talisman Bought Transfers is collected centrally for the Inland Revenue by the Stock Exchange Centre but a company secretary is still responsible for seeing that such a transfer is properly completed as to the duty payable before he registers it.

A Talisman Sold Transfer need not specify the consideration or Sepon's address (Stock Transfer (Addition of Forms) Order 1979 (SI 1979 No 277), art 3(1)). A Talisman Bought Transfer need not be executed under hand but is sufficiently executed by Sepon if it bears a facsimile of Sepon's corporate seal, authenticated by the actual or facsimile signature of a director or the secretary of Sepon (ibid, art 3(2)).

If a Talisman Sold Transfer relates to only some of the shares represented by a share certificate a balance certificate is requested on the Talisman Sold Transfer. When the secretary registers the transfer he will issue a balance certificate in the name of the transferor. This is issued via The Stock Exchange to the transferor's broker: the shares represented thereby are never transferred into Sepon's name.

The system also includes arrangements for the settlement of claims to dividends and the like in respect of shares sold.

5.1.5 Certification of transfers by The Stock Exchange

Although the Talisman system has much reduced the amount of certification work undertaken by The Stock Exchange, The Stock Exchange Centre still certifies transfers of companies' securities arising from transactions on the Exchange in certain circumstances.

(Before the introduction of Talisman certification work arising from such transactions was mostly performed by The Stock Exchange as an alternative to certification by the company.) The Centre can certify Talisman Sold Transfers against a balance certificate requested in respect of a previous transaction provided the Talisman Sold Transfer for that previous transaction has not been despatched by the Centre to the company for registration or against a Talisman Bought Transfer provided it has not been similarly despatched.

Where a holding is passing to two or more transferees, brokers transfer forms may still be used and certified in certain circumstances. Where brokers transfers are used a stock transfer form is completed as if for a non-market transaction, save that the words in italics are left in and the lower part of the form (where details of the transferee would be inserted) is cancelled. Brokers transfers completed as to Part 1 are then certified by The Stock Exchange Centre or by the secretary (usually the former) by being produced with the stock transfer and the certificate(s). If certification is by the secretary he retains the certificate(s) for the shares concerned and the stock transfer until he receives the brokers transfers for registration. If certification is by the Centre it forwards the certificate(s) and stock transfer to the secretary. Having been certified the brokers transfers are then delivered to the buying brokers who insert particulars of the transferees in Part 2, place their stamp upon them and lodge them with the company secretary for registration in the normal way.

5.1.6 Summary of variants of Stock Exchange transactions

In the case of Stock Exchange transactions, therefore, the secretary will most often receive for registration Talisman Sold Transfers accompanied by certificate(s) and Talisman Bought Transfers, but less frequently he may receive certified Talisman Sold Transfers, ordinary stock transfers or brokers transfers. Transfers will always be accompanied by certificate(s) or certified (either by the secretary or The Stock Exchange Centre). Where transfers are certified the certificate(s) will already have been lodged with the secretary.

5.1.7 Scrutinising of transfers

All transfers should be carefully scrutinised. The form of transfer must comply with the requirements summarised above and must be properly executed.

Sometimes transfers may be executed by a person who signs

on behalf of the transferor; and in such a case the secretary must see that the power of attorney by which the authority is given is in order. Transfers of shares standing in the names of joint holders must be executed by all the holders. The secretary should check that the form is correctly dated and either sufficiently stamped (see 5.1.9) or in the case of a Talisman Bought Transfer properly completed as to the duty payable.

Where the directors have power to refuse registration of a transfer the secretary should, in appropriate cases (eg where the shares are partly paid) and if possible, make inquiries as to the status of the transferee, for transfers of shares which are not fully paid should not be allowed to bankrupts, minors or 'men of straw'.

It is also important to consider the position of the transferor, for if calls are in arrear it may be desirable to refuse the transfer until payment has been made. The Articles may also give a lien on the shares for debts due to the company, although the Yellow Book prohibits this for fully paid shares of listed companies. In particular, if there is a call or lien outstanding, the transfer should be refused if a receiving order has been made or a bankruptcy petition filed against the transferor and it is even advisable in such circumstances to delay a transfer if notice has been received of an act of bankruptcy committed by the transferor within the previous three months.

If a transfer, duly signed by a transferor, is received for registration after the death of the transferor, registration may not on that account be refused, unless probate or letters of administration have previously been registered, in which case the shares should be registered in the name of the executor or administrator.

5.1.8 Refusal to register a transfer

In the absence of contrary provisions in the Articles, a shareholder is entitled to transfer his shares to whomsoever he pleases, and even to transfer partly paid shares to a pauper on the eve of liquidation (*Parker's Case* (1867) 2 Ch App 685); but the directors may be given power to refuse to register transfers at their discretion. Table A, for example, empowers directors to refuse to register any transfer of shares which are not fully paid if they disapprove of the transferee or if the company has a lien on the shares (reg 24), and similar provisions appear in most Articles. Fully paid listed shares, however, must be free from any restriction on the right of transfer.

Where such a power to refuse to register a transfer is given, it must be exercised by the directors in good faith, in the interests of the company and not for purely personal motives, but the burden of proving lack of good faith lies upon the person disputing their decision (*Re Coalport China Co* [1895] 2 Ch 404).

Articles often give the directors power to refuse to register a transfer without giving reasons for the refusal. If such a power is exercised, the secretary should in reply to inquiries asking why the transfer has been rejected call attention to the provisions of the Articles and steadfastly refrain from giving the reasons for the rejection, for the court will not draw unfavourable inferences from such refusal but if reasons are given will consider them.

The exercise of the power requires the passing of a resolution at a board meeting, so that where one of three directors died and only one of the surviving directors objected to the person to whom the deceased director's shares had been transferred, registration was permitted as, the voting at the board meeting having been equal, no resolution refusing the transfer had been passed (*Re Hackney Pavilion* [1924] 1 Ch 276). The right to exercise the power may be lost by undue delay (*Re Swaledale Cleaners Ltd* [1968] 1 WLR 432).

If a receiving order or charging order is made, or an injunction issued against the transferor, any transfer must, of course, be refused, and if a stop notice is formally served on the company a transfer should not be registered until at least eight days after notice of its lodgment has been given to the person who issued the stop notice (see 4.7).

Notice of a refusal to register a transfer must be given to the transferee within two months after the date on which the transfer is lodged with the company (s 183(5)).

5.1.9 *Stamp duty*

Once TAURUS is introduced, stamp duty on transfers of shares, including shares in unlisted companies, will be abolished. Until then, the following will apply.

The secretary should check that transfers are properly stamped. Under s 17 of the Stamp Act 1891 any person whose office it is to enrol, register or enter in any rolls, books or records any instrument and who enters one which is not duly stamped is liable to a fine, although this has not increased in recent years from the amount of £10.

The consideration being stated on the form of transfer, it is usually easy to ascertain whether the proper duty has been paid, but if the amount of the consideration is substantially less than the market value of the shares, the secretary should ask the person lodging the transfer to obtain an adjudication of the duty by the Commissioners of Inland Revenue. The rate of duty on transfers on sale of stock or marketable securities (including a company's shares and any loan stock or debenture stock with an equity element) is 50p for every £100 or part of £100 of the consideration (Finance Act 1963, s 55(1A) as inserted by the Finance Act 1986). In any case of doubt, the stamping of the document with an adjudication stamp relieves the secretary of liability.

Under the Stamp Duty (Exempt Instruments) Regulations 1987 (SI 1987 No 516) certain kinds of transfer are exempt from stamp duty if a certificate, duly signed and specifying the category of transfer concerned, is included in, endorsed on or attached to the transfer. The following are the more important transfers to which this applies:

(1) a transfer on the retirement of a trustee or on the appointment of a new trustee;
(2) a transfer to the beneficiary named in the will of property which is the subject of a specific legacy;
(3) a transfer to the person entitled of property included in the residuary estate of a testator or in the estate of an intestate;
(4) an appropriation of property in satisfaction of various entitlements under wills or settlements;
(5) a transfer by a liquidator of property of the company in liquidation to shareholders in satisfaction of their rights;
(6) a transfer operating as a voluntary disposition inter vivos.

The following types of transfer are liable to a fixed duty of 50p if endorsed with a duly signed certificate that they are such:

(1) a transfer by way of security for a loan or re-transfer to the original transferor on repayment of a loan;
(2) certain transfers to a mere nominee of the transferor, or from a mere nominee to the person for whom he has held the property, or from one nominee to another nominee of the same beneficial owner.

Relief from stamp duty is available on certain intra-group transfers (s 42 Finance Act 1930, as amended) and corporate reconstructions and mergers (s 75 et seq, Finance Act 1986).

5.1.10 Stamp duty reserve tax

This tax, introduced by the Finance Act 1986 and called 'SDRT' for short, is a tax on transactions rather than documents and is not strictly a stamp duty. A detailed explanation of it would be outside the scope of this book. Further reference may be made to the Finance Act 1986, Part IV, as amended, the Stamp Duty Reserve Tax Regulations 1986 (SI 1986 No 1711) and *Stamp duty reserve tax: notes for guidance* published by the Inland Revenue. Moreover, SDRT will be abolished along with stamp duty upon the introduction of TAURUS. Until then, however, the following brief outline may assist.

SDRT applies, at the rate of 50p for every £100 or part of £100 of the amount or value of the consideration, where there is an agreement to transfer chargeable securities for money or money's worth. It does not apply to the initial issue of securities and does not apply if an instrument of transfer is entered into and, if chargeable to stamp duty, is duly stamped within two months of the agreement. Typical examples of circumstances where SDRT is payable are where a person:

(1) buys shares and resells them before they are transferred into his name (eg, where he buys and resells them within a stock exchange account); or

(2) buys renounceable letters of acceptance or allotment.

'Chargeable securities' includes shares in a company and also convertible loan capital which is convertible into shares.

SDRT is payable by the purchaser. It does not apply to a transaction which bears stamp duty, and SDRT may be repaid or cancelled where an instrument of transfer is duly stamped with ordinary stamp duty after the two month period. There are special exemptions for Stock Exchange market makers and broker-dealers.

SDRT is also payable, at 1.5 per cent of the value involved, where chargeable securities are converted into depositary receipts or are transferred or issued into certain clearance systems.

5.2 Transmission

5.2.1 General

Transmission of shares, which is the vesting of shares in a new holder otherwise than by execution of an instrument of transfer, occurs on the death or bankruptcy of the registered holder. As to bankruptcy see 4.8.5.

5.2.2 Transmission on death

On the death of a sole shareholder his shares vest in his personal representatives (ie his executors or administrators), who are usually the only persons to be recognised by the company as entitled to the shares and who become entitled to all dividends payable and will be liable for all sums due in respect of the shares to the extent of the deceased holder's assets.

If the shares of the company are not listed on The Stock Exchange, the secretary may first learn of the death of a member from a request for a valuation of the shares at the date of death. The secretary should write stating the price or prices at which the last transactions, at arm's length, before the date of death, were recorded.

A personal representative may either (a) allow the shares to remain registered in the name of the deceased, or (b) apply to have his own name entered as registered holder, or (c) transfer the shares (s 183(3) and reg 30). In private companies, Articles frequently include special provisions regarding the disposal of shares passing by transmission.

Whichever course is adopted, evidence of the title of the personal representative must be produced to the company. Production of a grant of probate, letters of administration or any document which is in law sufficient evidence thereof (eg, an office copy of a grant of probate or letters of administration) must be accepted as evidence of title notwithstanding anything in the Articles to the contrary (s 187). A note of the death, the name and address of the executor or administrator, and of the production should be entered in the register and on the share certificate. The Yellow Book provides that a listed company may not charge a fee for registering a death; other companies may charge such a fee if authorised by the Articles, although it is rare to do so. The secretary usually signifies that the relevant document has been produced to him by placing a rubber stamp on it with his signature or initials and the date.

If the personal representative's request for the shares to be placed in his own name is accepted, a new account should be opened in the register in his name, without reference to his representative capacity, for the fiduciary nature of his title should not appear on the register. Appendix 5 has a specimen letter of request. This need not be stamped, and is applicable only where the shares are to be placed in the name of the sole personal representative or the names of all of them where more than one. Where this course is adopted, the personal representative on registration becomes fully liable, even beyond the extent of the deceased's assets, for all sums due in respect of the shares. On such registration a new share certificate must be issued to the personal representative. The directors may refuse to comply with the request where the Articles give them power to refuse to register a transfer; but if the Articles contain no power of veto, the directors cannot refuse to register an executor as a member (*Scott v Frank F Scott (London) Ltd* [1940] Ch 794). Where the company takes power to limit the number of shareholders in a joint account, The Stock Exchange requires in the case of listed shares that up to four persons may be registered.

A personal representative has power to transfer shares notwithstanding that he is not a member of the company (s 183(3)), but unless the shares have been placed in his own name, his description on the transfer should indicate the capacity in which he signs, eg James Smith, of 1 Brown Street, London, Grocer, executor of Sam Smart. A personal representative can also notwithstanding that he is not a member institute an application to the court under s 459(1) for relief on the grounds of unfairly prejudicial conduct (s 459(2)) (see 4.16.1).

5.3 TAURUS

The methods of transfer of listed securities will be changed, commencing with a pilot scheme in mid-1993, with the introduction of a computer-based system of procedures for paperless share transactions devised by The Stock Exchange and known as TAURUS (Transfer and Automated Registration of Uncertificated Stock). Regulations have been made (the Uncertificated Securities Regulations 1992 — the 'Regulations') which provide the legal framework for the new systems, but The Stock Exchange is yet to publish its rules for their operation. Until then, no practical guidance as to how market dealings will take place can be given, but it is possible to describe some of the more significant changes which will be made to laws which are outlined elsewhere in this book.

5.3.1 General

Once The Stock Exchange has set up its TAURUS systems, a London listed company may, with its shareholders' and The Stock Exchange's permission, convert all of its ordinary shares (and/or all of its other securities or all securities of a particular class) into 'uncertificated securities' (regs 75 and 78). Whilst a company will continue to maintain a register of members, the register can be updated only at periodic intervals on instructions from designated 'controllers'. (A company must appoint at least one controller who could be its present registrars, but acting in a separate capacity.) This right on the part of a controller to direct that the register be altered is called an 'entitlement'. Entitlements are in turn held and exercised by controllers on behalf of individual 'account holders' who would under the present laws and systems correspond to the holders and transferees of shares.

As in the past, the members eligible to receive dividends and other distributions and documents, such as notices of meetings, and to vote at and attend meetings, will be determined by reference to the register maintained by the company (Sched 3). The register must be updated at least once in every period of five weeks and is likely to be updated for other events such as dividend record dates.

5.3.2 Transfers

Transfers of uncertificated securities will no longer take place by means of documents of transfer accompanied by certificates of title. Rather, title to securities will be transferred by changes to the register of members effected by means of notifications by controllers: account holders or their brokers will notify their controllers of the details of any transfers and such controllers will notify the company that the transferee's shareholding has increased and/or that the transferor's shareholding has decreased (reg 18 and Part V). The company will not, therefore, be obliged any longer to check the validity of documents of transfer or to match transferor with transferee (save in the case of special procedures applicable to off-market transfers).

As mentioned above, The Stock Exchange has yet to formulate its practical procedures inter alia for market dealings within this framework.

5.3.3 Certificates

As the name suggests, a company with uncertificated securities will no longer need to issue certificates in respect of those securities and certificates will cease to be prima facie evidence of a member's entitlement to the securities (reg 48). Instead, the register of members maintained by the company will be prima facie evidence that the persons named in it have title to the securities registered against their names (reg 17). The record of account holders maintained by a controller will also be prima facie evidence that entitlements recorded as being held for a person are in fact held for that person (reg 28).

5.3.4 Disclosure of interests in securities

The 'entitlements' of a controller will not be regarded as an interest in securities for the purposes of Part IV of the Act but the interests of account holders in 'entitlements' will.

5.3.5 Stamp Duty

Once TAURUS is introduced, stamp duty on transfers of shares will be abolished.

5.3.6 Example

To summarise the effect of the regulations by example:

Exco has 100,000 shares in issue which it wishes to convert into uncertificated securities. It has 50 shareholders. Exco appoints two controllers (Controller 'A' and Controller 'B') having initially 50,000 entitlements each. Controller A has 20 account holders (including Mr Smith) and Controller B has 30 account holders (including Mr Jones).

Mr Jones sells 100 of his shares and Mr Smith buys 100 shares. Mr Jones is under an obligation to notify Controller B that his shareholding has decreased by 100 shares and Mr Smith will notify Controller A that his shareholding has increased. Controllers A and B will notify Exco that Controller B has 100 entitlements fewer than it previously had, and Controller A will notify an increase of 100 entitlements. This will be noted immediately in Exco's record of entitlements. Controller A will also notify the company that Mr Smith's shareholding has increased by 100 and Controller B will notify the company that Mr Jones' shareholding has decreased by 100. At the next update of the register, Mr Smith will be registered as holding an additional 100 shares and Mr Jones' registered shareholding will be decreased by 100.

Chapter 6

Meetings

6.1 General

As a general rule a valid meeting of a company cannot be held unless the meeting was summoned by the proper summoning authority, and this proper authority is the board of directors (*Re Wyoming State Syndicate* [1901] 2 Ch 431). In other words, a meeting summoned by some of the members or some of the directors without the sanction of the board (or ratification by the board prior to the meeting) is not a properly constituted meeting and any decisions it may make will not bind the company. The first step to be taken towards the effective summoning of a meeting is, therefore, to obtain from the board of directors authority to summon the meeting. This should be done by placing a proposal for the summoning of the meeting before a properly constituted meeting of directors (see 6.9).

The general principle stated above is subject to the following modifications:

(1) the directors must convene an extraordinary general meeting on the requisition either of members holding at least one-tenth of paid-up capital carrying voting rights (s 368—see 6.3) or of an auditor whose notice of resignation contains a statement of circumstances which he considers should be brought to the notice of members or creditors of the company (s 392A).

(2) if a public company's net assets are half or less of its called-up share capital the directors must within 28 days of the earliest day on which any of them knows this convene an extraordinary general meeting for a date not less than 56 days from that day to consider whether any, and if so what, measures should be taken to deal with the situation (s 142).

(3) if the Articles do not make other provision in that behalf, a valid meeting may be summoned by any two or more

members holding not less than one-tenth of the issued share capital or if the company does not have a share capital, not less than five per cent in number of the members of the company may call a meeting (s 370).

(4) where Table A applies, if there are not within the United Kingdom sufficient directors to call a general meeting, any director or member may call a general meeting (reg 37).

(5) if the annual general meeting is not held within the prescribed period specified by s 366 (unless an election has been made pursuant to s 366A — see 6.2.1), the Department of Trade may call or direct the calling of the meeting on the application of any member (s 367).

(6) if for any reason it is impracticable to call a meeting or to conduct it in the manner prescribed by the Articles or the Act, the court may give directions (s 371).

6.2 Annual General Meetings

6.2.1 General

Every company must hold an annual general meeting in each year unless it is a private company which has made an election under s 366A as described (in 6.10) below; but the first of these meetings need not be held in the year in which the company is incorporated or in the following year, provided that it is held within 18 months after the date of incorporation (s 366). If, therefore, a company was incorporated on 1 December 1987, no meeting need be held in 1987 or in 1988, but one must be held not later than 31 May 1989. Not more than 15 months may elapse between two consecutive annual general meetings (ibid) and a company listed on The Stock Exchange is required to issue its report and accounts, which will normally be circulated with the notice of annual general meeting, within six months of the end of the relevant financial period (section 5, Chapter 1 of the Yellow Book).

If default is made in complying with the statutory requirements, any member of the company may apply to the Department of Trade, which may direct the meeting to be called. In this event, subject to any directions by the Department, the meeting, if not held in the year in which it should have been held, will not be deemed to be the annual general meeting for the year in which it is held, unless a resolution that it shall be so treated is passed by the meeting (s 367(4)). A copy of any such resolution must be filed within 15 days.

A private company may, by 'elective resolution' in accordance with s 379A, dispense with the holding of annual general meetings (s 366A(1)). However, a member may, within three months before the end of any year, require an annual general meeting to be held (s 366A(3)). Such requisition will not affect the election's applicability to any subsequent year. For a description of the so-called 'Elective Régime' see 6.10 below.

6.2.2 Ordinary business of meeting

The 'ordinary' business of an annual general meeting may be set out in a company's Articles and normally includes:

(1) to receive or consider and adopt the accounts, the directors' report and the auditors' report on the accounts. This item of business is often described as considering, adopting or approving the accounts although s 241(1) (which a company can disapply by elective resolution pursuant to s 252) merely requires the directors to lay the accounts before the company in general meeting and does not require them to be adopted or approved or even considered. The accounts laid by the directors are still the company's statutory accounts even if the company in general meeting votes not to approve them. The laying of the accounts is usually done at the annual general meeting, but it can be done at an extraordinary general meeting and may have to be as s 244 generally requires the accounts to be laid before the company in general meeting within seven months if it is a public company, or within ten months if it is a private company, of the end of the relevant accounting reference period.

(2) to declare a dividend. This is usually done in general meeting because the Articles normally provide that dividends, apart from interim dividends, must be declared in general meeting (see reg 102). This item is not an obligatory part of the business of an annual general meeting and may be done at an extraordinary general meeting.

(3) to elect or re-elect directors. This item is usually included in the business of an annual general meeting because the Articles often provide that some of the directors shall retire at each annual general meeting and that the company may

then re-elect them or elect new directors (see regs 73 and 74).

(4) to appoint auditors. At each general meeting at which accounts are laid in accordance with s 241, auditors must be appointed to hold office from the conclusion of that meeting until the conclusion of the next such general meeting (s 384(1)). Again, a private company may pass an elective resolution to dispense with the obligation to appoint auditors annually (s 386).

(5) to fix the auditors' remuneration or determine the manner in which it shall be fixed. This must be done in general meeting unless the company is a private company which has dispensed with the laying of accounts (s 385). Often the general meeting merely resolves that the auditors' remuneration shall be fixed by the directors.

A specimen notice convening an annual general meeting will be found in Appendix 5.

It should be noted that Table A no longer includes a provision stating what constitutes the ordinary business of an annual general meeting and company secretaries may wish to adopt an article similar to reg 52 of the Table A incorporated in the Companies Act 1948.

6.2.3 Special business of meeting

Special business (ie any business other than ordinary business falling to be dealt with at the annual general meeting) may also be conducted. The Articles will normally require such business to be stated as such in the notice of meeting. As to special notice, see 6.4.3.

6.2.4 Procedure at meeting

Typical procedure at an annual general meeting would therefore be as follows:

(1) the secretary may read the notice convening the meeting (see Appendix 5), but provided no-one objects this notice is usually taken as read.

(2) the chairman may make a statement supplementing the directors' report.

(3) the adoption of the directors' and auditors' reports and the accounts is proposed and the chairman invites and answers questions.

(4) the declaration of the dividend recommended by the directors is proposed.

(5) directors are appointed or reappointed.

(6) auditors are appointed or reappointed (see 9.2).

(7) special business mentioned in the notice is transacted.

(8) the chairman declares the meeting closed.

The register of directors' holdings (see 8.9.1) must be produced at the beginning of the annual general meeting and must remain open and accessible to any person attending the meeting (Sched 13, Part IV, para 29).

6.3 Extraordinary General Meetings

The directors are invariably empowered by the Articles to convene an extraordinary general meeting of the company whenever they think fit.

Such a meeting will be summoned in the same manner as an annual general meeting but the period of notice will depend on the type of resolution to be passed (see 6.4.2).

Section 368, however, provides that directors must convene an extraordinary meeting if so required by the holders of not less than one-tenth of such of the paid-up capital of the company as carries the right of voting, or, where there is no share capital, by members representing not less than one-tenth of the voting rights. If the directors do not proceed to convene a meeting within 21 days of receipt of a requisition (such meeting to be held within 28 days of the notice convening it), the requisitionists may themselves convene the meeting.

A requisition under s 368 must be in writing signed by the requisitionists and must state the objects of the meeting. It may consist of one document signed by all the requisitionists or of several similar documents signed by one or more of them, and must be deposited at the company's registered office.

Any reasonable expenses of the requisitionists are repayable by the company which may retain sums so repaid out of any fees or other remuneration due or to become due to the directors who were at fault, but no other penalty is imposed on directors who fail to convene a meeting when required by requisition.

As to the requisitioning of an extraordinary general meeting by a resigning auditor pursuant to s 391, see 9.5.

6.4 Notice

6.4.1 Persons entitled to receive notice

Care must be taken to give notice of a meeting to all persons entitled to receive such notice, for failure to do this may render the meeting invalid; though if all persons entitled to attend do so and unanimously waive the irregularity, the failure to give the necessary notice can be overcome (*Re Express Engineering Works Ltd* [1920] 1 Ch 466 and see further 6.6.3); and see also reg 39 and *Re West Canadian Collieries Ltd* [1962] Ch 370 and *Musselwhite v Musselwhite (CH) & Son Ltd* [1962] Ch 964.

The basic principle is that every member of the company is entitled to notice of a meeting, but the Articles may take away this basic right from certain classes of members, eg from holders of preference shares in certain circumstances, or from holders of shares on which calls have not been paid, or from members who have given no address within the United Kingdom.

Notice of all general meetings must be given to the company's auditors (s 390(1)).

Regulation 38 provides that notice shall be given to all the members, all persons entitled to a share by the death or bankruptcy of a member, the directors and the auditors. Regulations 112 and 116 contain exceptions: for example, in the case of joint holders of a share notice shall be given to the joint holder whose name stands first in the register of members in respect of the joint holding and notice so given shall be sufficient notice to all the joint holders. A member whose registered address is outside the United Kingdom and who gives to the company an address in the United Kingdom at which notices may be given to him shall be entitled to have notices given to him at that address, but otherwise such a member is not entitled to be sent notices.

In the case of a meeting at which the company's objects are to be altered, notice must be given to certain holders of debentures (see 1.3.3).

6.4.2 Period of notice

See 6.6.3 below in relation to short notice. In the absence of the special circumstances described there, the following applies:

(1) In the case of an *annual general meeting*, not less than 21 days' notice in writing must be given; and this is so even where

the Articles purport to allow a shorter period (s 369(1)). Regulation 38 prescribes 21 days' notice in writing at the least. An adjourned meeting may be summoned by a lesser period of notice, however, if the Articles so provide, and in any case if all the persons entitled to attend and vote at the meeting so agree, the meeting can be held even where less than 21 days' notice has been given (s 369(3)). This agreement need not be obtained at the meeting, so that if, for any reason, it is desired to summon an annual general meeting within 21 days, this can be done, provided that all persons entitled to attend and vote agree in advance.

(2) In the case of *meetings other than the annual general meeting*, not less than 14 days' notice in writing is necessary, except in the case of an unlimited company, when seven days' notice will suffice (s 369(1)), or of a meeting at which a special resolution is to be passed, when 21 days' notice is needed (s 378(2)). By agreement of a majority in number of members having the right to attend and vote, being a majority holding not less than 95 per cent in nominal value of shares giving the right to attend and vote, a valid meeting (not being an annual general meeting) can be summoned by a lesser period of notice (s 369(3) and (4) and reg 38). Shareholders of a private company can elect that this percentage be reduced to 90 per cent (see 6.10.3 below);

(3) In construing the above rules, both the day on which the notice is served or deemed to be served, and the day on which the meeting is held will usually be excluded from the period required (see for example reg 38 which requires 21 days' *clear* notice). Where Table A applies, if notice is posted to members on the first day of a month by first class post, the first, second and third days of that month must be excluded since Table A provides that notice shall be deemed to be effected 48 hours after it is posted (reg 115). The fourth day of the month is, therefore, the first of the 21 days' notice required for summoning an annual general meeting. The 24th is the last of the 21 days; and, since the day on which the meeting is to be held must also be excluded, the meeting cannot properly be held before the 25th.

(4) The periods of 21 and 14 days specified in s 369 are statutory minimum periods. Articles may require longer periods of notice, but cannot authorise shorter periods.

6.4.3 Special notice

'Special notice' is required for a resolution for (i) filling a casual vacancy in the office of auditor or reappointing an auditor appointed by the directors to fill a casual vacancy (s 388); (ii) the removal of a director or the appointment at the same meeting of a new director instead of the one removed (s 303(2), see 8.5); and the appointment or approval of the appointment of a director who is over the age limit (s 293(5), see 8.4).

Notice of the intention to move such a resolution must be given *to* the company not less than 28 days before the meeting at which it is to be moved. But if, after such notice is given, a meeting is held within 28 days, the notice is deemed to have been properly given (s 379). This latter provision prevents the directors thwarting a member who gives special notice of a resolution by holding a meeting within 28 days of the special notice being given.

Notice of the resolution must be given by the company at the same time and in the same manner as the notice of the meeting; but if this is not practicable the notice may be given by newspaper advertisement or in any other mode allowed by the Articles not less than 21 days before the meeting (s 379(2)).

Provided that special notice is given the meeting itself can be held at short notice.

6.4.4 Contents of notice

The Articles will usually contain certain provisions as to the contents of the notice. Under reg 38 the notice must specify the time and place for the meeting and the general nature of the business to be transacted and, in the case of an annual general meeting, must specify the meeting as such. Sufficient detail must be given to enable members to determine whether or not it is desirable for them to attend.

In addition, the following detailed information must be given:

(1) in the case of an annual general meeting, the notice must state specifically that the meeting is to be the annual general meeting (s 366(1)).

(2) if extraordinary or special resolutions are to be passed, the notice must state specifically that they are to be proposed as extraordinary or special resolutions (s 378). Such resolutions should be set out in full.

(3) if the company has a share capital, the notice must state with reasonable prominence that a member entitled to attend and vote is entitled to appoint a proxy or, where that is allowed (see s 372(3)), one or more proxies to attend and

vote instead of him, and that a proxy need not also be a member of the company (s 372(1)).

In drafting notices, it is always wise to err on the side of caution and to give rather more than less information than may be absolutely necessary, for the inadequacy of the notice may invalidate the proceedings at the meeting. Thus, notice of intention to alter the company's Articles should always state the nature of the contemplated alterations (*Normandy v Ind Coope & Co Ltd* [1908] 1 Ch 84); a notice of intention to increase capital must specify the amount of the proposed increase (*MacConnell v Prill (E) & Co Ltd* [1916] 2 Ch 57). A notice 'to elect directors' is sufficient notice to permit the election of directors up to the maximum permitted by the Articles (*Choppington Collieries Ltd v Johnson* [1944] 1 All ER 762) but is not good practice. Any interests of directors must be clearly disclosed (*Kaye v Croydon Tramways Co Ltd* [1898] 1 Ch 358).

In the case of listed companies, proofs of all notices of meetings, circulars (other than Class 1 circulars), proxy forms and other documents to be sent to shareholders must be submitted to the Quotations Department of The Stock Exchange (except for the annual accounts and the notice convening the annual general meeting if only routine business is to be conducted) and copies submitted when issued.

6.4.5 Members' notices and statements

Although, in general, it is for the directors to determine what business is to be put before a meeting, the members of a company have power to require the directors to give notice of certain resolutions which they desire to have put to the *annual general meeting*.

The members who desire to exercise this right must deposit at the company's registered office a requisition signed by the requisitionists, or two or more copies which between them contain the signatures of all the requisitionists. This requisition must be deposited not less than six weeks before the meeting; and with it must be deposited or tendered a sum reasonably sufficient to meet the company's expenses in giving effect to it (although the company may subsequently resolve in general meeting to bear these expenses itself). The requisition must be made by members who have not less than one-twentieth of the total voting rights of all the members having at the date of the requisition the right to vote at the meeting, or by not less than 100 members holding shares in the company on which there has been paid up an average sum, per member, of not less than £100 (ss 376 and 377).

On receiving such a requisition, the company must give notice of the desired resolution to members of the company entitled to have notice of the meeting by serving them with a copy of the resolution in any manner permitted for service of notice of the meeting, and in the same manner and, as far as practicable, at the same time as notice of the meeting; but, where it is not practicable to serve the notice at the same time as the notice of the meeting, it must be served as soon as practicable thereafter.

The requirement that the requisition must be deposited with the company not less than six weeks before the meeting might give rise to the possibility that its effect might be avoided by summoning a meeting to be held within six weeks of the deposit; but s 377(2) provides that if, after a copy of a requisition is received, an annual general meeting is called for a date six weeks or less after the copy has been deposited, the copy shall be deemed to have been properly deposited for the purposes of that meeting.

Notice of the desired resolution must be given also to members not entitled to notice of the meeting by giving notice of the general effect of the resolution in any manner permitted for giving such members notice of meetings of the company (s 376(3) and (4)).

In addition to requisitioning notices of resolutions to be put before the annual general meeting, members may require the company to circulate to members entitled to have notice of *any general meeting* a statement of not more than 1,000 words with respect to the matter referred to in any proposed resolution or the business to be dealt with at the meeting. The requisition for this purpose must be deposited in the same manner as that for a notice and must be made by the same number of members; and the statement must be circulated by the company in the same manner in which notice of a requisitioned resolution is served, except that it need not be notified to members who are not entitled to notice of the meeting. But the deposit of the requisition must be made at least one week instead of six weeks before the meeting (s 377(1)). The company is not bound to circulate a statement which the court is satisfied is designed to obtain 'needless publicity for defamatory matter' (s 377(3)).

6.5 Proceedings at Meetings

6.5.1 Proxies

Every member of a company having a share capital who is entitled to attend and vote at meetings is entitled to appoint a person, not necessarily a member of the company, as his proxy to attend and vote instead of him (s 372(1)); any clause in the Articles purporting to take away this right is void. Unless the Articles otherwise provide, a member of a public company (but not of a private company in the absence of provision in the Articles) may appoint two or more proxies (by implication from s 372(2)(b)). In the case of a private company a proxy appointed to attend and vote instead of a member has the same right as the member to speak at the meeting, notwithstanding anything to the contrary in the Articles (s 372(1)). But a public company proxy may not speak unless authorised by the Articles. A proxy is entitled to vote only on a poll (see 6.5.5) unless the Articles provide otherwise. As to representatives of bodies corporate which hold shares, see 4.8.1. A proxy may be (i) special, appointing a person to vote (normally as the appointor directs in the proxy) on the specific resolution(s) set out in the notice of the meeting, or (ii) general, appointing a person to vote as he thinks fit on all business coming before the meeting. Proxies can authorise a person to attend a single meeting, a number of meetings or any meetings held while the proxy remains in force. Proxies do not now have to be stamped even if they are for more than one meeting.

The form of proxy will normally be regulated by the Articles (see eg regs 60 and 61): see also Appendix 5 for a specimen form.

The Articles may state that proxies to be used at a meeting must be deposited at the registered office of the company or some other place a certain period before the meeting (see, eg, reg 62); but any provision in the Articles which purports to require a proxy or any other document necessary to show the validity of the appointment to be deposited more than 48 hours before the meeting or adjourned meeting is void (s 372(5)) and the period prescribed by Articles is normally 48 hours, although occasionally a shorter period is found.

Where the Articles contain such a requirement for the deposit of proxies before the meeting, and the meeting is adjourned, the question whether a proxy deposited after the first holding of the meeting, but not less than the requisite period before it reassembles after adjournment, can be used is a question of construction. If the Articles require the proxy to be deposited not less than 48 hours before 'the meeting or any adjournment thereof', the proxy can be used at the adjournment; but if the Articles require the deposit to be made not less than 48 hours before 'the meeting', a proxy deposited after the first holding of the meeting cannot be used at the adjournment (*McLaren v Thomson* [1917] 2 Ch 261). A misprint or other palpable mistake in a proxy does not entitle a company to reject the proxy (*Oliver v Dalgleish* [1963] 1 WLR 1274).

The Articles may authorise the directors to send out with notices of meetings proxy forms with or without the names of suggested donees inserted therein; and, even in the absence of specific power in the Articles, the directors may do this if they believe it to be in the interests of the company (*Peel v LNWR* [1907] 1 Ch 5). But if invitations in this or any other form to appoint as proxy a person or one of a number of persons are issued at the company's expense they must be issued to all, and not some only, of the members entitled to be sent notice of and to vote at the meeting by proxy: this rule does not however prevent the issue to a member at his request in writing of a form of appointment naming a proxy or a list of persons willing to act as proxies, if the form or list is available on request in writing to every member entitled to vote by proxy (s 372(6)). Companies whose securities are listed on The Stock Exchange are required to send out two-way proxy forms to shareholders and debenture holders entitled to attend and vote in the case of all resolutions other than merely procedural resolutions (section 5, chapter 2, para 36 of the Yellow Book). A proxy can cast in favour of a resolution the votes of shareholders who do not indicate how their votes should be cast (*Oliver v Dalgleish* [1963] 1 WLR 1274). A proxy form subject to The Stock Exchange's requirements must state that if it is returned without an indication as to how the proxy shall vote on a particular matter the proxy will exercise his discretion as to whether he votes and if so how. Such proxy forms must state that a shareholder is entitled to appoint a proxy of his own choice and must provide a space for the name of such a proxy.

A proxy may usually be withdrawn or revoked by the donor at any time before the donee has cast his vote (but see *Holman v Clegg* (1957) 101 SJ 216). It may be revoked by the donor attending the meeting in person or by depositing at the registered office of the company a written revocation (reg 63), although some Articles provide that a vote given in accordance with a proxy shall be valid notwithstanding revocation provided that no notice of such revocation shall have been received at the registered office, say, one hour before the meeting. If the donor attends the meeting in person, his vote must be accepted even if the Articles state that a proxy shall be revocable only by the deposit of a written revocation (*Cousins v International Brick Co Ltd* [1931] 2 Ch 90).

6.5.2 The quorum

Even where a meeting has been properly summoned, its activities may be ineffective if, when it assembles, it is not properly constituted.

In the first place, its acts can have no effect unless the necessary *quorum* is present. The number of members required to be present in order to constitute a quorum is usually fixed by the Articles. Table A requires the presence of two persons entitled to vote on the relevant business, each being a member or a proxy for a member or a representative of a corporation (reg 40). If no version of Table A applies and the Articles do not provide otherwise, the quorum is two members (s 370(4)) or, in the case of single member private companies, one member. Proxies are not members personally present, unless they hold shares in their own right; but the representative of another body corporate which is a shareholder is a member personally present. Articles often provide that the quorum must be present 'at the time when the meeting proceeds to business'. If this or similar wording applies, a reduction in numbers below a quorum before a vote is taken will not invalidate the resolution (*Re Hartley Baird Ltd* [1955] Ch 143). Otherwise however a meeting cannot continue if members withdraw leaving no quorum (*Henderson v Louttit* [1894] 21 Rettie (Ct of Sess) 674).

Table A provides that if no quorum is present within half an hour of the time fixed for a meeting, or if during a meeting such a quorum ceases to be present, it shall, if convened on the requisition of members, be dissolved, but otherwise shall stand adjourned to the same day in the next week and at the same time and place or to such time and place as the directors determine (reg 41). It has been held as a general rule that a single person cannot constitute a meeting (see eg *Re London Flats* [1969] 1 WLR 711 and *Jarvis Motors (Harrow) Ltd v Carabott* [1964] 1 WLR 1101) although this rule may no longer be good law (see below). In particular, the following exceptions apply:

(1) it has been held that one member can constitute a class meeting (*East v Bennett Bros Ltd* [1911] 1 Ch 163).

(2) A meeting called by the Department of Trade or the court may, if so directed, consist of one person only (ss 367(2) and 371(2)).

(3) Section 2 of the Companies (Single Member Private Limited Companies) Regulations 1992 (SI 1992 No 1699) provides that any enactment or rule of law will be modified as necessary to accommodate single member companies. Accordingly, those companies may clearly have meetings of the one member and provisions to the contrary in the Articles (eg reg 40 of Table A) are deemed modified accordingly. Arguably the conceptual change underlying this provision also challenges the logic of the cases cited above so as to permit (should the Articles also permit) such meetings in other cases.

The court may order a meeting to be held if the quorum provisions would give the minority shareholders a vote disproportionate to their shareholding (*Re HR Paul & Son Ltd* (1973) 118 SJ 166).

6.5.3 *The chairman of a meeting*

Where the Articles contain provisions for the appointment of a chairman of a meeting, they must be complied with if the meeting is to be properly constituted (see eg regs 42 and 43). If the Articles do not contain any provisions as to who shall act as a chairman of a meeting and if no version of Table A applies, any member elected by the members present may be the chairman (s 370(5)); and, where the chairman stops or improperly adjourns a meeting contrary to the wishes of a majority, the meeting may elect a new chairman in his place for the purpose of continuing the proceedings (*National Dwellings Society v Sykes* [1894] 3 Ch 159).

It is the duty of the chairman to preserve order and to see that the proceedings are properly conducted in accordance with the Act and the Articles and otherwise in accordance with the wishes of the meeting. He will (subject to any resolution passed by the meeting) decide all incidental questions arising at the meeting which require immediate decision, and in particular ascertain the sense of the meeting on any resolution coming before it (*Second Consolidated Trust Ltd v Ceylon AT & R Estates Ltd* [1943] 2 All ER 567). He may, when he considers that a matter has been discussed sufficiently, move that the question be now put (*Wall v London & Northern Assets Corporation* [1898] 2 Ch 469).

6.5.4 Adjourned meetings

Where Table A (reg 45) applies, the meeting can be adjourned only with the consent of the members present and must be adjourned if they so decide. In the absence of such a regulation, any meeting may be adjourned at the discretion of the chairman, but in exercising this discretion the chairman must act in good faith (see *John v Rees* [1970] Ch 345—adjournment in case of disorder). The chairman should adjourn only for the purpose of enabling the meeting to conduct its business more efficiently. Unless the Articles provide to the contrary, the chairman is not bound to adjourn a meeting if he considers it unnecessary.

Where a meeting is adjourned, the Articles must be consulted to ascertain whether or not notice of the adjourned meeting must be given. Table A requires seven clear days' notice to be given only where the meeting is adjourned for 14 days or more (reg 45). If the Articles are silent on the point, no notice is necessary (*Kerr v Wilkie* (1860) 1 LT 501). Where the Articles prescribe that notice shall be given, the notice need not state the purpose for which the original meeting was called unless the Articles require this (as reg 45 does) (*Scadding v Lorant* (1851) 3 HL Cas 418).

An adjourned meeting is a continuation of the original meeting, and proxies given for the original meeting may be used at the adjournment, unless they are revoked before they are used. As to whether proxies filed between the original and the adjourned meeting can be used, see 6.5.1. As to whether a meeting which breaks up is adjourned, see *Jackson v Hamlyn* [1953] Ch 577.

A resolution passed at an adjourned meeting is deemed to have been passed on the date on which it is, in fact, passed (s 381).

6.5.5 Persons entitled to vote

The Articles will usually determine who shall and who shall not be entitled to attend and vote at meetings of the company (see eg *Bushell v Faith* [1970] AC 1099); but, if they contain no other provision, in the case of a company originally having a share capital every member has one vote in respect of each share or each £10 of stock he holds and in any other case every member has one vote (s 370(6)). Where Table A applies, the personal representative of a deceased shareholder who has not had himself registered as the holder of the shares (see 5.2) may not vote at a meeting (reg 31), though he is entitled to receive notice of the meeting (reg 116). In addition, no member may vote unless all calls in respect of his shares have been paid (reg 57). The receiver, committee or curator bonis of a member of unsound mind may vote provided that evidence of the authority of the person claiming an entitlement to vote is deposited at the registered office, or such other place as the Articles specify for the deposit of forms of proxy, at least 48 hours before the meeting or adjourned meeting (reg 56).

Articles usually provide that in the case of joint holders the vote of the senior who tenders a vote, in person or by proxy, shall be accepted to the exclusion of the others, seniority being determined by the order of the holders' names in the register (reg 55).

The chairman does not have a casting vote unless the Articles give him one (see reg 50).

Generally a subsidiary may not exercise voting rights in respect of shares which it holds in its holding company (see s 23 and 4.8.1).

Care should be taken to ensure that only those entitled to attend and vote do so and for this reason officials of the company should be posted at the door of the meeting room. Those attending should be asked their names and these should be checked against the register of members and a list of persons appointed as proxies. It is usual for members and proxies attending a general meeting to be asked to sign their names in a book kept for the purpose.

6.5.6 *Voting by show of hands*

Primarily the voting on a resolution is by show of hands, in which event each person entitled to vote has one vote irrespective of the number of shares he may hold. A proxy may not vote on a show of hands unless he is a member in his own right or the Articles state that he may (s 372(2)(c)) (and see reg 54).

6.5.7 *Voting by poll*

Except on the question of the election of a chairman or an adjournment of the meeting, the members of a company have a statutory right to demand that a poll be taken (s 373(1)). This right may be exercised after a vote by show of hands has been taken (and the Articles may permit a demand for a poll before a vote by show of hands—reg 46 and *Holmes v Keyes* [1959] Ch 199). Any provision in the Articles which purports to take away this right to demand a poll is void.

The demand for a poll may be made:

(1) by at least five members having the right to vote at the meeting; or

(2) by a member or members representing at least one-tenth of the total voting rights of all the members having the right to vote at the meeting; or

(3) by a member or members holding shares in the company conferring a right to vote at the meeting, being shares on which an aggregate sum has been paid up equal to at least one-tenth of the total sum paid up on all the shares conferring that right (s 373(1)(b)).

If the Articles provide that a poll may be demanded by a smaller proportion of the members than those listed above, a demand made by such smaller proportion is effective; but no larger proportion may be required by the Articles. Where Table A applies, a poll may be demanded by the chairman or by two members present in person or by proxy (reg 46).

A proxy for a member has the same right as the member to join in a demand for a poll (s 373(2)).

The Articles may provide for the manner in which the poll shall be taken. Table A provides that it shall be taken in such manner as the chairman directs (reg 49) and that except on the election of a chairman or a question of adjournment (on which the poll must be taken immediately) the chairman may direct at what time the poll shall be taken (reg 51), ie forthwith, later on the same day or on another day, provided it is not more than 30 days after the poll is demanded. Unless the Articles otherwise provide, however, the voters must attend and record their votes and the chairman cannot direct that voting cards shall be sent out to them (*McMillan v Le Roi Mining Co Ltd* [1906] 1 Ch 331). Where a future day for the poll is fixed, the chairman should specify the hours during which voting shall take place. If this is not done, the lists cannot be closed until midnight, unless all possible votes are previously recorded.

On a poll a member entitled to more than one vote need not use all his votes or cast all the votes he uses in the same way (s 374).

The secretary should make preparations for a poll. Forms of proxy which have been deposited should be scrutinised carefully and a list of members and their proxies made out in a form such as the following:

Name of member	Name of proxy	No of shares	Remarks	Votes	
				For	Against

It is the practice to require the voting cards to express the number of shares held by the voter or the person or persons on whose behalf he is acting as proxy. Scrutineers should be appointed to watch the counting of the votes and in particular to ensure that votes of a member lodging a valid proxy who attends and votes in person are not counted twice.

6.6 Resolutions

The cases in which the different types of resolution are required are summarised in Appendix 4.

6.6.1 Ordinary resolutions

Except where the Act or the Memorandum or Articles require something to be done by extraordinary resolution or by special resolution, a meeting may express its will by ordinary resolution. This is a resolution in favour of which a majority of members entitled to vote and voting either in person or by proxy cast their votes. If the voting is by show of hands, a majority in number of those present in person and voting will suffice; but where a poll has been demanded the votes to which shareholders are entitled must be established from the Articles (normally one vote per share).

6.6.2 Extraordinary and special resolutions

A resolution is an *extraordinary* resolution when it has been passed by a majority of not less than three-fourths of such members as (being entitled so to do) vote in person or, where proxies are allowed, by proxy at a general meeting of which notice specifying the intention to propose the resolution as an extraordinary resolution has been duly given (s 378(1)).

A resolution is a *special* resolution when it has been passed by such majority as is required for the passing of an extraordinary resolution and at a general meeting of which not less than 21 days' notice specifying the intention to propose the resolution as a special resolution has been duly given (s 378(2)).

A special resolution is required to sanction certain matters required by the Act. For example, the following matters require special resolutions:

(1) Changing the name of the company (s 28(1)).
(2) Alteration of the objects in the Memorandum (s 4, see 1.3.1).

(3) Disapplication of the pre-emption provisions contained in s 89 (s 95).

(4) Reduction of company's capital (s 135).

(5) Authorisation of the off-market purchase of a company's own shares (s 164).

(6) Approval of the purchase or redemption of a company's own shares out of capital (s 173).

(7) Decision to wind up a company either by the court or voluntarily (Insolvency Act 1986 ss 84(1)(b) and 122(a)).

The main differences between these two types of resolutions are therefore that a meeting to pass an extraordinary resolution (provided that it is not the annual general meeting) may be summoned by 14 days' notice (or seven days' if the company is unlimited) (see 6.4.2), whereas a meeting to pass a special resolution must be summoned by 21 days' notice, whether or not it is the annual general meeting.

6.6.3 Short notice and written resolutions

1 Short notice A meeting can be convened on short notice (ie notice of any length at all) if, in the case of an annual general meeting, all the members entitled to attend and vote agree and in other cases, if it is agreed by a majority in number of the members having the right to attend and vote, being a majority together holding not less than 95 per cent (or 90 per cent if an appropriate elective resolution has been passed—see 6.10.3(4) below) in nominal value of the shares giving that right (s 369(3) and (4) and s 378(3) and see reg 38) if all the members of the company are present and agree, any defect in the notice may be waived (*Re Oxted Motor Co* [1921] 3 KB 32; *Re Bailey, Hay & Co* [1971] 1 WLR 1357). (See however r 4.54 of the Insolvency Rules 1986 in relation to a minimum period of notice of 21 days for a resolution for a creditors' voluntary winding-up.)

In all other cases, if all the shareholders agree that a resolution passed on short notice shall be treated as valid, the court will not be ready to hear a shareholder say that the resolution is not valid (*Re Pearce, Duff & Co Ltd* [1960] 1 WLR 1014). In *Parker & Cooper Ltd v Reading* [1926] Ch 975 and *Re Duomatic Ltd* [1969] 2 Ch 365, it was held that ratification of directors' acts given by all members entitled to attend and vote at general meetings, but without a meeting being held, is as binding as a resolution in general meeting. In *Cane v Jones* [1980] 1 WLR 1451 it was held that an agreement between all members was effective to vary a company's Articles although there was no meeting or written resolution.

2 *Written resolutions*   If the Articles permit, a written resolution signed by all members entitled to notice of and to attend and vote at general meetings will (subject to any provision of the Act requiring a meeting to be held—see eg ss 142 and 366) be as valid as a resolution passed at a general meeting.

In addition, s 381A provides for written resolutions in lieu of a general or class meeting to be passed, without a period of notice, if signed by all the members of the company who at the date of the resolution would be entitled to attend and vote at such meetings.

There are a number of general points to note on this section, which was introduced by the 1989 Act:

(1) Every member has a right of veto.

(2) It can be used only by a private company.

(3) The signatures need not be on a single document provided each is on a document which accurately states the terms of the resolution. It should be noted that the documents distributed to the shareholders need not be identical and accordingly the resolution could be included in an individual letter to shareholders.

The date of the resolution is the date when the resolution is signed by or on behalf of the last member to sign. As only the members who would be entitled to vote at a general meeting need to sign the resolution, the signature of any one of joint shareholders will suffice. Likewise, where a shareholder dies and his shares are disenfranchised until the personal representatives are registered as members, the holding can be properly ignored until such time as the personal representatives are registered. If, however, the composition of shareholders changes whilst the resolution is doing the rounds it will be necessary to get the new member to sign the resolution.

The procedure for the passing of written resolutions is subject to review by the company's auditors. Section 381B provides that a copy of any resolution that is to be proposed must be sent to the auditors. If the proposed resolution concerns the auditors 'as auditors' then the auditors may, within a seven-day period, give notice to the company stating that the resolution ought to be considered by an appropriate meeting of the company. Accordingly, even though a resolution has been passed it will not be effective until the expiry of the seven-day period unless the auditors have previously notified the company of their intention not to require a meeting.

The written resolution procedure cannot be used in two specified circumstances (as set out in Pt I of Sched 15A):

(1) An ordinary resolution under s 303 removing a director before the expiration of his period of office.

(2) An ordinary resolution under s 391 removing an auditor before the expiration of his term of office.

Schedule 15A specifies that various additional documents have to be sent with the written resolution in specified instances in order for the resolution to be validly passed. The general rule is that whenever documents are required to be despatched with the notice of meeting or displayed prior to a resolution being passed, the documents concerned must be sent to shareholders at or before the time the resolution is sent to him for his signature. Details of the resolutions referred to in Pt II of Sched 15A are set out in the Table II (see overleaf).

A record of the resolution (and of the signatures) is to be entered into the company's minute book. Such record if purporting to be signed by a director or secretary is evidence of the resolution and all the procedural requirements are deemed to have been complied with unless the contrary can be shown.

It will be necessary for such resolutions to be filed at Companies House, within 15 days of their being passed, if they are, in effect, passing an extraordinary or special resolution. Section 381A(6) expressly states that any reference in an enactment to a special, extraordinary or elective resolution is deemed to include a written resolution having the same effect. Furthermore s 381A(5) provides that any reference in an enactment to a resolution being passed is deemed to be a reference to the date when all the members sign or, if later, the date when the auditors give or are deemed to have given their approval.

The procedure contained in the Act is broader than that under the common law or reg 53:

(1) It applies whether or not a company has reg 53 or a similar Article in its Articles of Association.

(2) It puts beyond doubt that the written resolution can effect

Table

Resolution	Documents to be supplied with written resolution
Special resolution under s 95(2)—disapplication of pre-emption rights to specific allotments of equity securities	Written statement from directors specifying information set out in s 95(5): —reasons for making recommendation; —amount to be paid to the company in respect of the equity securities; —directors' justification of that amount.
Special resolution under s 155(4) or (5)—permitting a private company to give financial assistance in certain circumstances	Documents specified in s 157(4)(a): —directors' statutory declaration with auditors' report.
Special resolution under s 164(2), (3) and (7)—authorising, varying or revoking authority for the company to make an off market purchase of its own shares or varying an existing contract so approved	Documents referred to in s 164(6): —a copy of the purchase contract; —a copy of variation to the terms of the contract. (A member holding shares to which the resolution relates need not sign.)
Special resolution under s 173(2)—approving redemption or purchase of own shares out of capital	Documents specified in s 174(4): —directors' statutory declaration and auditors' report. (A member holding shares to which the resolution relates need not sign.)
Ordinary resolution under s 319—approval of directors' service contract of more than five years	The service contract itself—s 319(5).
Ordinary resolution under s 337—provision of a director with funds to meet expenditure incurred for the purposes of the company or for him to properly perform his duties	Matters to be disclosed pursuant to s 33(4): —purpose of the expenditure incurred; —the amount of funds to be provided by the company; —the extent of the company's liability under any transaction which is or is connected with the thing in question.

a special or extraordinary resolution as expressly stated in s 381A(6).

(3) Section 381A(4) states that the written resolution is to be treated as if it had been passed at a general meeting and any reference in any enactment to a meeting at which a resolution is passed or to members voting in favour of the resolution shall be construed accordingly. Therefore a written resolution under s 381A can be used to pass a resolution where the Act would normally require a physical meeting to be held, such as s 121, provided the requirements of Sched 15A, Pt II are complied with.

3 General matters applicable to notices The notice convening a meeting to consider an extraordinary or special resolution should state the actual wording of the resolution to be passed. (In theory a notice giving the *full* substance of such a resolution might suffice, but it is difficult to see how one can be sure of doing this without giving the actual wording.) Notice of a special or extraordinary resolution having been given, no amendment of substance, however small, is possible unless it is simply to correct a clerical error (*Re Moorgate Mercantile Holdings Ltd* [1980] 1 All ER 40 and see *Re Williare Systems plc* [1987] BCLC 67): but an *ordinary resolution* may be amended at the meeting at which it is proposed, provided that the amendment is reasonably within the scope of the business as described and does not impose further obligations on the company (*Torbock v Lord Westbury* [1902] Ch 871).

6.6.4 Elective resolutions

An elective resolution is a resolution passed at a general meeting of shareholders held on at least 21 days' notice and agreed to by all shareholders entitled to attend and vote at the meeting in order to dispense with certain administrative provisions of the Act (see 6.10 below).

6.6.5 Filing of resolutions at the Companies Registry

Within 15 days of the passing of, inter alia, any of the following resolutions, a printed copy, signed by an officer of the company, must be filed with the Registrar, who will record:

(1) special resolutions (s 380(4)(*a*)).

(2)   extraordinary resolutions (s 380(4)(b)).

(2a) elective resolutions by private companies (s 379A).

(3)   resolutions or agreements agreed to by all the members of a company which, but for such agreement, would have had to be passed as special or extraordinary resolutions (s 380(4)(c)).

(4)   resolutions or agreements agreed to by all members of a class of shareholders which, but for the agreement, would have had to be passed by a particular majority or in a particular manner, and resolutions and agreements which bind all members of a class of shareholders though not agreed by them all (s 380(4)(d)).

(5)   a directors' resolution on the Secretary of State's direction under s 31(2) to change a company's name which previously did not have to include 'Limited' so that it ends with 'Limited' (s 380(4)(e)).

(6)   resolutions in respect of authority to allot relevant securities (s 380(4)(f)).

(7)   resolutions of directors by reason of a public company's acquisition of its own shares to re-register it as a private company (s 380(4)(g)).

(8)   resolutions in respect of authority for market purchases by a company of its own shares (s 380(4)(h)).

(9)   resolutions to wind up voluntarily (s 380(4)(j)).

(10) resolutions increasing the authorised capital (s 123(3)).

(11) a resolution by a public company under s 104 to approve an agreement to acquire a non-cash asset from its founders within its first two years as a public company (s 111(2)).

The Companies Registry has issued a leaflet specifying the various forms of 'printing', eg typewritten or produced in durable and reliable form by photocopying, approved by the Registrar.

Where Articles have been registered a copy of every resolution or agreement which must be filed under s 380(1) (which includes all the types of resolution listed above except (10) and (11)) and which is in force must be embodied in or annexed to every copy of the Articles issued subsequently (s 380(2)).

Where the company is operating under Table A and no Articles have been registered, a copy of every such resolution or agreement must be forwarded to any member on request, but a fee of not more than 5p may be charged (s 380(3)).

Where, in any case other than a special resolution altering the objects clause in a company's Memorandum of Association (the filing requirements in relation to which are regulated by s 6), a company is required to send to the Registrar a document making or evidencing any alteration in its Memorandum or Articles, there must be sent with such document a printed copy of the Memorandum or Articles as altered (which should have endorsed thereon a certificate signed by, for example, a director or the secretary that it is a true copy of the altered Memorandum or Articles) (s 18).

6.7 Minutes

6.7.1 Minute books

Section 382(1) provides that minutes of all proceedings at general and board meetings must be entered in books kept for the purpose.

Any minute of such a meeting purporting to be signed by the chairman of that meeting or the next one is evidence of the proceedings (s 382(2)).

The minutes do not provide conclusive evidence, however, unless the Articles so provide (*Kerr v Mottram (John) Ltd* [1940] Ch 657) but the burden of disproving the truth of their contents is on those who dispute their correctness. Until the contrary is proved, every meeting of which minutes have been properly made and signed is deemed to have been duly convened, and all proceedings had at the meeting to have been duly had (s 382(4)).

Where loose-leaf books are used for minutes, adequate safeguards should be adopted against substitution of leaves (s 722(2)). For example, the loose-leaf pages should be numbered consecutively and the minutes should be numbered consecutively throughout the book and not in a separate series for each meeting. When the minutes of a meeting are signed, eg, by the chairman of the next meeting, he should sign at the end of the minutes and initial or sign all (if any) preceding pages which include those minutes.

In *Hearts of Oak Assurance Co Ltd v James Flower & Sons* [1936] Ch 76, the court refused to accept a loose-leaf minute book as evidence but this was before the predecessor to s 722(2) was enacted.

The minutes may be kept in non-legible form provided that they can be reproduced in legible form (s 723).

6.7.2 *Keeping of minutes*

Care and accuracy should be observed in recording the proceedings of both general and board meetings, for it is reasonable to assume that proceedings not mentioned in the minutes did not occur.

Careful notes should be taken during the meeting and the full minutes prepared and written into the minute book as soon as possible after it.

In writing up minutes the secretary should endeavour to include every matter of a material nature, without including excessive detail.

Thus a minute of a resolution at a board meeting approving transfers of shares might be worded as follows:

'Resolved that transfers numbered 84 to 97 be registered and that the seal be affixed to the new certificates needed, numbered 153 to 166.'

A specimen of the minutes of the first meeting of the directors of a newly incorporated company is given in Appendix 1.

Minutes of a resolution passed at a general meeting should state the nature of the resolution, ie whether it is an ordinary, extraordinary or special resolution, and *the number of votes for and against* where these are announced by the chairman. Where figures are not announced it should be recorded that a resolution was passed unanimously, or by the requisite majority, as the case may be. In addition, it should be stated whether the voting was by poll or show of hands. It is not usual to state the number of votes at a board meeting, but directors voting against a resolution may ask for their dissent to be recorded.

If minutes are not kept, the company and every officer in default is liable to a fine (s 382(5)).

6.7.3 *Reading of minutes*

In practice, minutes of a board meeting are usually signed by the chairman of the next meeting. They are usually circulated to board members a reasonable period before the next meeting rather than read aloud at that next meeting. Any alterations should be made before the minutes are signed and should be initialled by the chairman. A resolution should be passed authorising any alterations. Before signing, the chairman should put the minutes to the meeting for confirmation.

The minutes of general meetings are usually read and signed at the next succeeding *board* meeting, it being neither necessary nor advisable to wait for the next general meeting which may not be held for a year or more.

6.7.4 Inspection of minutes

Section 383 provides that the minute book of proceedings at general meetings must be kept at the registered office, and that any member may:
(1) inspect the same without charge during prescribed hours (currently at least two hours in each business day); and
(2) require a copy to be supplied within seven days of request at the prescribed charge (currently 10 pence per 100 words).

When a general meeting is held at some place other than the registered office, strict compliance with the above section will prevent the secretary from having the minute book with him at the meeting. In such a case he should have at hand copies of the minutes of recent general meetings.

Members are not entitled to inspect the minutes of directors' meetings, but reports made to the directors by accountants or solicitors for the purposes of the company may be inspected (see *Gouraud v Edison Gower Bell Telephone Co of Europe* (1888) 57 LJ Ch 498, and *Dennis & Sons Ltd v West Norfolk Farmers Manure & Chemical Co-operative Co Ltd* [1943] Ch 220).

6.8 Class and Section 425 Meetings and Voluntary Arrangements

6.8.1 General

In certain circumstances, it may be necessary to summon a meeting of a class of shareholders. Such meetings are usually summoned either (*a*) where a variation of class rights is involved under the Articles or s 125, or (*b*) under s 425. In addition the Insolvency Act 1986 provides for meetings of the company (and its creditors) to consider voluntary arrangements (see ss 1(1) and 3 Insolvency Act 1986).

6.8.2 Class meetings under s 125

In the case of a class meeting summoned under s 125, the

provisions of the Articles as to general meetings of the company apply, so far as applicable, subject to the following qualifications:

(1) a quorum shall be two persons holding or representing by proxy at least one-third of the issued shares of the class, except that at an adjournment one holder of shares of the class or his proxy suffices.

(2) any holder of shares of the class present in person or by proxy may demand a poll.

Notice of such meetings must be given to all members of the class concerned, whether or not they are entitled to receive notice of a general meeting.

The statutory regulations concerning proxies (see 6.5.1) apply to meetings of a class of members of a company (s 372(7)).

6.8.3 Section 425 meetings

Under s 425, where a compromise or arrangement is proposed between a company and (a) its creditors or any class of them, or (b) its members or any class of them, the court may on summary application order a meeting of the group concerned to be summoned. The order of the court which authorises the summoning of the meeting will determine the nature of the notice and the form of proxy to be sent out with the notice; but any reasonable form of proxy may be employed if a shareholder thinks fit not to use the form sent out with the notice, and a proxy cannot be rejected on the ground that it has not been deposited at the company's registered office within the time specified in the notice (*Re Dorman Long & Co Ltd* [1934] Ch 635). If the arrangement is approved by a majority in number representing three-fourths in value of those members of the group who are present and vote either personally or by proxy at the meeting, and the sanction of the court is obtained, the compromise or arrangement will become binding on the company and all creditors and members concerned when an office copy of the court order has been delivered to the Registrar. (See also 4.14)

6.8.4 Voluntary arrangements

Section 1 of the Insolvency Act 1986 provides for proposals to be put to the company and its creditors for a composition in satisfaction of its debts or a scheme of arrangement of its affairs ('voluntary arrangements'). Any such meeting of the company is convened in accordance with the provisions of ss 2 and 3 of the Insolvency Act. (See also 11.1)

6.9 Board Meetings

A company's Articles usually contain regulations for the summoning, constitution and conduct of board meetings. Table A and most special Articles leave such matters largely to the discretion of the directors by providing that they may regulate their meetings as they think fit (reg 88). This gives the board the power to issue standing orders for the conduct of their meetings.

Regulations 88 to 98 of Table A or the relevant Articles should be studied.

Table A gives the directors the power of delegating any of their powers to committees (reg 72). This enables the work of the board to be done by some of its members only. But any act of a committee must have behind it the sanction of a properly constituted board meeting. In other words, the acts of a committee will not have the effect of an act of the board unless the committee was appointed by a properly constituted board meeting. If Table A is excluded and the Articles do not authorise the directors to delegate their powers to committees, they may not do so (*Re Leeds Banking Co, Howard's Case* (1866) 1 Ch App 561). In the case of listed companies, The Stock Exchange will require the Articles to provide that a committee must include a majority of directors.

An attendance book may be signed by all directors present at each meeting of the board. Where the meeting is attended by other officials of the company, such as the auditors, they may also sign.

Agenda papers should be prepared by the secretary for both general and board meetings, setting out briefly the matters with which the meeting is to deal.

6.10 The Elective Régime

6.10.1 General

The 1989 Act introduced the concept of an elective resolution which, if passed, allows a company to dispense with certain requirements of the Act described below.

6.10.2 The elective resolution

At least 21 days' notice is required of a meeting at which an elective resolution is proposed and it must be agreed to by all the members of the company entitled to attend and vote at the meeting (s 379A). There are a number of points to note about elective resolutions:

(1) Any member can veto such a resolution and accordingly it will be appropriate only for shareholder/management companies or wholly owned subsidiaries of private or public companies.

(2) It can be passed by means of a unanimous written resolution passed in accordance with the provisions of ss 381A–382A (see 6.6.3).

(3) It can be used only for private companies and accordingly ceases to have effect if the company is re-registered as a public company.

(4) It can be revoked by an ordinary resolution.

(5) Such a resolution can be passed or revoked notwithstanding any provision in the company's Memorandum or Articles of Association.

(6) It (or a resolution revoking an elective resolution) is required to be filed at Companies House within 15 days of its being passed.

6.10.3 Requirements that can be dispensed with

1   Companies Act 1985, section 80   Section 80 requires that the directors of a company have the consent of members prior to the issue of any shares. The authority must state the maximum number of securities over which it is given and its duration, the maximum length of which is five years (see 3.1.1).

An elective resolution passed pursuant to s 80A will enable the authority to be given for any fixed period exceeding five years or for an indefinite period of time. The authority may be revoked or varied in general meeting and a fixed period can be renewed. If an election is subsequently revoked and the s 80 authority was given for an indefinite period or for more than five years then the authority will expire forthwith if the authority was given more than five years ago; otherwise the authority will continue to have effect until the expiry of five years (s 80A(7)).

Section 80 authority can be given only in relation to existing share capital and, therefore, even if the directors have authority to issue shares pursuant to s 80 for an indefinite period of time any subsequent increase in share capital will necessitate a new authority to be obtained.

2 *Annual general meetings* The general rule under s 366 is that an AGM must be held in each year, the first AGM must be held within the first 18 months of incorporation and not more than 15 months must elapse between the date of one AGM and another. A private company may elect to dispense with the holding of AGMs required by s 366 and this is intended to complement the provisions concerning written resolution so that shareholders need never physically meet during the year.

The election has effect for the year in which it is given and for subsequent years. Accordingly, it must be given within the first 18 months of incorporation if it is intended to dispense with the first AGM. An elective resolution does not affect any liability already incurred for non-compliance with the requirements of the Act in previous years (s 366A).

This provision is not, however, as radical as it first appears: merely because a company dispenses with the AGM does not mean that it can dispense with all the business to be conducted at the AGM—other elective resolutions will be required to effect this. Furthermore, it is possible for any single shareholder to require the holding of an AGM (without revoking the elective resolution— which would require an ordinary resolution) by giving notice to the company not later than three months prior to the end of the year in which an AGM would otherwise be required to be held. This is obviously desirable protection for minority shareholders since once consent had originally been obtained for the passing of the elective resolution, the directors could be forever safeguarded from being challenged on the management of the company.

The section contemplates only a general power dispensing with AGMs and does not seem to provide for a specific resolution, for example not requiring AGMs for the first five years. Accordingly, it would be necessary to revoke the elective resolution after the time that it was no longer intended to apply.

If an election ceases to have effect, the company is not required to hold an AGM in that year if the revocation takes effect less than three months before the end of the year in which the AGM would otherwise require to be held.

3 Laying of accounts and reports The general rule is that the directors of a company are required to lay copies of the company's annual accounts and directors' report before the general meeting (s 241). The period allowed for laying and delivering reports and accounts for a private company is ten months after the end of the relevant accounting reference period (s 244).

A private company may elect to dispense with the laying of accounts and reports before the company in general meeting (s 252). Clearly this goes hand in hand with the election to dispense with the AGM and usually both elections will be made at the same time. If this election has not been made and the requirement to dispense with an AGM has been made then it will be necessary to convene a general meeting for the purpose of laying accounts, so reducing the effectiveness of dispensing with AGMs.

Once the election becomes effective the requirement to lay accounts before the AGM is complied with by sending to shareholders these accounts, together with, in cases of qualified accounts (ie where the auditors cannot say, without qualification, the accounts give a true and fair view of the state of affairs of the company), a statement explaining the qualification not less than 28 days before the end of the period allowed for laying accounts. In addition to the accounts a statement must be included setting out the member's right to require a meeting. The election has effect in relation the accounts in respect of the financial year in which the election is made and subsequent financial years. Revocation, likewise, applies to the accounts in the financial year that the revocation is made.

Within the 28-day period from the date on which accounts were sent out, any member or auditor may, by notice in writing to the company at its registered office, require a meeting to be held for the purpose of laying the accounts (s 253(2)). If the directors do not convene a meeting within 21 days from the date of the notice the member or auditor can convene the meeting himself within a three-month period. It is expressly provided that the directors have not duly convened a meeting if they convene a meeting for a date more than 28 days after the date of the notice convening it. Any reasonable expenses of the member convening the appropriate meeting in default of the directors are to be paid by the company and reclaimed from the directors. It should be noted that an election to dispense with the laying of reports and accounts or with the holding of an AGM must be stated in the annual return.

4 Short notice provisions Sections 369(4) and 378(3) enable a general meeting (other than an AGM), whether or not a special or extraordinary resolution is proposed, to be held on short notice provided at least 95 per cent of members so agree. The 1989 Act enables shareholders to elect that this figure can be reduced to an amount of not less than 90 per cent. The exact percentage can be left undefined to be determined by the general meeting at a later date.

5 Dispensation with appointment of auditors A private company may elect to dispense with the obligation to appoint auditors annually. This, again, will go hand in hand with the election not to hold an AGM and to dispense with the laying of accounts at a general meeting. The general rule is that auditors are to be appointed at: (i) the general meeting at which accounts are laid (s 385); or (ii) if an election dispensing with the laying of accounts has been made, at a general meeting convened within a 28-day period of the accounts being despatched to members (s 385A). When the election to dispense with appointing auditors is in force the auditors are deemed to be reappointed for each succeeding financial year on the expiry of the time for appointing auditors. The usual safeguard has been included—a member may, by notice in writing to the company, propose that the appointment of auditors be terminated and the directors are required to convene a meeting, within 14 days, for a date not more than 28 days after the date that the notice was given in order to consider the appropriate resolution. If the directors do not convene a meeting within 14 days the member may do so himself within three months of that date. If a resolution is so passed then the auditors will not be reappointed when next they would be and if a notice is deposited within 14 days of the accounts being sent out to members then any deemed reappointment shall not have effect for that financial year. A member can exercise this right only once a financial year.

If the election is revoked then the auditors continue in office until the general meeting at which the accounts are laid or until another appointment under s 385A.

6 Other matters Section 117 of the Companies Act 1989 permits the Secretary of State by regulations to make provisions enabling private companies to elect to dispense with compliance to

Companies Act requirements provided that these relate 'primarily' to the internal administration and procedure of companies. No regulations have, at present, been made under this section.

Chapter 7

Annual Return, Accounts and Reports

7.1 Annual Return

7.1.1 General

At least once in every year a company must make a return (Form 363) to the Registrar of Companies containing the particulars set out in s 364 and s 364A. The timescale for submitting an annual return has been substantially altered by the Companies Act 1989. The annual return has to be made up to a date in each year which is the anniversary of the company's incorporation, signed by a director or the secretary of the company and returned to the Registrar within 28 days after the date to which it is made up. If administratively more convenient, such as where a company has a number of subsidiaries, the annual return can be made up to a date less than 12 months from the date of the company's incorporation or last annual return, as the case may be, so that all the annual returns of companies within the group can be prepared with effect from the same date. Another important procedural change is that the Registrar will now send to companies a 'shuttle' annual return (Form 363s) which will have been completed with such information as is contained on the company's file at Companies House. Accordingly, the administrative burden of completing Form 363 will be substantially reduced since it will now be necessary only to check the accuracy of the information and add any recent information.

7.1.2 Contents of the annual return

In general, the amount of information required to be included in the annual return has been greatly reduced by the Companies Act 1989.

The particulars are required to be included in the annual return and are as follows:

(1) The address of the registered office.

(2) (a) The address at which the register of members is kept if this is not the same as the registered office.

(b) The address at which a register of holders of debentures is kept if this is not the same as the registered office.

(3) The type of company it is and its principal business activities.

(4) The name and address of the company secretary and the directors.

(5) In the case of individual directors, his nationality, date of birth and business occupation and, in the case of both individual and corporate directors, such particulars of other directorships as are required to be contained in the company's register of directors (see 8.8.1).

(6) If the company has elected to dispense with the laying of accounts before the general meeting and/or the holding of an annual general meeting under the elective régime provisions (see 6.10), a statement to that effect.

(7) The total number of issued shares of the company and their aggregate nominal value.

(8) If there are different classes of shares, the nature of the class (eg preferred or deferred) and the total number and aggregate nominal value of issued shares of that class.

(9) A list of the names and addresses of members and those who have ceased to be members since the last return (or, in the case of the first return, since the incorporation of the company) and if the names are not alphabetically listed, an appropriate index.

(10) The number of shares of each class held by each member and the number of shares of each class transferred since the last return (or, in the case of the first return, since the incorporation of the company).

If the information referred to in paras (9) and (10) has been given in either of the two immediately preceding returns then it is only necessary to include particulars of persons ceasing to be or becoming members and details of shares transferred since the date of the last return.

7.1.3 *Annual return of company with no share capital*

A company which has no share capital is required to file a Form 363 save that the information contained in paragraphs (7) to (10) is not required to be included.

7.2 Preparation, Presentation and Registration of Accounts

The considerable volume of legislation which deals with a company's accounts can be divided into three topics: (i) the keeping of accounting records; (ii) the presentation of accounts to the members; and (iii) the registration of accounts.

7.2.1 *Keeping of accounting records*

Section 221 provides that every company shall cause accounting records to be kept sufficient to show and explain the company's transactions. The accounting records must disclose with reasonable accuracy at any time the financial position of the company at that time and enable the directors to ensure that any balance sheet and profit and loss account prepared under the Act complies with the Act's requirements. It should be noted that the accounting records need not give a true and fair view of the state of affairs of the company. In particular accounting records must contain (*a*) daily entries of all receipts and expenditures of money, (*b*) a record of the assets and liabilities of the company and (*c*) where the company's business involves dealing in goods, statements of (i) stock held by the company at the end of each financial year, (ii) stocktakings used or to be used to prepare any statement of stock referred to in (i), and (iii) all goods (except goods sold in ordinary retail trade) sold and purchased including details of buyers and sellers. A parent company which has a subsidiary undertaking in relation to which the above requirements do not apply (ie because it is incorporated outside the UK) is required to take reasonable steps to secure its subsidiary keeps such accounting records as to enable the directors of the parent to compile accounts in accordance with the requirements of the Act.

The accounting records must be kept at the registered office or at such other place as the directors think fit and must at all times be open to inspection by the officers of the company; but if they are kept at a place outside Great Britain, there must be sent to and kept in a place in Great Britain such accounts and returns with respect to the business dealt with in the books outside Great

Britain as will disclose with reasonable accuracy the financial position of the business at intervals not exceeding six months and enable the company's balance sheet and profit and loss account to be prepared in accordance with the Act's requirements. A private company must keep such accounting records for three years and a public company for six from the date on which they are made (s 222).

Although accounts have to be open for inspection by the company's officers (which includes directors, managers and the secretary) in *Conway v Petronious Clothing Co* [1978] 1 WLR 72 it was held that the right of inspection was available only to enable an officer to fulfil his duty. Accordingly, an order for inspection was refused to a director pending the result of a general meeting convened to consider a resolution for his dismissal.

Severe penalties, including imprisonment, are laid down for a defaulting officer where a company fails to comply with the requirements of the Act for the keeping of accounting records.

7.2.2 Duty to prepare, lay and deliver accounts by reference to accounting reference periods

Unless an appropriate elective resolution has been passed (see 6.10) by ss 241 and 242, the directors of every company are under a duty in respect of each financial year to lay before the company in general meeting and deliver to the Registrar of Companies accounts for that year. For this purpose a company's accounts for a financial year comprise the profit and loss account, balance sheet, directors' report, auditors' report and, if the company has subsidiaries and has to prepare group accounts (see 7.3), those group accounts (s 262).

The period for which a profit and loss account is prepared is called a 'financial year' whether it is a year or not (s 223). A company's first financial year begins with the first day of its first accounting reference period and ends with the last day of that period or such other date not being more than seven days after the end of that period as the directors may determine. Subsequent financial periods begin with the day immediately following the end of the company's previous financial year and end with the last day of its next accounting reference period or such other date, not more than seven days before or after the end of that period, as the directors may determine.

The directors of a parent company shall secure that, except where in their opinion there are good reasons against it, the financial year of each of its subsidiary undertakings coincides with the company's own financial year.

See however 7.4.3 below for exemptions for small and medium-sized companies from the obligation to deliver full accounts to the Registrar.

The directors of an unlimited company are not normally required to deliver accounts to the Registrar (see 12.1).

Determination of accounting reference period   To ascertain the period for which a profit and loss account is to be prepared (and therefore the financial year) one must first ascertain a company's accounting reference period.

Basically:

(1) a company can give notice on Form 224 to the Registrar within 9 months of its incorporation specifying any date in the calendar year as its accounting reference date and if it does not do so its accounting reference date will be the last day of the month in which the anniversary of its incorporation falls;

(2) a company's first accounting reference period is the period which begins with its incorporation and ends with its accounting reference date falling more than 6 months but not more than 18 months after its incorporation; and

(3) each succeeding year ending with the accounting reference date is an accounting reference period (s 224).

A company can during any accounting reference period ('the current accounting reference period') give notice to the Registrar on Form 225(1) specifying a new accounting reference date on which the current accounting reference period and subsequent accounting reference periods are to end (s 225(1)). A company can also after the end of an accounting reference period ('the previous accounting reference period') give notice on Form 225(2) specifying a new accounting reference date on which the previous accounting reference period and subsequent accounting reference periods are to be treated as ending or having ended, but this second type of notice:

(1) can be given only if the company is a subsidiary undertaking or parent undertaking of another company and the new accounting reference date coincides with that of such other company unless the period for laying and delivering accounts

in relation to the previous accounting reference period has already expired (s 225(5) and see 7.2.3); or

(2) an administration order under Part II of the Insolvency Act 1986 is in force.

Neither type of notice has effect if it would extend the current or previous accounting reference period to more than 18 months (s 225(6)). A notice has no effect if it would extend the current accounting reference period and is given within five years of the end of a previous accounting reference period which was so extended unless:

(1) the company is a subsidiary undertaking or parent undertaking of another company and the new accounting reference date coincides with that of such other company, or

(2) where an administration order under Part II of the Insolvency Act 1986 is in force; or

(3) the Secretary of State permits (s 225(4)).

There is no minimum for the duration of a shortened accounting reference period (other than the first) and there is no restriction on the number of times a company may shorten its accounting period.

7.2.3 *Period allowed for laying and delivering accounts*

The period allowed for laying accounts before the company in general meeting and delivering them to the Registrar in relation to any accounting reference period is, in the case of a private company, ten months or, in the case of a public company, seven months after the end of that accounting reference period (s 244). Where, however, a company carries on business or has interests outside the United Kingdom, the Channel Islands and the Isle of Man and notice to that effect claiming an extension of the period for laying and delivering accounts is given to the Registrar on Form 244 then the period is extended by three months. A separate notice is needed for each period for which the claim is made. Special provisions apply where the effect of a notice given under s 225 is to shorten an accounting reference period. In such a case, the period for laying and delivering accounts is the later of (i) the period specified above and (ii) three months from the date that notice is given under s 225. The Secretary of State may extend the period for laying and delivering accounts if for any special reason he thinks fit to do so (s 244(5)).

Penalties and default orders If the requirements of the Act as to the laying and delivering of accounts are not complied with before the end of the period allowed then each director of the company is guilty of an offence and liable to be fined unless he can prove that he took all reasonable steps for securing that those requirements would be fulfilled within that time (s 241). If the directors fail to make good any default within 14 days of notification the court may make a default order, on application by any member or creditor of the company or by the Registrar, requiring the directors to make good the default within such time as may be specified in the order (s 242).

The company itself may also be liable to a penalty for failure to deliver the accounts (s 242A):

Length of Delay	Public Company	Private Company
Up to 3 months	£500	£100
More than 3 months but less than 6 months	£1,000	£250
More than 6 months but less than 12 months	£2,000	£500
More than 12 months	£5,000	£1,000

7.2.4 Duty to supply copies of accounts

A copy of the company's accounts (comprising the documents referred to at 7.2.2) must, not less than 21 days before the date of the general meeting before which they are to be laid, be sent to: (i) every member of the company; (ii) every holder of debentures of the company; and (iii) all other persons so entitled to receive notice of general meetings, eg the auditors (s 238(1)).

This general rule is subject to the following modifications:

(1) copies need not be sent (i) to a person who is not entitled to notices of meetings if the company is unaware of his address; (ii) to more than one of the joint holders of shares or debentures none of whom is entitled to receive notices of meetings; or (iii) in the case of joint holders of shares or debentures some of whom are and some of whom are not entitled to receive notices of meetings, to those who are not so entitled (s 238(2)).

(2) if copies are sent less than 21 days before the meeting, they shall nevertheless be deemed to have been duly sent if it

is so agreed by all the members entitled to attend and vote at the meeting (s 238(4)).

(3) where a company has no share capital, copies need not be sent to members or debenture holders who are not entitled to notice of the meeting (s 238(3)).

Any member of a company and any holder of debentures is entitled to be furnished on demand, within seven days and without charge, with a copy of the last accounts of the company (s 239).

A company with listed securities is also required to send to the holders or insert as paid advertisements in two national daily newspapers half-yearly interim reports not more than four months after the end of the period to which the report relates (section 5, chapter 2, para 23, Yellow Book).

7.3 Group Accounts

7.3.1 General

In general, in addition to preparing individual accounts, where at the end of its financial year a company is a parent company, it must prepare group accounts comprising a consolidated balance sheet and profit and loss of the company and its subsidiary undertakings (s 227(1)). Group accounts are, however, not necessary where (i) the company is at the end of its financial year the wholly owned subsidiary of another body corporate incorporated in the EEC (the 'parent undertaking') (because that other body corporate, or a third one further up a chain of ownership, will prepare group accounts) (s 228(1)), or (ii) where the parent undertaking holds more than 50 per cent of the shares and notice requesting the preparation of group accounts has not been served on the company by shareholders holding in aggregate more than half of the remaining shares or five per cent of the total shares.

These exemptions are conditional upon the company complying with the detailed requirements set out in s 228(2). In particular that the company is included in consolidated accounts for a larger group drawn up to the same or an earlier date in the same financial year by a parent undertaking established in the EEC. In addition, the company must note its exemption to produce group accounts and name its parent undertaking in its own accounts and deliver to the Registrar with its own accounts, copies of its group accounts, the parent undertaking's annual report and an auditors' report thereon. The exemption is not available to any company whose securities are listed on a stock exchange with the EEC.

Moreover, group accounts need not deal with a subsidiary if

(1) severe long-term restrictions substantially hinder the exercise of the rights of the parent company over the assets or management of that undertaking;

(2) the information required for the preparation of group accounts cannot be obtained without disproportionate expense or undue delay;

(3) the interest of the parent company is held exclusively with a view to resale and the subsidiary has not previously been included in group accounts;

(4) the activities of one or more subsidiary undertakings are so different from the other companies within the group that their inclusion would be incompatible with the obligation to give a true and fair view; and

(5) the subsidiary undertaking is not material for the purpose of giving a true and fair view.

However, where group accounts are not submitted or any subsidiaries are excluded from them, the particulars prescribed in Sched 5, Part I must be given in a note to the accounts.

7.3.2 Form of group accounts

Where group accounts are required, they must consist of a consolidated balance sheet dealing with the state of affairs of the company and all the subsidiary undertakings which must be dealt with and a consolidated profit and loss account dealing with the profit or loss of the company and those subsidiary undertakings (s 227(2)).

The overriding principles to be borne in mind are that the group accounts must (as explained below at 7.4.1) give a true and fair view of the state of affairs and profit or loss of the company and its subsidiary undertakings dealt with as a whole, so far as concerns the members of the company (s 227(3)), and must comply with the requirements of Sched 4A. In particular group accounts must combine the information contained in the separate balance sheets and profit and loss accounts of the companies included in the consolidation though with such necessary adjustments as may be appropriate in accordance with generally accepted accounting principles or practice (Sched 4A, para 2(1)).

7.3.3 *Financial year of holding companies and subsidiaries*

A parent company's directors must secure that, except where in their opinion there are good reasons against it, the financial year of each of its subsidiary undertakings shall coincide with the company's own financial year (s 223(5)).

Where the financial year of a subsidiary undertaking does not coincide with that of its parent, the group accounts are to be made from the accounts of the subsidiary undertaking ending not less than three months before those of the parents or from interim accounts as at the end of the parent's financial year end (Sched 4A, para 2(2)).

In this event, whether or not the affairs of a subsidiary undertaking are dealt with in the group accounts, a note to the parent company's own accounts or, where group accounts are prepared, the group accounts must state, in respect of the subsidiary undertakings whose financial years do not coincide with that of the company, the reasons why the company's directors do not think such coincidence necessary and the dates on which such subsidiary undertakings' financial years ended (the earliest and latest such dates being sufficient if there are several) (Sched 5, paras 4, 19).

7.4 Form and Content of Accounts

7.4.1 *General*

Sections 226 and 227 and Scheds 4, 4A, 5 and 6 lay down the form and content of the accounts of an individual company and of group accounts, which will each include balance sheet, profit and loss account and information to be given in notes to the accounts. However where a banking, insurance or shipping company is involved the accounts may instead comply with ss 255 and 255A–E and Sched 9: accounts so prepared are called special category accounts. References to a company's profit and loss account include in the case of a company not trading for profit its income and expenditure account (s 262(2)).

The overriding requirement in ss 226 and 227 is that the balance sheet and the profit and loss account of a company give a true and fair view of, respectively, the state of the company's affairs and its profit or loss for the financial year and that group accounts give a true and fair view of the state of affairs and profit or loss of the undertakings dealt with by those accounts as a whole so far as concerns members of the company. If compliance with the detailed requirements of Sched 4 or 4A and all other requirements of the Act whether as to the accounts of an individual company or as to group accounts would not provide sufficient information to give a true and fair view, any necessary additional information must be provided in the accounts or notes to them. If, owing to special circumstances, compliance with such requirements would prevent the giving of a true and fair view, even if additional information were provided, the directors may so far as necessary depart from them: if they do so, particulars of the departure, the reasons for it and its effect must be given in a note to the accounts.

Under Sched 4 a balance sheet must be compiled in one of the two formats and a profit and loss account in one of the four formats set out in the Schedule. The detailed provisions of Sched 4 are not listed here. Once one format for the balance sheet or profit and loss account has been adopted, it must be followed in later years unless in the opinion of the directors there are special reasons for a change: any such change and the reasons for it must be explained in a note to the accounts which include it (Sched 4, para 2). Certain modification of the format is allowed as specified in Sched 4: for example, when the special nature of the company's business requires, the directors shall adapt the arrangement and headings and subheadings in respect of items which are given Arabic numbers in the formats (Sched 4, para 3(3)). Various notes to the formats must be observed. Preliminary expenses, expenses of and commission on the issue of shares or debentures, and costs of research must not be treated as assets in a balance sheet (Sched 4, para 3(2)).

Schedule 4 Part II sets out certain accounting principles and rules, including one set called the 'historical cost accounting rules' and another called the 'alternative accounting rules'. The latter allow departures from the historical cost accounting rules to reflect current cost accounting principles. Part III lists information which, if not given in the accounts, must be provided in notes to them. Part IV contains provisions which apply where the company is a parent company or subsidiary undertaking and Part V provisions which apply where it is an investment company. Part VI, which specified information to be given in notes to the accounts where advantage has been taken of merger relief, has been repealed by the Companies Act 1989. In Part VII there are a number of rules which apply in the interpretation of the previous Parts of the Schedule.

In the preparation of a company's accounts, due regard should also be had to the recommendations contained in each Financial Reporting Standard which is from time to time prepared by the Accounting Standards Committee and approved by the Committee's constituent accountancy bodies (and to the publications of the International Accounting Standards Committee). Financial Reporting Standards are intended to supersede Statements of Standard Accounting Practice but until the relevant standard is introduced reference will still have to be made to the applicable statement. A secretary will normally be guided in respect of the application of these rules by the company's auditors.

7.4.2 Approval and signing of Accounts

The balance sheet, once the accounts have been approved by the board, must be signed by a director to evidence such approval and a copy of any balance sheet delivered to the Registrar must similarly be signed (s 233(1) and (2)). Every copy of the balance sheet which is laid before the company in general meeting or otherwise circulated, published or issued is required to state the name of the person who signed the balance sheet (s 233(2)). Failure to comply with the above requirements will result in the company and every officer who is in default guilty of an offence and liable to a fine.

7.4.3 Accounting exemptions for small and medium-sized companies

Sections 246 to 249 and Sched 8 (which may be amended by statutory instrument) enable small and medium-sized companies to deliver modified accounts to the Registrar. The relaxations extend also to the requirements relating to notes to the accounts and documents to accompany accounts. Full accounts, disregarding the relaxations, must still be prepared, audited, reported on by the auditors and laid before the company in general meeting. The relaxations extend both to a company's individual accounts and to group accounts but the rules relating to individual accounts must be considered before those relating to group accounts. Accordingly, the following paragraphs relate to individual accounts except where otherwise indicated.

A company qualifies as a small or medium-sized one in a financial year if in that year it satisfies at least two of three qualifying conditions. These conditions are that turnover, 'balance sheet total' (broadly, total assets) and average number of employees must not exceed certain limits. The limits are:

	Small company	Medium-sized company
Turnover	£2,000,000	£8,000,000
Balance sheet total	£975,000	£3,900,000
Average number of employees	50	250

In its first financial year a company can deliver accounts modified as for a small or medium-sized company if in that year it qualifies as, respectively, a small or medium-sized one (s 247(1)(a)). In later years the position is more complicated. Basically, it can deliver accounts for a financial year modified as for a small or medium-sized company if in both that year and the preceding one it qualified as, respectively, a small or medium-sized company (s 247(1)(b)). However, having once become entitled to deliver accounts modified as for a small or medium-sized company, it is still entitled to do so despite not qualifying in one year as a small or medium-sized company (but in the next year will be so entitled only if it qualifies in that year) (s 247(2)).

The exemptions cannot however apply to a company which is:

(1) a public company;
(2) a banking or insurance company;
(3) an authorised person under the Financial Services Act 1986; or
(4) (subject as mentioned below) a member of an 'ineligible group'.

A banking company means a company authorised under the Banking Act 1987 and an insurance company means an insurance company to which Part II of the Insurance Companies Act 1982 applies. A group is ineligible if it includes:

(a) a company within (1), (2) or (3) above;
(b) a body corporate which is not a company but which can lawfully exercise power under its constitution to offer its shares or debentures to the public (ie a body corporate which is not a company but which in its ability to offer its securities to the public is equivalent to a public company).

However a company which is exempt from the obligation to appoint auditors under the provisions relating to dormant companies (see 9.2) is entitled to deliver modified accounts as a small company notwithstanding that it is a member of an ineligible group (s 250(4)(*d*)).

Moreover, a parent company need not prepare group accounts (see 7.3) if the group (meaning the parent company and its subsidiary undertakings) constitutes, respectively, a small or medium-sized group—ie if, in essence, the group would qualify as, respectively, a small or medium-sized company assuming it were a single company. This is subject to two modifications:

(i) additional requirements must be complied with for 'gross' turnover and balance sheet total, ie without making the set-offs and other adjustments required by Schedule 4A and

(ii) the aggregate balance sheet total for a small group is £1 million as opposed to £975,000 for a small company (s 249(3)).

Abbreviated individual accounts delivered to the Registrar must state on the balance sheet immediately above the signatures of the directors that the directors rely on the exemptions contained in Sched 8 for small or medium-sized companies and a statement of the grounds on which the company is entitled to those exemptions (Sched 8, para 7).

Such modified accounts delivered to the Registrar must be accompanied by a special report of the auditors stating that in their opinion:

(1) the company is entitled to deliver abbreviated accounts in respect of the financial year, as claimed in the directors' statement, and

(2) any accounts are properly prepared as such in accordance with Sched 8 (Sched 8, para 8).

The auditors must previously have provided the directors with a report as to whether (1) and (2) above are the case.

The main features of the relaxations for individual accounts for a small company are:

(*a*) a modified balance sheet showing figures by reference to only the main headings of the full accounts need be delivered (save that certain information about sums due has to be disclosed in the balance sheet or a note);

(*b*) the profit and loss account and directors' report need not be delivered;

(*c*) the information required to be given in notes to the accounts is reduced;

(d) the information required by Sched 6 about the salaries and similar benefits of directors and higher paid employees need not be delivered;

(e) no requirement to state in the notes whether the accounts have been prepared in accordance with applicable accounting standards and to identify any material departure therefrom. Accordingly, small and medium-sized companies do not have to comply with Financial Reporting Standards and Statements of Standard Accounting Practice.

Under the relaxations for individual accounts for a medium-sized company a profit and loss account modified as stated in Sched 8 para 5 may be delivered to the Registrar instead of the full one and the information concerning turnover required by Sched 4 para 55 need not be given. It is still necessary to produce a full directors' report and balance sheet.

7.4.4 Publication of accounts

Section 240 contains certain rules relating to the publication of accounts. Publishing accounts means publishing, issuing or circulating them or otherwise making them available for public inspection in a manner calculated to invite members of the public generally or any class of them to read them (s 240(4)).

Where a company publishes its statutory accounts it must publish with them the auditors' report indicating whether the accounts have been prepared in accordance with the statutory provisions and whether they provide a true and fair view of the company's financial position (s 240(1)).

If a company publishes accounts other than those prepared in accordance with the Act, then such accounts must be accompanied by a statement indicating that they are not the statutory accounts, whether statutory accounts have been delivered to the Registrar, whether the auditors have reported on the statutory accounts and if so whether the report was qualified or contained a statement under s 237(2) or (3) (see 7.6) (s 240(3)). It is not permissible to publish with the non-statutory accounts any auditors' report on the statutory accounts. Further, a company which is required to prepare group accounts for a financial year must publish its group accounts at the same time as it publishes its individual accounts.

A company is regarded as publishing non-statutory accounts if it publishes any balance sheet or profit and loss account relating to a financial year of the company or a group, or purporting to deal with any such financial year, otherwise than as part of its accounts required to be delivered to the Registrar pursuant to s 242.

To constitute a balance sheet or profit and loss account there must be a series of figures, albeit only a few figures, connected by addition or subtraction and demonstrating the amounts of assets and liabilities or profit or loss. A mere statement of profits cannot therefore be a profit and loss account. A preliminary announcement of the results for a financial year will almost certainly constitute non-statutory accounts if it includes the information required by The Stock Exchange to be given by listed companies in accordance with the Yellow Book, but an advertisement setting out a summary of the figures included in such a preliminary announcement may or may not constitute non-statutory accounts depending on its contents.

It is considered that the statement required by s 240(3) need not deal with comparative figures for a preceding year which are included in any publication of non-statutory accounts; in other words, although the statement required by s 240(3) must indicate whether the new figures are statutory accounts, whether they have been audited, etc, the statement need not indicate these matters in respect of the figures for the preceding year. Statutory accounts have to include comparative figures for the preceding year but this does not make them accounts for the preceding year: the same principle should apply to non-statutory accounts.

Financial statements for a past year or series of past years contained in prospectuses, offer documents or other company circulars will often constitute non-statutory accounts for those years.

Section 240(3) does not apply to announcements of interim (half-yearly or quarterly) results as these do not relate to or purport to deal with a financial year of the company, only with part of a financial year.

7.4.5 Information required by Schedule 5

Section 231 and Sched 5 require certain information on related undertakings to be given in the notes to a company's accounts. Sched 5 is divided into two parts: Part I deals with companies not required to prepare group accounts and Part II relates to where group accounts are to be prepared.

The information required to be given in Sched 5 is detailed and the principal items are set out below. However, information does not have to be given in respect of certain undertakings where:

(1) the undertaking is established under the law of a country outside the UK or carries on business outside the UK and the directors believe that the disclosure of the information would be seriously prejudicial to the business of the undertaking, its parent or any subsidiary undertaking and the Secretary of State agrees. This exemption does not apply to information relating to the value of the parent's investment in the subsidiary or the number, description and amount of shares in and debentures of the parent held by or on behalf of the subsidiary;

(2) the number of undertakings is such that the directors believe compliance with Sched 5 would result in information of an excessive length being given, then information need be given only in respect of those undertakings whose results or financial position the directors believe principally affected the figures shown in the accounts and those undertakings excluded from consolidation under s 229(3) or (4) (see 7.3.1). This exemption does not apply to information required to be given regarding arrangements attracting merger relief.

Information to be given in respect of companies not required to prepare group accounts

(a) Subsidiary undertakings

The following information is required to be given in respect of subsidiary undertakings:

(i) the name of the subsidiary;

(ii) the country of incorporation where incorporated outside Great Britain and if incorporated in Great Britain, whether it was incorporated in England and Wales or Scotland;

(iii) if unincorporated its principal place of business;

(iv) the reason why group accounts are not required to be prepared, identifying any undertakings falling within the exemptions specified in s 229 (see 7.3.1);

(v) the identity of each class of shares held by the parent and the proportion of nominal value of the shares of that class represented by those shares;

(vi) the aggregate amount of its capital and reserves at the end of its financial year together with the profit and loss for that year, but this information is not required to be given where (a) group accounts are not required to be prepared because the parent is included in the accounts of a larger group pursuant to s 228; or (b) the undertaking is not required by the Act to deliver a copy of its accounts to the Registrar (ie a company incorporated outside the UK), has not published its balance sheet within the UK and the parent's holding is less than 50 per cent of the nominal value of the shares; or (c) if the information is not material;

(vii) where the financial years of any undertaking do not coincide with that of the parent, the reasons for that and the date on which the financial year of the undertaking ended;

(viii) any qualification in the auditors' report on the subsidiaries' accounts unless such qualification is covered by the parent's accounts or is immaterial;

(ix) the total investment of the company in the shares of the subsidiary;

(x) the number, description and amount of shares in and debentures of the parent held by the subsidiary.

(b) Information to be given in respect of undertakings other than subsidiary undertakings

Information has to be given about undertakings in which the parent has a significant holding. A significant holding is a holding of ten per cent or more of any class of shares or where the amount of the holding exceeds one-tenth of the amount of the company's assets. The information which is required to be given (by reference to paragraph numbers of information to be given about subsidiary undertakings, see p 175) is (i), (ii), (iii), (v) and (vi). In the case of information required to be given about the undertaking's capital and reserves and profit and loss, such information is required only where the parent holds 20 per cent or more of the nominal value of the shares in the undertaking. A parent does not have to give this information in the same circumstances as in the case of subsidiary undertakings, save that in order for the exemption in (vi)(a) to apply it is necessary for both the parent's accounts to be included in the accounts of a larger group and the investment in all undertakings where the parent has a 20 per cent holding to be shown in the notes to the accounts by way of equity method of valuation.

Arrangements attracting merger relief   Where the parent has issued shares in consideration for the issue transfer or cancellation of shares in another company (the 'other company') in circumstances where it is not required to transfer any premium payable on its shares to share premium account in accordance with s 131 (see 3.11) full details must be given about the transaction. In particular details of the other company, the shares acquired and issued must be given and the accounting treatment adopted by the company in respect of the shares acquired must be specified. Furthermore, any profit or loss attributable to the sale of shares in the other company or fixed assets held by the other company or its subsidiary undertakings must be identified if it arose during the current financial year or the two preceding years. Similarly, if shares in the other company or its fixed assets are transferred to another member of the group and that members' shares are sold then that part of the profit or loss attributable to such shares or assets has to be separately identified.

Information about parent undertaking   Where the company is a subsidiary undertaking, information has to be given relating to the parent undertaking of the largest group of undertakings for which group accounts are drawn up and of which the company is a member and the smallest such group. For example, if company C is a wholly owned subsidiary of company B which is a wholly owned subsidiary of company A then in drawing up accounts of company C, information would have to be given about company A (the parent of the largest group) and company B (the parent of the smallest group). The information which has to be given is as follows:

(i) The name of the parent;
(ii) The country of incorporation where incorporated outside Great Britain and if incorporated in Great Britain, whether it was incorporated in England and Wales or Scotland;
(iii) If it is unincorporated, the address of its principal place of business;
(iv) If copies of group accounts are available to the public, the address from which such accounts can be obtained.

Where the ultimate parent is not required to produce group accounts then the information referred to in paras (i) and (ii) is required to be given.

Information to be given in respect of companies required to prepare group accounts
(a)   Subsidiary undertakings. The following information is required to be given in respect of subsidiary undertakings (by reference to

the paragraph numbers on information to be given on subsidiary undertaking where group accounts are not required to be prepared. See p 175):

(i), (ii), (iii), (v) (this information has to be given both in respect of the parent company and the group), (vii), (viii) (in respect of subsidiary undertakings excluded from the consolidation), (x).

In addition, the information contained in paragraph (vi) has to be given but is required only in respect of subsidiary undertakings not included in the consolidation and does not have to be given where the group's investment in the undertaking is included in the accounts by way of the equity method of valuation or in the circumstances set out in (vi)(b) or (c)).

It is also necessary to identify in the notes which of the relevant provisions of s 258(2) or (4) applies in order for the subsidiary undertaking to be treated as such. This is not necessary where it is a subsidiary undertaking by virtue of the parent holding a majority of the voting rights in the undertaking and the parent holds the same proportion of the shares in the undertaking as it holds voting rights.

(b)　Joint ventures.　In respect of joint ventures (undertakings managed jointly with another undertaking whose accounts are not consolidated in the same group) the following information has to be given:

  (i) name of the undertaking;

  (ii) address of the principal place of business of the undertaking;

  (iii) the factors on which joint management of the undertaking is based;

  (iv) the proportion of the capital of the undertaking held by group companies;

  (v) the financial year-end of the undertaking if it does not coincide with that of the company.

(c)　Associate undertakings.　An associated undertaking is an undertaking in which a member of the group has a participating interest (ie one held on a long-term basis for the purpose of securing a contribution to its activities by the exercise of control or influence arising from or related to that interest) and over whose operating and financial policy it exercises a significant influence and which is not a subsidiary undertaking or a joint venture. It is presumed that a company does exercise significant influence if it holds 20 per cent or more of voting rights in another undertaking (Sched 4A, para 20).

The following information has to be given (by reference to the paragraph numbers on information to be given on subsidiary undertakings where group accounts are not required to be prepared, see p 175):

(i), (ii), (iii), (v) (this information has to be given both in respect of the parent company and the group).

(d)   Significant holdings of parent company or group.   Significant holding has the same meaning as that set out above in respect of Part I of Sched 5 (see p 175). The information which is required to be given where the parent company has a significant holding in an undertaking (by reference to paragraph numbers of information to be given about subsidiary undertakings where group accounts are not required to be prepared, see p 175) is (i), (ii), (iii), (v) (in respect to shares of the undertaking held by the parent) and (vi) (where the parent holds 20 per cent or more of the shares in the undertaking). In the case of information required to be given about the undertaking's capital and reserves and profit and loss, a parent does not have to give this information where the conditions of (vi)(b) or (c) are satisfied. Where it is other members of the group, rather than the parent that has a significant holding in an undertaking, the information in (v) and (vi) is to be given on a group basis.

(e)   Arrangements attracting merger relief. Information about parent undertaking.   Same information to be included as set out in Part I of Sched 5, see pp 176–7.

7.4.6 Information required by Schedule 6
Information as to remuneration of directors and higher paid employees

Section 232 and Schedule 6 require information relating to directors to be included by way of note to the accounts.

The following particulars must be given in a note to a company's accounts:

(*a*) The aggregate amount of the directors' emoluments

This amount includes any emoluments paid to or receivable by a person in respect of his services as director of the company or in respect of his services, while director of the company, as director of any subsidiary undertaking, or otherwise in connection with the management of the affairs of the company or any subsidiary undertaking; and must distinguish between (a) emoluments for services as a director, whether of the company or its subsidiary undertaking; and (b) other emoluments (para 1).

The term 'emoluments' in this context includes fees and percentages, sums paid by way of expenses, allowances in so far as charged to United Kingdom income tax, any contributions paid in respect of him under any pension scheme, and the estimated money value of any other benefits received by him otherwise than in cash. In addition, emoluments in respect of a person's accepting office, ie golden hellos, have to be disclosed.

(b) Particulars of directors' emoluments and waivers

Where the company is a parent company or a subsidiary undertaking or where the amount disclosed in (a) above exceeds £60,000, the following particulars must be given:

(i) the emoluments of the chairman or, if in a financial year there have been more than one, the emoluments of each of them while chairman, unless, in all cases the chairman's duties were wholly or mainly discharged outside the UK (para 3);

(ii) the number (if any) of directors who had no emoluments or whose several emoluments amounted to £5,000 or less and the number (if any) whose emoluments fell within each of the £5,000 brackets above that amount (other than directors who discharge their duties wholly or partly outside the UK) (para 4(2));

(iii) the emoluments of the most highly paid director included in (ii), if more than the chairman (para 4(3));

(iv) the number of directors who have waived rights to receive emoluments and the aggregate amount of the said emoluments (para 6).

For the purposes of paras 3 and 4, unlike (a) above, one does not include contributions paid in respect of a director under any pension scheme (para 5).

(c) The aggregate amount of directors' or past directors' pensions

For the purposes of this requirement, the expression 'pension' includes any superannuation allowance or gratuity or similar payment (para 13(3)(a)). The amount to be shown does not include any pension paid or receivable under a pension scheme (as defined below) if the scheme is such that contributions under it are substantially adequate for the maintenance of the scheme; but, subject to this, must include any pension paid or receivable in respect of any such services of a director or past director as are mentioned under heading (a) above, to or by him or, on his nomination or by virtue of dependence on or other connection with him, any other person (para 7(2)). Accordingly, if contributions a company pays to an occupational pension scheme were adequate to fund the pension, it would not be necessary to disclose the payment of such pensions. Pensions payable over and above this amount would be disclosable.

The expression 'pension scheme' mentioned above means a scheme for the provision of pensions in respect of services as director or otherwise which is maintained in whole or in part by means of contributions; and the expression 'contribution' means any payment (including an insurance premium) paid for the purposes of a scheme by or in respect of persons rendering services in respect of which pensions will or may become payable under the scheme, except that it does not include any payment in respect of two or more persons if the amount paid in respect of each of them is not ascertainable (para 13(3)(c)).

The amount shown must distinguish between pensions in respect of services as director, whether of the company or its subsidiary undertakings, and other pensions (para 7(3)). A subsidiary undertaking includes an undertaking which is a subsidiary undertaking at the time the services were rendered, even though it is not a subsidiary of the company at the reporting date (para 13(2)(b)).

(d) The aggregate amount of any compensation to directors or past directors in respect of loss of office

The figure must include sums paid to or receivable by a director or past director for loss of office as director of the company, or for loss, while director of the company or on or in connection with his ceasing to be a director, of any other office in connection with the management of the company's affairs or of any office as director or otherwise in connection with the management of the affairs of a subsidiary undertaking. Compensation includes benefits otherwise than in cash and it is necessary to include, in respect of non-cash compensation, the nature of the compensation and its estimated monetary value. Furthermore, compensation for loss of office includes sums paid as consideration for or in connection with a person's retirement from office. The figures shown must distinguish (*a*) between compensation in respect of the office of director, whether of the company or a subsidiary undertaking, and compensation in respect of other offices, and (*b*) between sums paid by or receivable from, respectively, the company, its subsidiary undertakings and others (paras 8 and 10(3)).

(*e*) Sums paid to third parties in respect of directors' services

It is necessary to disclose the aggregate amount of any consideration paid to or receivable by third parties for making available the services of any person as a director of the company or while a director of the company as a director of any of its subsidiary undertakings or otherwise in connection with the management of the affairs of the company or any of its subsidiary undertakings. The reference to a third person is to a person other than the director, the company or any of its subsidiary undertakings or any person connected with the director or any body corporate controlled by him.

The following rules apply for the purposes of paras 1, 7, 8 and 9 (cases (*a*), (*c*), (*d*) and (*e*) above):

(1) In each case it is necessary to include all relevant sums paid by or receivable from the company, its subsidiary undertakings and anyone else, except sums to be accounted for to the company, to any subsidiary, or under s 314 or 315 (see 8.5.2) to past or present members of the company or any subsidiary undertaking (para 10(2)).

(2) The figures must show the aggregate of the sums receivable in respect of a financial year, whenever paid; or, in the case of sums not receivable in respect of a period, the sums paid during the financial year; save that:

(*a*) where, as mentioned above, a payment is not included because the person receiving it is liable to account for it, and the liability is subsequently released (in whole or in part), or is not enforced within two years; or

(*b*) where any expenses or allowances are charged to United Kingdom income tax after the end of the relevant financial year;

such sums must be shown in the first accounts in which it is practicable to show them and shall be distinguished from the amounts included apart from this rule (para 11).

(3) Generally the term 'subsidiary undertaking' means a subsidiary undertaking as defined by s 258 (see 1.4.5); but, for the

above purposes only, if a director of the company was also a director of another undertaking by virtue of the company's nomination, direct or indirect, that other body corporate is to be deemed to be a subsidiary undertaking whether or not it falls within the terms of s 258. For the purpose of the requirements concerning emoluments and pensions, only subsidiaries which were such at the time the services were rendered need be taken into account; and as regards compensation for loss of office, only subsidiaries which were such immediately before the loss of office need be considered (para 13(2)(b)).

Any director of a company and any person who is or has within the previous five years been an officer of a company must give notice to the company of any particulars required for the purpose of complying with cases (a) to (d) above (s 232(3)).

Information as to loans to and transactions with directors, persons connected with directors and officers   Certain details of such matters must be given in a note to a company's accounts or to group accounts prepared by a holding company as explained at 8.14.2.

7.4.7 Banking and insurance companies and groups

Banking and insurance companies are able to prepare individual accounts in accordance with the requirements of Part I of Sched 9 rather than Sched 4 (s 255(1)). Similarly, the parent company of a banking or an insurance group is able to prepare group accounts in accordance with Part II of Sched 9 (s 255A(1)). A banking group is defined as a group where the parent is a banking company or at least one of the undertakings within the group is an authorised institution under the Banking Act 1987 and the predominant activities of the group are such as to make it inappropriate to prepare group accounts in accordance with the formation in Part I of Sched 4 (s 255A(3)). An insurance group is defined as a group where the parent company is an insurance company or the predominant activity is insurance business and activities which are a direct extension of or ancillary to insurance business (s 255A(4)). Accounts of banking and insurance companies which are prepared under these provisions must indicate that they have been so prepared.

The detailed requirements of Sched 9 are not listed here but they are generally less detailed than those of Sched 4.

Where banking or insurance company accounts are prepared in

accordance with s 255 various rules as to eg accounts and disclosure of certain matters in the directors' report continue to apply as they did before the Companies Act 1981. For example:

(1) the directors' report must continue to state certain particulars as specified in Sched 10, eg, particulars of shares and debentures issued during the year (s 255C) and;

(2) the information normally required to be given by Sched 5 about subsidiaries and other bodies corporate in which the company has a significant holding (see 7.4.4) is not needed.

7.4.8 Insurance companies

Insurance companies will need to have regard to Part II of the Insurance Companies Act 1982.

7.4.9 Revision of defective accounts

The directors are able to prepare revised accounts if the accounts do not comply with the requirements of the Act (s 245). In addition the Secretary of State is able to give notice to the directors questioning them as to whether the accounts comply with the Act and if the directors give no satisfactory explanation in response the Secretary of State may make an application to the court (ss 245A, 245B).

7.5 Directors' Report

7.5.1 General

The directors' report, which is comprised in the company's accounts for the purposes of the rules requiring such accounts to be laid before the company in general meeting and filed, must contain a fair review of the development of the business of the company and its subsidiary undertakings during the financial year and of their position at its end and state the amount, if any, which the directors recommend shall be paid by way of dividend and the amount (if any) which they propose to carry to reserves (s 234(1)).

7.5.2 Further contents

The directors' report must also state or contain:

(1) the names of the persons who, at any time during the financial year, were directors of the company (s 234(2));

(2) the principal activities of the company and its subsidiary

undertakings in the course of that year and any significant change in those activities in that year (s 234(2));

(3) particulars of any significant changes in the fixed assets of the company or any of its subsidiary undertakings which have occurred in the year and of any substantial difference in the market value of any land (as at the end of the year) from the amount at which it is included in the balance sheet which in the directors' opinion is of such significance that it should be brought to the attention of members or holders of debentures (Sched 7 para 1);

(4) as respects each person who was a director at the end of the year, particulars of his interests at the end of the year and at the beginning of the year (or, if he was not a director then, when he became a director) according to the register of directors' holdings whether in relation to the company's shares or those of any other body corporate in the same group (see 8.8.1) (Sched 7 para 2) and whether according to the register he or his immediate family had any right to subscribe for shares or debentures in the company or any member of the group. In both cases, these details may be given in a note to the accounts instead of in the directors' report (Sched 7 para 2A and 2B);

(5) if the company (not being a wholly owned subsidiary of a company incorporated in Great Britain) has, or the company and its subsidiaries have between them, in the financial year given more than £200 for political and/or charitable purposes a statement, in the case of each of the purposes for which money has been given, of the amount given for that purpose, and, in the case of political purposes, certain additional particulars (Sched 7 para 3);

(6) if the company has purchased or maintained insurance for any officer or auditor in respect of liabilities to the company pursuant to s 310(3)(a) (see 8.13.4) then this fact has to be stated (Sched 7 para 5A);

(7) particulars of any important events affecting the company or any of its subsidiary undertakings which have occurred since the end of the year (Sched 7 para 6(a));

(8) an indication of likely future developments in the business of the company and its subsidiary undertakings and of their activities (if any) in the field of research and development (Sched 7 para 6(b) and (c));

(9) various particulars concerning any shares in the company

bought or otherwise acquired by the company itself or its nominee, or acquired by any other person with financial assistance from the company in circumstances such that the company has a beneficial interest in the shares, or which are made subject to a lien or other charge in favour of the company (Sched 7 paras 7 and 8);

(10) in the case of companies employing more than 250 people, a statement describing such policy as the company has applied during the financial year:

    (a) for giving full and fair consideration to applications for employment by disabled persons, having regard to their particular aptitudes and abilities,

    (b) for continuing the employment of and arranging appropriate training for those who become disabled while employed by the company, and

    (c) otherwise for the training, career development and promotion of disabled employees (Sched 7 para 9);

(11) in the case of companies of such classes as may be prescribed in regulations, such information as may be prescribed about the arrangements in force that year for securing the health, safety and welfare at work of employees of the company and its subsidiary undertakings, and for protecting other persons against risks to health or safety arising out of or in connection with the activities at work of those employees (Sched 7 para 10) (as at 1 July 1992, no such regulations had been made);

(12) in the case of companies employing an average of more than 250 persons during the financial year, a statement describing the action taken during the year to introduce, maintain or develop arrangements to:

    (a) provide employees systematically with information on matters of concern to them as employees,

    (b) consult employees or their representatives on a regular basis,

    (c) encourage employees' involvement in the company's performance through an employees' share scheme or otherwise, and

    (d) achieve a common awareness by all the employees of the financial and economic factors affecting the performance of the company,

leaving aside persons employed to work wholly or mainly outside the United Kingdom (Sched 7 para 11).

7.5.3 Listed companies

Listed companies are required by the Yellow Book to circulate with each annual report certain additional information in relation to themselves and their subsidiary undertakings and associated companies (if any). Companies whose shares are traded on the Unlisted Securities Market must similarly circulate with each annual report the information specified in the general undertaking applicable to such companies. For example, by Stock Exchange requirements a listed company or a company whose shares are traded on the Unlisted Securities Market must include in its annual report and accounts particulars of any authority given by shareholders to the board to buy the company's own shares existing at the end of the year and also, in the case of such purchases made otherwise than through the market or by tender or partial offer to all shareholders, particulars of the names of sellers of such shares bought, or proposed to be bought, by the company during the year (section 5, chapter 2, para 21(p)). (Particulars of purchases made during the year must be disclosed in accordance with s 234(4) and Sched 7 Part II.) The other Stock Exchange requirements in respect of matters to be included in the annual accounts are set out in section 5, chapter 2, para 20 of the Yellow Book.

7.5.4 Approval and signing of directors' report

Similar rules apply to the approval and signing of the directors' reports as apply to the accounts themselves ie the report must be approved by the board, signed by a director or, in this case, the secretary and the name of the person who signed the report must appear on the report before it is circulated, published or issued to any person (s 234A).

7.6 Auditors' Report

7.6.1 General

The company's auditors are required to make a report to the members on all annual accounts (defined as individual and any group accounts required by ss 226 and 227), copies of which are to be laid before the company in general meeting or would be so laid if an appropriate elective resolution was not in force (s 235), but see 9.2, below in relation to dormant companies. By s 261(2) a report on a company's annual accounts or its balance sheet or profit and loss account extends to any notes to the accounts in question giving information required by the Act and required or allowed to be given in a note to the accounts.

If a company publishes any of its statutory accounts, they must be accompanied by the auditors' report (s 240(1)), and such report is comprised in a company's accounts for the purposes of the rules that such accounts be laid before the company in general meeting and delivered to the Registrar (ss 241(1), 242(1)).

7.6.2 Contents

The auditors' report must state:

(1) whether in the auditors' opinion the annual accounts have been properly prepared in accordance with the Act and whether in their opinion a true and fair view is given:

    (a) in an individual balance sheet, of the state of the company's affairs as at the end of the financial year;

    (b) in an individual profit and loss account, of the company's profit or loss for the financial year;

    (c) in the case of group accounts, of the state of affairs as at the end of the financial year and profit or loss for the financial year of the undertakings included in the consolidation as a whole, so far as concerns members of the company (s 235(2));

(2) the auditors are required to consider whether the information given in the directors' report is consistent with the annual accounts and, if not, to indicate as such in their report.

In preparing their report the auditors must carry out such investigations as will enable them to form an opinion as to the following:

(1) whether proper accounting records have been kept by the company and proper returns adequate for their audit have been received from branches not visited by them; and

(2) whether the company's individual accounts are in agreement with the accounting records and returns;

and if the auditors are of the opinion that any of these are answerable in the negative they must state that in their report (s 237).

If the auditors fail to obtain all the information and explanations which, to the best of their knowledge and belief, are necessary for the purposes of their audit, they must state that in their report (s 237(3)).

Furthermore, if the details required by Sched 6 (concerning directors' emoluments, pensions and compensation, the numbers of higher-paid employees, loans to and other transactions with directors, persons connected with directors and officers (see 7.4.6)) are not duly given in notes to the accounts, the auditors must state them in their report, so far as they reasonably can (s 237(4)).

7.7 Summary Financial Statements

The Companies Act 1989 introduced a procedure whereby companies listed on The Stock Exchange are able to send to their members a summary financial statement instead of full accounts (ie those required to be circulated pursuant to s 251(1)).

7.7.1 When summary financial statements can be used

The detailed procedures are set out in The Companies (Summary Financial Statement) Regulations 1990 (the 'Regulations'). In order for a company to be able to send out summary financial statements the following conditions must be met:

(i) There must be no provision in a company's memorandum or articles of association requiring that full accounts be sent or forbidding the sending out of summary financial statements.

(ii) The company must have ascertained that the shareholder does not wish to receive full accounts and reports. The wishes of a shareholder may be ascertained in one of two ways:

(a) by a *relevant notification* received from the shareholder not later than 28 days before the first date on which copies of the full accounts are to be sent to shareholders in relation to any financial year indicating that he wishes to receive summary financial statements and which has not been impliedly countermanded by the failure to respond to a relevant consultation;

(b) by the shareholder failing to respond to an opportunity given to the member to elect to receive copies of the full accounts as part of a *relevant consultation*.

The procedure for the contents of a relevant consultation is set out in paragraph 6(3) of the Regulations and provides that it must state (i) in the future the shareholder will be sent a summary financial statement instead of the full accounts unless he notifies the company to the contrary and (ii) in a prominent position, that failure to reply has important consequences. The notification must be accompanied by a copy of the full accounts, a copy of the summary financial statement in respect of the same financial year as the full accounts and a postage prepaid printed card or form upon which the shareholder is able to indicate by marking a box whether he wishes to receive full accounts for the next financial year or indefinitely.

(iii) The period for allowed for laying full accounts must not have expired.

(iv) The summary financial statement must have been approved by the board and the original statement signed by a director.

(v) The name of the director who signed the statement must be stated.

(vi) The following statement must be included in a prominent position:

> 'This summary financial statement does not contain sufficient information to allow for a full understanding of the results and state of affairs of [the company] [the group and the state of affairs of the company or of the group]. For further information the full annual accounts, the auditors' report on those accounts and the directors' report should be consulted'.

(vii) It must contain a conspicuous statement of the right for the shareholders to demand, free of charge, a copy of the last full accounts.

(viii) It must be accompanied by a postage prepaid printed card or form upon which the shareholder is able to indicate by marking a box whether he wishes to receive full accounts for the next financial year or indefinitely.

7.7.2 Form and content of summary financial statement

The contents of a summary financial statement is set out in Sched 1 of the Regulations (other than for banking or insurance companies which have to comply with Scheds 2 and 3 respectively) and comprise three main areas:

(i) Directors' report

The statement has to contain the whole of, or a summary of, that portion of the directors' report which contains the following:
— the business review;
— important post-balance sheet events;
— likely future developments in the business;
— list of the names of the directors.

(ii) Summary profit and loss account
— turnover;
— income from shares in group undertakings and participating interests, or where group accounts are to be prepared, income from interests in associated undertakings;
— other interest receivable and similar interest and income payable and similar charges;
— the profit or loss on ordinary activities before and after taxation;
— tax on profit or loss on ordinary activities;
— minority interests (where group accounts are prepared);
— extraordinary income and charges after tax and after, where group accounts are prepared, the deduction or addition, as the case may be, of minority interests;
— profit or loss for the financial year;
— the aggregate amount of dividends paid and proposed.

In addition the aggregate amount of directors' emoluments is to be shown under an appropriate heading.

In respect of every item shown in the profit and loss account the corresponding amount shall be shown for the immediately preceding financial year.

(iii) Summary Balance Sheet

The statement must contain a summary balance sheet and, where group accounts are required to be prepared, a consolidated balance sheet and shall show, in so far as it can be derived from the full balance sheet, a single amount for each of the headings to which letters are assigned in the format set out in Part I of Sched 4 (with, in the case of group accounts, minority interests), but:

(a) where an alternative position is permitted for any item in the format, the summary balance sheet shall use the position used by the full balance sheet;

(b) in the case of format 2, heading C under 'Liabilities', two figures must be shown, one figure for amounts falling due within one year and one figure for amounts falling due after one year.

In respect of every item shown in the summary balance sheet the corresponding amount shall be shown for the immediately preceding financial year.

Chapter 8

Directors

8.1 Appointment of Directors

Every company is required to have a director as well as a secretary, and if there is only one director, that sole director cannot also be the secretary (s 283(2)). Moreover, every public company registered since 1 November 1929 must have at least two directors (s 282). A company may be a director (see s 289(1)(*b*)) but a corporation the sole director of which is secretary to the company may not be a sole director (s 283(4)).

The first directors of a company are sometimes named in and appointed by the Articles but, whether or not this is the case, the statement of particulars to be delivered on application for registration of a company (Form 10) must contain the name and relevant particulars of the persons who are to be the first directors of the company (s 10) (and any appointment by the Articles is void unless the person appointed is also named in the statement of particulars (s 10(5)).

The appointment of directors other than the first directors is usually provided for in the Articles. Table A gives the power of appointment to the company in general meeting, but allows the existing directors to fill a casual vacancy or to appoint an additional director until the next annual general meeting (reg 79). If a Stock Exchange listing is desired, the Articles must state that a director appointed to fill a casual vacancy or as an addition to the board shall hold office only until the next annual general meeting and shall then be eligible for re-election (section 9, chapter 1, para 4.2 of the Yellow Book).

In the case of a public company, two or more directors may not be appointed by a single resolution at a general meeting unless this procedure is first approved by the meeting without any vote being given against it (s 292(1)). If this requirement is not observed, the resolution appointing two or more directors is void, and no provision for the automatic reappointment of retiring directors in default of another appointment will take effect. However a special resolution altering the Articles may be passed in the ordinary way although it involves the appointment of two or more persons as directors (s 292(4)).

The Articles may contain provision for a director to appoint an alternate to act for him in circumstances specified in the Articles (see eg regs 65 to 69 Table A). A specimen notice of an appointment of an alternate director is contained in Appendix 5.

8.2 Retirement of Directors

Table A provides that directors shall retire by rotation (see regs 73 to 76) and similar provisions are often found in Articles not incorporating Table A. Great care must be taken in applying the provisions of the Articles, for considerable difficulties may ensue if these are not strictly observed.

Where there is provision in the Articles for the automatic reappointment of a retiring director if the vacancy caused by his retirement is not filled at the general meeting, this provision will operate even if the meeting resolves that he shall not be reappointed (*Grundt v Great Boulder Proprietary Gold Mines Ltd* [1948] Ch 145— though see reg 75 which provides to the contrary). The provision will not operate where a resolution to appoint directors has been rendered void under s 292(2) or where the retirement is under s 293 see 8.4.

Articles may also provide that a director shall vacate office in certain events (see reg 81), and may make provision for resignation; but even if there is no provision for this latter event, it seems that even a verbal resignation may have effect (*Latchford Premier Cinema Ltd v Ennion* [1931] 2 Ch 409), though the company may, in such a case, be entitled to damages for breach of a service agreement.

Where Articles give a director the power of assigning his office (in practice this is very unusual) an assignment must be sanctioned by special resolution of the company (s 308). An appointment of a new director by will of a deceased director is an assignment for this purpose.

8.3 Managing Director

The directors are frequently given power by the Articles to appoint one of their number managing director and to delegate to him such of their powers as they think fit (see reg 84). The terms of his appointment and his remuneration will (subject to the Articles) be fixed by the directors, and the latter usually takes the form of a salary with or without a director's fee and with or without a bonus related to profits. A provision contained in the Articles under which a person is appointed managing director does not in itself constitute a contract between him and the company, and he should, for his protection, enter into an agreement with the company after it has been incorporated (*Read v Astoria Garage (Streatham) Ltd* [1952] 2 All ER 292). The court has however on occasions implied a collateral contract on the terms of the Articles but this will provide little protection if the Articles give shareholders the right to remove directors. A managing director is not usually subject to retirement by rotation or counted in arriving at the number to retire although the position should always be checked in the Articles. On ceasing to be a director he automatically ceases to be managing director but it would normally be an implied term of any service agreement entered into that the company would not remove him from his office as a director (*Shindler v Northern Raincoat Co Ltd* [1960] 1 WLR 1038).

8.4 Age limit for Directors

Section 293 lays down two general rules, namely: (*a*) that no person can be appointed a director if at the time of his appointment he has attained the age of 70; and (*b*) that a director shall vacate office at the conclusion of the annual general meeting commencing next after he attains the age of 70; but these general rules are subject to a number of important modifications:

(1) they do not apply to a private company unless it is a subsidiary of a public company (or a company registered in Northern Ireland as a public company) (s 293(1)(*b*));

(2) if the company was first registered after the beginning of the year 1947, the section has effect subject to the provisions of the company's Articles, so that compliance with the Articles will be required if it provides for an earlier or later retirement date (s 293(7));

(3) if the company was registered before the beginning of the

year 1947, the section has effect subject to any alterations of the company's Articles made after the beginning of 1947; and if at the beginning of the year 1947 the Articles contained provisions for the retirement of directors under the age limit or for restricting the appointment of directors over a given age, the section does not apply to directors to whom such provisions apply (ibid);

(4) the main rules will not prevent the appointment of a director over 70 years of age or require him to retire on attaining that age if his appointment is or was made or approved by the company in general meeting; but special notice (see 6.4.3) is required for such appointment or approval; and the notice both to and by the company must state or must have stated the age of the person to whom it relates (s 293(5)).

Where a director does retire under the section, no provision for automatic reappointment will operate; and if the meeting at which he retires does not fill the vacancy, it may be filled as a casual vacancy (s 293(4)).

If a director who retires under s 293(3) is reappointed (as he may be under s 293(5)) or another director is appointed in the place of a director so retiring, the retiring director or new director must be treated, for the purpose of determining the time at which he or any other director is due to retire, as if he had become a director on the day on which the retiring director was last appointed before his retirement (s 293(6)). Except in this case, however, the retirement of a director out of turn under s 293(3) is to be disregarded in determining when other directors retire (ibid).

8.5 Removal of Directors

8.5.1 General

Notwithstanding anything in the Articles or in any agreement with the director, a company may by ordinary resolution remove a director before the expiration of his period of office (s 303).

Special notice (see 6.4.3) must be given of any resolution for the removal of a director or for the appointment of any person in place of a director so removed. Accordingly, if a shareholder wishes to remove a director he must give 28 days' notice of his intention to move the resolution to the company before the meeting is held. Where a majority of the board is, or is likely to be, hostile to the proposed resolution, the notice should be accompanied by a requisition of an extraordinary general meeting in accordance with the requirements of s 368 (see 6.3). The directors, in convening the necessary meeting, must give members notice of the resolution at the same time as the notice of the meeting. There are no special requirements for the notice of the meeting which can be held on 14 days' notice (unless the Articles provide for a longer period). There is an anti-avoidance provision contained in the section which provides that if the directors attempt to frustrate a member's proposal by calling a meeting prior to the expiry of the 28 day period the notice will still be deemed to have been properly given. On receiving notice of an intended resolution to remove a director, the company must forthwith send a copy of the resolution to the director, who is entitled to be heard at the meeting (ss 303(2) and 304(1)).

The director may, moreover, make representations in writing and request that they be notified to members of the company, in which event the company must, if it is not too late, state in any notice of the resolution given to members that representations have been made, and send a copy of the representations to every member to whom notice has been sent. If a copy is not sent, because the notice is received too late or because of the company's default, the director may require the representations to be read out at the meeting (s 304(3)). The representations need not be sent to members or read out at the meeting if on the application of the company or the person claiming to be aggrieved the court is satisfied that the procedure is being abused to secure needless publicity for defamatory matter (s 304 (4)). If a vacancy created by the removal of a director is not filled at the meeting by which he is removed, it may be filled as a casual vacancy (s 303(3)). Removal of a director from office under s 303 may give rise to a claim for compensation or damages by the director, and the right to pursue any such claim is expressly preserved by s 303(5).

It is arguable that a meeting convened to consider a resolution to remove a director pursuant to s 303 cannot be held on short notice since this would be inconsistent with the directors' right to send written representations to the members.

In the case of wholly owned subsidiary companies in a group of companies it is not unusual to include a provision in the company's Articles enabling the holding company to appoint and remove directors by notice in writing to the company.

Despite the clear intention of the legislative expressed in s 303 to prevent directors entrenching themselves on the board by provision in the Articles, it has been expressly recognised by the judiciary in *Bushell v Faith* [1970] AC 1099 that weighted voting rights can be attached to shares so as to enable the holder to defeat any resolution to remove him as a director.

It is possible to avoid the need for special notice by inserting a provision in the Articles to permit shareholders to remove a director by means of special or extraordinary resolution. In such a case, although 21 or 14 days' notice of the meeting would need to be given, no special notice is required and nor does the director get rights to send a circular to shareholders or speak at the relevant meeting. Furthermore, the meeting can be held on short notice (see 6.6.3). However, a note of caution should be sounded—the use of this procedure may, if challenged in court, be viewed as an attempt to subvert the intention of Parliament. Although this risk is small, given the court's approach in *Bushell v Faith*, nevertheless there must still be a concern that this course of action would be subject to challenge.

It is clear that the written resolution procedure contained in s 381A (see 6.6.3) or any such procedure contained in a company's Articles cannot be used to pass an ordinary resolution under s 303 (see Sched 15A, Part I, para 1). If a director is being removed pursuant to a special resolution in accordance with the procedure set out in the Articles, then a written resolution should be able to be used.

8.5.2 Compensation for loss of office

It is not lawful for a company to make to any director any payment by way of compensation for loss of office, or as consideration for or in connection with his retirement from office, unless particulars of the proposed payment (including the amount thereof) are disclosed to the members of the company and the proposal is approved by the company (s 312). However, if the sum is a bone fide payment by way of damages for breach of contract or by way of pension (including any superannuation allowance, superannuation gratuity or similar payment) in respect of past services disclosure and approval under s 312 (or under ss 313 and 314—see below) is not required (s 316(3)). When disclosure is required, it must be made to all the members while the payment is still a proposal: where no disclosure is made to, eg, preference shareholders, the directors can be liable for misapplication of the company's funds (*Re Duomatic Ltd* [1969] 2 Ch 365).

It is also not lawful for any such payment to be made to any director by the company or by any other person in connection with the transfer of the whole or any part of the undertaking or property of the company unless similar disclosure and approval has taken place (s 313). A sum paid in breach of this rule is held by the recipient on trust for the company.

If any such payment is proposed in connection with a transfer of all or any of the shares in the company, being a transfer resulting from one of four types of offer, it is the duty of the directors to whom payments are to be made to take all reasonable steps to secure that particulars of the proposed payment are included in or sent with any notice of the offer given to any shareholder. The four types of offer are (a) an offer made to the general body of the shareholders; (b) an offer made by or on behalf of some other body corporate with a view to the company becoming its subsidiary or a subsidiary of its holding company; (c) an offer made by or on behalf of an individual with a view to his obtaining the right to exercise or control the exercise of not less than one-third of the voting power at any general meeting of the company; and (d) any other offer which is conditional on acceptance to a given extent (s 314).

If a director fails to take such reasonable steps, or if any person, who has been properly required by such director to include particulars in or send them with such notice fails to do so, he is liable to a fine of £400 (s 314(3)), and if the requirements as to such payments have not been complied with, or if the making of the proposed payment is not approved before the transfer of any shares in pursuance of the offer, any sum received by the directors is deemed to have been received by them in trust for the persons who have sold their shares as a result of the offer (s 315(1)).

The making of the proposed payment must be approved by a meeting summoned for the purpose of the holders of the shares to which the offer relates, and of all other holders of shares of the same class; and if this does not include all members of the company and there are no provisions in the Articles for summoning and regulating such a meeting, the provisions of the Act and the Articles relating to general meetings shall apply subject to any modification ordered by the Department of Trade (s 315(2)). If at such a meeting a quorum is not present, and after the meeting has been adjourned to a later date, a quorum is again not present, the payment to the director will be deemed to have been approved (s 315(3)).

Payments falling within ss 312 to 316 will normally be taxable in the hands of the recipient (ss 148 and 188 of and Sched 11 to the Income and Corporation Taxes Act 1988) to the extent that they exceed £30,000.

8.6 Directors' Qualification

Articles may provide that a director shall hold a certain number of shares in the company. Where the Articles do require shares to be held, the number of shares so required must be obtained within two months of the director's appointment or such shorter time as may be prescribed by the Articles; and if they are not obtained within such period, or the director ceases at any time to hold the necessary number of shares after appointment, his office is to be vacated. In such an event, the person so vacating office cannot be reappointed until he has acquired the requisite qualifying shares. Any director who continues to act after his office has thus been rendered vacant is liable to a fine which increases daily (s 291).

In construing the Articles, attention must be paid to the expressions used, for the acquisition of shares may be made a condition precedent to appointment, eg where the Articles state that no person may be appointed a director unless he 'shall have acquired' a certain number of shares. In this event, an appointment before the shares are acquired is ineffective from the outset, and the statutory two months of grace are not available. Articles may require the qualifying shares to be held by the director 'as beneficial owner'; but, in the absence of such a requirement, the holding of sufficient shares as trustee for some other person is sufficient (*Howard v Sadler* [1893] 1 QB 1). Furthermore, a provision that qualification shares shall be held by a director 'in his own right' does not mean that it is necessary for him to be the beneficial owner. The fact that the director has received the shares as a present from promoters does not disqualify him (*Re Innes & Co Ltd* [1903] 2 Ch 254). Unless the Articles otherwise provide, it is sufficient if the shares are held jointly with another person (*Grundy v Briggs* [1910] 1 Ch 444), but the holding of a bearer warrant will not qualify (s 291(2)).

8.7 Disqualification of Directors

(1) The Articles may provide for certain circumstances in which directors become disqualified (see eg reg 81). An undischarged bankrupt may not act as a director except with the permission

of the court which adjudged him bankrupt (Company Directors Disqualification Act 1986 s 11).

(2) The court has power, pursuant to the Company Directors Disqualification Act 1986, to make a disqualification order restraining persons from acting as directors or being involved in any way, whether directly or indirectly in the promotion, formation or management of a company. The table below summarises the principal circumstances in which the court may make such an order:

Offence	Disqualification Period	Company Directors Disqualification Act 1986
Conviction of an indictable offence in connection with the promotion, formation, management or liquidation of a company, or with the receivership or management of a company's property	15 years or 5 years if the disqualification order is made by a court of summary jurisdiction	s 2
Persistently in default in relation to provisions of the companies legislation requiring any return, account or other document to be filed, delivered or sent to the Registrar of Companies.	5 years	s 3
Participation in fraudulent or wrongful trading or any other fraud in relation to the company or any breach of duty as an officer, liquidator, receiver or manager.	15 years	ss 4, 10
Summary conviction on three occasions within the last five years for breach of the companies legislation referred to in (2) above	5 years	s 5

The court is *required* to disqualify a director where it is satisfied that he is or has been a director of a company which has at any time become insolvent and that his conduct as a director makes him unfit to be concerned with the management of a company (s 6 1986 Act) and may do so following an investigation of the company's affairs in certain circumstances by an inspector appointed by the Secretary of State (s 8 1986 Act). The minimum period of disqualification is two years (in the case of s 6) and the maximum 15 years. The liquidator, administrator or administrative receiver are under a statutory duty to report any director who they believe is liable to be disqualified under s 6.

The court, in order to determine whether a person is unfit to be concerned in the management of a company, is to have regard to the matters set out in the schedule to the Act. These include such matters as whether the director has been guilty of any mis-feasance or breach of fiduciary duty in relation to the company and any misappropriation or retention of the company's money.

In *Re Lo-Line Electric Motors Ltd* (1988) 4BCC 415 the judge recognised that although the power to disqualify was not funda-mentally penal it did involve a substantial interference with freedom and it followed that the rights of the individual had to be fully protected. Ordinary commercial misjudgment did not in itself justify disqualification. In the normal case the conduct complained of had to display a lack of commercial probity, although in an extreme case of gross negligence or total incompetence, disqualification could be appropriate.

(3) The acts of a director are valid notwithstanding any defect that may afterwards be discovered in his appointment or qualifi-cation (s 285). Similarly, acts done by a person as a director are valid notwithstanding that it is afterwards discovered that his appointment has been terminated because he has attained the age of 70 (s 293(3)).

8.8 Details of Directors and Secretaries

8.8.1 Company register

Every company is required by s 288 to keep at its registered office a register of directors and secretaries containing the following particulars:

(1) Particulars as to directors
    (a) in the case of an individual, his present first name and surname, any former name or surname (s 289(2)), his

usual residential address, his nationality, his business occupation (if any), particulars of other directorships (see below) and his date of birth;

(b) in the case of a corporation, its corporate name and registered or principal office (s 289(1)(b)).

Where a director holds or has held directorships in other companies, these must also be recorded in the register; but it is not necessary to record directorships held outside the preceding five years; or in dormant companies; or in companies of which the company is the wholly-owned subsidiary, or which are the wholly-owned subsidiaries either of the company or of another company of which the company is the wholly-owned subsidiary. For this purpose the expression 'company' includes any body corporate incorporated in Great Britain; a body corporate is deemed to be the wholly-owned subsidiary of another if it has no members except that other and that other's wholly-owned subsidiaries and its or their nominees; and a company is dormant during any period in which no significant accounting transaction occurs (see s 250(3)), s 289(3)).

For the purposes of s 288, a person in accordance with whose directions or instructions the directors are accustomed to act is deemed to be a director and officer of the company (s 288(6)) and consequently his details are to be kept in the register of directors.

(2) Particulars as to secretaries

(a) in the case of an individual, his present Christian name and surname, any former Christian name or surname (s 289(2)), and his usual residential address;

(b) in the case of a corporation or a Scottish firm, its corporate or firm name and registered or principal office (s 290(1)(b)).

The particulars contained in the registers must also be included in the annual return (see 7.1).

The register of directors and secretaries is governed by the Companies (Inspection and Copying of Registers, Indices and Documents) Regulations 1991, No 1998 (see 10.2.4).

Listed companies must notify the Quotations Department of The Stock Exchange without delay of any changes in the directorate (section 5, chapter 2, para 41 of the Yellow Book).

8.8.2 Filing of particulars relating to directors and secretaries

The statement of particulars to be delivered to the Registrar on application for registration of a company (Form 10) must contain the relevant particulars of the first directors and secretary and their respective written consents to act (s 10(2)). It should be noted that Form 10 requires a director to disclose all directorships held within the preceding five years, whether or not current. Notification of any changes of directors or secretary, or of any changes in their registered particulars, must be given to the Registrar (on Form 288) within 14 days of the change; such notification must specify the date of the change and contain a written consent to act signed by each person named as having become a director or secretary (s 288(2)).

8.9 Directors' Shareholdings and Dealings

8.9.1 Company register

Every company must keep a register showing as respects each director of the company (1) the number of shares of each class in, and the amount of debentures of each class of, the company or any other body corporate, being the company's subsidiary or holding company, or a subsidiary of the company's holding company, in which he (or his spouse or infant child—s 328(1)) is interested (s 325) and (2) particulars of the occurrence of certain events relating to such shares or debentures including any change in the registered interests (s 325). The rules set out in Sched 13 have effect for the interpretation of, and otherwise in relation to, this provision (s 324(3)). There are certain exceptions (see SI 1985 No 802)—in particular where the company is a wholly-owned subsidiary of a company incorporated outside the UK, interests in shares or debentures of the foreign company are not required to be kept.

The register need not include particulars of shares in any body corporate which is the wholly-owned subsidiary of another body corporate (s 324(6)) nor is a director required to provide any particulars to a company of interests in shares or debentures of its holding company where he is a director of that company and such company holds all the shares of the company and is required to keep a register under s 325.

A director is bound to notify the company in writing of the subsistence of relevant interests and of the occurrence of most of the events requiring to be recorded in the register (s 324(1)), the company itself being bound to insert in the register particulars of the granting to and exercise by a director (or his spouse or infant child) of a right to subscribe for shares or debentures of the company (s 325(3)). Notification must be given within five days of acquisition or of the occurrence of the relevant event (Sched 13 para 14). Inscription must take place within three days after notification or the event as the case may be (Sched 13 para 22).

For the purposes of the above requirements, any person in accordance with whose directions or instructions the directors of the company are accustomed to act (except by reason only of advice given by him in a professional capacity) is deemed to be a director of the company (ss 324(6), 325(6) and 741). A director may require that the nature and extent of his interest in any shares or debentures shall be indicated in the register (Sched 13 para 23) but nothing done for the purposes of s 324 affects the company with notice of, or puts the company upon inquiry as to, the rights of any person in relation to any shares or debentures (Sched 13 para 24).

The register must be kept at the place where the company's register of members is kept or at the company's registered office, except during the holding of the annual general meeting, when it must be produced at the commencement of the meeting and must remain open and accessible during the continuance of the meeting to any person attending the meeting (Sched 13 paras 25 and 29). Notice of the location of the register, and of any change in such location, must be given to the Registrar unless it has always been kept at the registered office (Form 325) (Sched 13 para 27). An index of the names mentioned in the register must be maintained unless the register is in a form which constitutes an index in itself (Sched 13 para 28). The register must be open to the inspection of any member of the company or the general public and copies thereof must be supplied in a similar way as the register of members (see 4.2.3 and 4.2.4).

Listed companies must notify the Stock Exchange by the end of the following day (weekends and bank holidays being ignored for this purpose) of any matter notified to the company under ss 324 or 328 in respect of its listed shares or debentures, and the Stock Exchange can publish such information in any manner it may determine (s 329). In a recent amendment to the Yellow Book, the Stock Exchange now requires disclosure to it of any dealings in shares by persons 'connected with' a director (within the meaning of s 346—see 8.12.3, Yellow Book, section 5, chapter 2, para 16).

8.9.2 *Restrictions on dealings in listed securities*

It is an offence for a director (including a shadow director) of a company (or his spouse or infant child (s 327)) to deal in options to buy or sell listed shares in, or listed debentures of, the company or its subsidiary or holding company or a subsidiary of its holding company (s 323) but there is an exemption in respect of buying rights to subscribe, and in respect of convertible debentures. If it appears to the Secretary of State that there are circumstances suggesting that s 323 (or, indeed, s 324) have been contravened, he may appoint inspectors to establish whether or not contraventions have occurred (s 446).

8.9.3 *Insider dealing*

Penal sanctions are also imposed by the Company Securities (Insider Dealing) Act 1985 (the 'CSIDA') against certain dealings in the securities of a company by individuals having unpublished price-sensitive information (s 10 CSIDA) in relation to those securities which was derived either from their present or past connection with the company (or a related company) or from someone so connected. The prohibition extends to dealings in securities of companies other than the one with which the individual (or his informant) is connected if the information relates to a transaction, actual or contemplated, between the two companies and also to dealings in one capacity by an individual contemplating a take-over offer for the company in another capacity.

The 'dealings' to which the prohibition applies are, in outline, dealings on a recognised stock exchange (s 1 et seq, CSIDA) and 'off-market dealings' in advertised securities (s 4, CSIDA).

The general conditions of liability are:

(1) that the individual knows that he is or was at any time in the preceding six months, or his informant is or was at any time in the six months preceding the obtaining of the information, connected with the relevant company (or is or was concerned in a take-over or other transaction, actual or contemplated, with the company. Individuals may be connected with a company as a director, officer or employee of the company or by virtue of a business or professional relationship giving rise to a position of confidence with such persons.);

(2) that the individual or his informant obtained the information by virtue of his connection;

(3) that it would be reasonable to expect the individual or his

informant not to disclose the information except for the proper performance of the functions attaching to his position; and

(4) that the individual or his informant knows the information is unpublished price-sensitive information (see s 10 CSIDA) in relation to the securities in question.

Any individual prohibited from dealing in any securities himself may not 'counsel or procure' any other person to deal in those securities or communicate the information to any other person if he knows or has reasonable cause to believe that that or some other person will make use of the information for the purpose of dealing (s 1(7),(8), CSIDA). Whilst companies as such are not subject to the CSIDA, since they are not 'individuals', a company is a 'person' for the purposes of the prohibition on counselling or procuring.

It is a defence to show that the individual acted otherwise than with a view to the making of a profit or the avoidance of a loss (whether for himself or another person) (s 3(1)(*a*) CSIDA), and there are also certain savings for liquidators, receivers, trustees and others. No offence is committed by taking advantage of inside information to refrain from dealing or advise another so to do.

Transactions in contravention of the CSIDA are not void or voidable for that reason alone (s 8(3)).

8.9.4 *Take-over Code and Stock Exchange provisions*

In relation to dealings in listed securities, the Code on Take-overs and Mergers and The Stock Exchange's Yellow Book should also be considered because the requirements they impose in some respects exceed those of the CSIDA. For example, Rule 4 of the Code imposes additional obligations with regard to secrecy of unpublished information and prohibits dealings of any kind (including option business and off-market transactions) in the securities of an offeree company by any person, not being the offeror, who is privy to confidential price-sensitive information concerning an actual or contemplated offer, prior to announcement of the offer or the termination of discussions.

The Stock Exchange has also issued a Model Code for securities transactions by directors of listed companies which, inter alia, prohibits dealings during the two months preceding the first announcement of annual and half-yearly results or dividends or distributions to be paid or passed. It also regulates dealings by a director's family and funds of which a director is trustee or beneficiary. The Model Code is to be regarded as a minimum standard of good practice, and listed companies are obliged by the continuing obligations provisions of The Stock Exchange Yellow Book to adopt their own rules in terms no less exacting.

The Institute of Directors has also published its own code of guidance on insider dealings as part of its revised *Guide to Boardroom Practice No. 6, Directors' Personal Liabilities, 1992.*

8.9.5 Publication of directors' names

A company's business documents need not state the names of its directors: but if, in the case of a company registered after 22 November 1916, a business letter contains in any form (except in the text or as a signatory) the name of any director, then the name of every other director must also be stated (s 305).

These requirements apply also to a company incorporated outside Great Britain which has a place of business in Great Britain, unless such place of business was established before 23 November 1916.

8.10 Remuneration of Directors

A director has no implied or statutory right to remuneration for his services as director, but invariably the right to remuneration is awarded by the Articles (see eg reg 82); and if it is not awarded by the Articles it may be granted by resolution of the company. A director will frequently also hold an executive position with the company, eg managing director or finance director, and as such will receive additional remuneration as an employee.

Where a director serves for a part of a year only, it is not clear whether he is entitled to a proportion of any annual remuneration awarded by the Articles (*Moriarty v Regent's Garage Co* [1921] 2 KB 766) unless the Articles (or the resolution in cases where the remuneration is fixed by the company in general meeting) provide that he is to be paid '*at the rate of £x* per annum', although it is probable that the Apportionment Act 1870 would be held to apply and the remuneration taken to accrue from day to day. Where the appointment of a director is invalid from the outset, he is not entitled to remuneration (*Woolf v East Nigel Gold Mining Co Ltd* (1905) 21 TLR 660); but it is otherwise where his original appointment is valid and he becomes disqualified subsequently (*Salton v New Beeston Cycle Co* [1899] 1 Ch 775).

Directors who are remunerated for their services are not entitled in addition to an allowance for travelling expenses unless the Articles so provide or the company so resolves (*Young v Naval, Military and Civil Service Co-operative Society of South Africa Ltd* [1905] 1 KB 687) (see reg 83); but out-of-pocket expenses may be reimbursed.

Particulars as to the remuneration of directors must be given in the company's published accounts (see 7.4.6).

It is unlawful to pay a director remuneration (whether as director or otherwise) free of income tax, or otherwise calculated by reference to or varying with the amount of his income tax, or to or with the rate or basic rate of income tax, and any provision in the Articles or in a contract for the payment of remuneration free of tax etc is to have effect as if it provided for payment, as a gross sum subject to tax, of the net sum for which it actually provides (s 311).

8.11 Directors' Service Agreements

A company must keep at an appropriate place (see s 318(1)) ie its registered office or principal place of business, or the place where its register of members is kept, copies of written service contracts of any director with the company or any subsidiary (and written memoranda of any unwritten ones), unless (*a*) the contract requires him to work wholly or mainly outside the United Kingdom, in which case only a memorandum of its terms as to duration need be made available (s 318(5)) or (*b*) the unexpired portion is less than twelve months or it can be terminated by the company within the next ensuing twelve months, without payment of compensation (s 318(11)). Notice of the place at which they are kept must be sent to the Registrar (Form 318) unless they have at all times been kept at the registered office. The inspection of the service contracts is governed by the Companies (Inspection and Copying of Registers, Indices and Documents) Regulations 1991, SI No 1998 (see 10.2.4).

The prior approval of the company in general meeting is needed before a contract is entered into under which a director will have security of employment for more than five years (s 319): an ordinary resolution is sufficient.

The following points should be noted:

(1) in the case of a director of a holding company, the requirement applies to any agreement for employment with the company or any subsidiary;

(2) it applies not only to contracts of employment in the strict

sense but also to contracts for the provision of services by the director;

(3) it applies whether or not the agreement is in writing;

(4) in case (1) the approval required is that of the holding company and that of the subsidiary, if partly owned; but no approval is required from a company incorporated abroad, whether it be an employing company or a holding company, or from a company which is a wholly-owned subsidiary of another company wherever incorporated;

(5) in certain circumstances, where a further agreement is entered into before the expiration of an existing agreement, the unexpired period of the existing agreement is to be added to the period of the further agreement in ascertaining whether the further agreement extends beyond five years;

(6) a term incorporated in a service agreement in contravention of s 319 is void and the agreement is deemed to include a provision entitling the company to terminate it on giving reasonable notice.

The provisions summarised above apply also to 'shadow directors' (ie any person in accordance with whose directions or instructions the directors of a company are accustomed to act—ss 318(6), 319(7) and 741).

The Stock Exchange Yellow Book requires that all service agreements not expiring or determinable within one year without payment of compensation must be available for inspection prior to and at the annual general meeting (section 2, chapter 5, para 42 Yellow Book).

8.12 Loans etc to Directors

Sections 330 to 347, taken together, construct an elaborate code of prohibitions and penalties in relation to loans and other financial transactions (under which credit is granted but which could not strictly be classified as loans) involving directors or persons connected with directors. These provisions are complex and difficult, even obscure. A comprehensive analysis of their ramifications would be inappropriate in a work of this nature but it is to be hoped that the following outline of the principal provisions will be of assistance. In any save a straightforward case, company secretaries would be wise to take professional advice; but it is necessary that the breadth of the provisions should be appreciated in order to be alert to the necessity for such advice in widely differing circumstances.

8.12.1 All companies

All companies are prohibited (s 330) from:

(1) making a loan to a director of the company or its holding company;

(2) entering into a guarantee or providing security in connection with a loan made by any person to such a director;

unless in the case of (1) above the aggregate of the 'relevant amounts' (see 8.12.3) does not exceed £5,000 (s 334).

It should be noted that 'company' for this purpose means a company incorporated under the Act or one of its predecessor Acts (s 735) and therefore does not extend to, for example, a wholly-owned but overseas incorporated subsidiary of a UK incorporated holding company.

Exceptions to the foregoing are:

(1) the provision for a director of funds to meet business expenditure if the prior approval of the company in general meeting is given (s 337) or, if such approval is not obtained, the relevant loan is to be repaid or any other liability arising under the transaction is to be discharged within six months from the conclusion of the next following annual general meeting;

(2) in the case of a money-lending company (see s 338(2)), a loan or guarantee in the ordinary course of business provided *either* the loan or guarantee is on an arm's length commercial basis *or* the loan made or guaranteed is a housing loan (ie a loan for the acquisition or improvement of a dwellinghouse for use as the only or main residence of the director, or for replacing a loan made by another for that purpose), such loans are ordinarily made to employees of the company on no less favourable terms and the aggregate of the relevant amount of the loan must not exceed £100,000;

(3) loans by a company to its holding company or the provision of a guarantee or security by a company in connection with a loan made to its holding company by any other person (s 336).

8.12.2 Relevant companies

These are public companies and any company which is a subsidiary of, or has a subsidiary or fellow subsidiary which is, a public company (s 331(6)). Again, the definition encompasses only companies incorporated under the Act and not foreign companies. In addition to the prohibitions applicable to all companies (see above), relevant companies are prohibited from:

(1) making or agreeing to make a *quasi-loan* (see 8.12.3) to a director of the company or its holding company or a loan or quasi-loan to any person *connected with* such a director, or entering into any guarantee or providing any security in connection with any such loan or quasi-loan or loan by any other person (s 330(3));

(2) entering into a *credit transaction* (see 8.12.3) for a director of the company or its holding company or any *connected person* or entering into a guarantee or providing any security in connection with such a credit transaction by any other person (s 330(4)).

Exceptions The same general exceptions apply to the additional prohibitions imposed on relevant companies as to the prohibitions imposed on companies generally—subject to special provisions and limitations, amongst which the following may be noted:

(1) the exception for business expenditure applies only if the aggregate of the relevant amounts does not exceed £20,000 (s 337(3));

(2) loans and quasi-loans under the exception for a money lending company are permitted in the case of a company which is not a recognised bank only if the aggregate of the relevant amounts does not exceed £100,000 (s 338(4));

(3) credit transactions are permitted if (*a*) the aggregate of the relevant amounts at the time of the transaction does not exceed £10,000, or (*b*) the transaction is entered into in the ordinary course of the company's business and the value of the transaction is not greater than, and the terms not more favourable than, would be offered to a person of equal financial standing not connected with the company (s 335(2));

(4) intra-group loan or quasi-loan guarantee or security arrangements which would otherwise be prohibited by reason only that a director of one member of the group is associated with another are permitted (s 333).

8.12.3 *General*

The following are the principal definitions applicable to the foregoing sections (insofar as not directly dealt with):

(1) A *quasi-loan* is a transaction under which one party ('the creditor') agrees to pay, or pays otherwise than in pursuance of an agreement, a sum for another ('the borrower'), or agrees to reimburse, or reimburses otherwise than in pursuance of an agreement, expenditure incurred by another party for another (likewise 'the borrower'):

  (*a*) on terms that the borrower (or a person on his behalf) will reimburse the creditor; or

  (*b*) in circumstances giving rise to a liability on the borrower (or any person on his behalf) to reimburse the creditor (s 331(3)).

For example the provision of a credit card which can be used for personal expenditure can constitute a quasi-loan.

(2) A *credit transaction* is a transaction under which one party (a) supplies goods or sells land under a hire-purchase agreement or a conditional sale agreement; (b) leases or hires land or goods in return for periodical payments; or (c) otherwise disposes of land or supplies goods or *services* on deferred payment terms (s 331(7)).

(3) *Services* means anything other than goods or land (s 331(8)).

(4) *Connected persons.* A person is connected with a director if such person (not being himself a director) is:

  (*a*) the spouse or minor child (legitimate or illegitimate) or stepchild of a director;

  (*b*) a body corporate with which the director is associated;

  (*c*) acting in the capacity of trustee of any trust (other than an employees' share scheme or a pension scheme) of which the director or his spouse or any minor child or stepchild or associated body corporate is a beneficiary or a possible beneficiary under a power conferred on the trustees; or

  (*d*) acting in his capacity as a partner of the director or of a person connected with the director by virtue of any of the foregoing subparagraphs.

For the purposes of (*b*) and (*c*) above, a director of a company is associated with another body corporate if he and persons connected with him are together interested in one-fifth of the equity share capital or entitled to exercise or control the exercise of one-fifth of the voting power at any general meetings of that body corporate (s 346(5)).

A whole section of the Act (s 339) is devoted to the manner in which '*relevant amounts*' are determined. In essence, the value of the proposed transaction and the outstanding value of all existing loans or other relevant arrangements to or with the person in whose favour a transaction is proposed and his connected persons must be aggregated.

Certain transactions which might otherwise enable the prohibitions to be evaded (eg the taking over by a company of loans, guarantees etc made or entered into by outside parties, or the company taking part in a collusive arrangement eg a back to back loan arrangement) are themselves prohibited (s 330(6) and (7)).

For the purposes of these restrictions on loans etc for directors and persons connected with them a shadow director is treated as a director (s 330(5)). A shadow director is a person in accordance with whose directions or instructions the directors of a company are accustomed to act (unless by reason only of advice given by him in a professional capacity).

See 8.14.2 for disclosure in a company's accounts of loans to or similar transactions for directors or persons connected with them.

8.13 Powers, Duties and Liabilities of Directors

8.13.1 Powers

The division of power between the board and general meeting depends on the construction of the Articles and where power of management is delegated to the board, the shareholders, through a general meeting, are unable to interfere.

The Articles will normally place the management of a company's affairs in the hands of the directors. Regulation 70 provides: 'subject to the provisions of the Act, the Memorandum and the Articles and to any directions given by special resolution, the business of the company shall be managed by the directors who may exercise all the powers of the company'.

Accordingly, directors will possess all the powers necessary to enable them to carry out their functions, eg to enter into contracts on behalf of the company, to engage or dismiss employees etc. The shareholders are able to intervene in the management of the company only where a special resolution can be passed. It is always open to the shareholders to remove the directors by ordinary resolution if they are unhappy with the management of the company (s 303 and see 8.5).

The directors' powers may, however, be restricted by the Articles. It may, for instance, be provided that certain acts shall not be done by them unless they first obtain the sanction of the company in general meeting; and, where there is such a provision in the Articles, failure to obtain such sanction may render the directors personally liable to the company. However in favour of a third party dealing with a company in good faith the power of the board of directors to bind the company or authorise others to do so is deemed to be free of any such limitation under the company's constitution and such a third party is not bound to enquire as to any such limitation and is presumed to have acted in good faith unless the contrary is proved (s 35A (see 1.3.2)). Even where there is such a limitation in the Articles, an act done without prior sanction may be ratified subsequently by the company, provided that where the act is beyond the capacity of the company by reason of a limitation in the Memorandum, the ratification must be by means of a special resolution (s 35(3)).

8.13.2 Fiduciary duties

A director's duties to his company are of a fiduciary nature, and are owed to the company itself, not to its shareholders individually or to creditors. It is the overriding duty of the directors to exercise their powers in good faith ie in the manner in which they consider it best in the interests of the company (see eg *Bamford v Bamford* [1970] Ch 212) and for a proper purpose (see eg *Howard Smith Ltd v Ampol Petroleum Ltd* [1974] AC 821 (PC)). In addition a director must not make a personal profit from the company (see eg *Cook v Deeks* [1916] 1 AC 554) and must not place himself in a position where his own interests and those of the company may conflict (see eg *Industrial Development Consultants v Cooley* [1972] 1 WLR 443). The interests of the company in this context means the interests of present and future shareholders: but s 309, whilst recognising that the duty is still owed to the company alone, requires the directors of a company to have regard, in the performance of their functions, to the interests of the company's employees in general as well as to the interests of its members. The Act further provides (s 719) that the powers of the company shall, if they would not otherwise do so, be deemed to include power to make provision, in connection with the cessation or the transfer to any person of the whole or part of the undertaking of the company or any subsidiary, for the benefit of persons employed or formerly employed by the company or by such subsidiary. This power may be exercised notwithstanding that its exercise is not in the best interests of the company, and, if so authorised by the Memorandum or Articles, may be exercised by a resolution of the directors (failing which provision it must be exercised as may be provided by the Memorandum or Articles, or otherwise by ordinary resolution of the company).

If the Articles do not restrict a power exercisable by the directors, they are not bound to follow directions given to them by the company in general meeting if they honestly believe that the course they themselves desire to adopt is best for the company (*Quin & Axtens Ltd v Salmon* [1909] AC 442); but the company can force its will upon them by altering the Articles by special resolution or by dismissing the offending directors by an ordinary resolution under s 303.

8.13.3 Duties of skill and care

Directors are also subject to certain duties regarding the degree of skill and care that they are required to exercise in the performance of their duties. An executive director's standard of care will in general be determined by his contract of service; non-executive directors are, however, subject to the common law rules which may be summarised as follows:

(1) a director need not exhibit in the performance of his duties a greater degree of skill than may reasonably be expected from a person of his knowledge and experience.

(2) a director is not bound to give continuous attention to the affairs of the company. He is not required to attend all board meetings, although he ought to attend when it is reasonable for him to do so.

(3) in respect of duties that, having regard to the exigencies of business, and the Articles, may properly be left to some other official, a director is, in the absence of grounds for suspicion, justified in trusting that official to perform such duties honestly (*Re City Equitable Fire Insurance Co Ltd* [1925] Ch 407).

The Insolvency Act 1986 has introduced a higher degree of skill and care on directors whose companies go into insolvent liquidation (see eg, 11.2.11).

Recently, the courts have begun to impose a higher duty of care on directors generally to reflect modern commercial life. For example in *Dorchester Finance v Stebbing* [1989] BCLC 498 it was held that two non-executive directors, who were chartered accountants, were liable to the company for negligence in that they signed blank cheques relying on the integrity of the managing director who counter-signed them. The court took into account the professional status of the directors and refused to recognise that they did not have a duty to supervise the management of the company.

8.13.4 Liabilities of directors

The liabilities of directors to the company and to outsiders who have dealings with the company are determined by the common law and the Act. At common law they may be liable to the company for eg negligence or breach of trust, and to outsiders for breach of warranty of authority. Under the Act the company is given statutory civil remedies for breaches of certain directors' duties as, for example, in relation to ss 320 to 322 (substantial property transactions involving directors—see 8.14) and s 330 (see 8.12), breach of which entitles the company to declare void any arrangement thereby entered into, to reclaim any gains or profits and to be indemnified against any loss or damage. There can also be liability to outsiders under the Act, as, for example, under the prospectus provisions (see 3.7.5) or under the listing particulars provisions of the Financial Services Act 1986 (see 3.5.3 and 3.5.4).

Failure by directors to observe many provisions of the Act and other statutes may give rise to criminal liability, as, for example, the prohibition on loans etc to directors under s 330 (see 8.12). This area is too extensive for treatment here but note that:

(1) Under s 450, any officer of a company who destroys, mutilates or falsifies, or is privy to destruction, mutilation or falsification of a document affecting or relating to its property or affairs, or makes or is privy to the making of a false entry in such a document, is, unless he proves that he had no intention to conceal the state of affairs of the company or to defeat the law, guilty of an offence. Further, any such person who fraudulently either parts with, alters, or makes an omission in any such document, is likewise guilty of an offence.

(2) Under s 19(1) of the Theft Act 1968, any officer of a body corporate, or any person purporting to act as such, who publishes or concurs in the publication of any written statement or account which to his knowledge is or may be

misleading, false or deceptive in a material particular, with intent to deceive members or creditors of the body corporate about its affairs is guilty of an offence punishable by up to seven years' imprisonment.

(3) It is an offence for an officer of a company to make a misleading statement to the company's auditor (s 389A—see further 9.6.2).

Except as provided in s 310 (and see reg 118), any provision (whether in the Articles or in any contract with the company or otherwise) for exempting any director or officer of the company or any person employed by the company as auditor from, or indemnifying him against, any liability for negligence, default or breach of trust is void. However, (i) s 310(3) permits a company to purchase and maintain for a director insurance in respect of liability which he may incur in connection with his office and which the company is prohibited from indemnifying him against pursuant to s 310(1); (ii) s 727 provides for relief to be given where the court considers that the director acted honestly and reasonably and in all the circumstances ought fairly to be excused.

Sections 206 to 219 Insolvency Act 1986 set out certain liabilities which may be incurred by a director in the event of the company being wound up. Directors should be particularly mindful of ss 213 and 214 (personal liability for fraudulent and wrongful trading—see 11.2.11) and secretaries should note the case of *Re Maidstone Buildings Provisions Ltd* [1971] 1 WLR 1085 (see 1.2.4).

A person dealing with a company is not generally obliged to satisfy himself that internal formalities have been complied with (*Royal British Bank v Turquand* (1856) 6 E & B 327). This rule does not apply in certain cases, eg where the person dealing with the company has actual notice of non-compliance, where there are circumstances which should have put him on inquiry or where he is an insider eg a director or the secretary of the company. The position of a third party dealing with the company is also assisted by s 35 and 35A (see 1.3.2).

8.14 Directors' Interests

8.14.1 Interests in contracts

A director should not allow his personal interests and his duties as a director to conflict. Accordingly, any interest in a contract with the company must be permitted by the Articles and disclosed in accordance with the Act. By s 317 it is the duty of a director who is in any way, whether directly or indirectly, interested in a contract or proposed contract with the company (or any transaction or arrangement with it, whether or not constituting a contract, entered into after 22 December 1980 (s 317(5)) to declare the nature of his interest at a meeting of the directors of the company. In the case of a proposed contract, the disclosure must be made at the meeting of the directors at which the question of entering into the contract is first taken into consideration, or if at that date the director was not interested in the proposed contract, at the next meeting of directors after he becomes interested. In the case of a contract in which a director becomes interested after it is made, he must declare his interest at the first meeting of directors held after he becomes interested. It is not sufficient for the disclosure to be made to a committee of the board, even if the committee is responsible for considering the contract in question (*Guinness plc v Saunders and Ward* [1988] 1 WLR 863).

A director may comply with the above requirements by giving general notice either (i) to the effect that he is a member of a specified company or firm and is to be regarded as interested in any contracts made with such company or firm or (ii) that he is to be regarded as interested in any contract made with a specified connected person (s 317(3)). Accordingly, it is not possible to give a general disclosure in respect of companies in which the director is also a 'director' and it is therefore necessary for a director to disclose such an interest at each board meeting which considers a contract with such a company.

For the purposes of s 317 a transaction falling within s 330 (loans etc to directors—see 8.12 above) and whether involving a director or a connected person must be treated as a transaction or arrangement in which he is interested (s 317(6)): this provision applies whether or not the transaction is in fact prohibited under s 330. Section 317 also applies to a 'shadow director' (see 8.12.3) who must declare his interest not at a meeting of the directors but by specific or general notice in writing (s 317(8)).

Even if the provisions of s 317 are complied with, a director will be entitled to benefit from a contract in which he is interested only if the provisions of the Articles are complied with. Table A provides that a director may retain any profit arising in respect of the contract but may not vote in respect of any contract in which he is interested, and shall not be counted in the quorum present at a meeting which considers such a contract, subject to the exceptions mentioned in regs 94 and 95. In some cases Articles prohibit directors from being interested in contracts and from voting, but the usual modern practice is to make provision similar to that in Table A or to extend it by providing that an interested director may still be counted in a quorum or vote.

Any arrangement under which a director of a company or its holding company (or a person connected with such a director— see s 346 and 8.12.3) is to acquire from the company, or dispose of to the company, any property or interest in property other than cash ('non-cash assets' which expression includes the grant, or extinction, of rights over any property—see s 739) having a value in excess of ten per cent of the company's relevant assets (but with a minimum of £2,000) or £100,000 must first be approved in general meeting by the company (unless a wholly-owned subsidiary) and, in the case of a director of a holding company or a person connected with him, the holding company. In the absence of such approval the arrangement is voidable by the company unless inter alia it is affirmed within a reasonable period by the company and (if applicable) its holding company in general meeting (s 320). These provisions do not apply where the company itself is a market maker and acquires or sells shares to a director through an independent broker (s 321(4)). Again, for the purposes of s 320 a shadow director is to be treated as if he were a director.

8.14.2 Disclosure in accounts of material interests

Section 232 requires inclusion in notes to the statutory accounts or group accounts prepared by a company in respect of any accounting reference period of particulars of transactions, arrangements and agreements of the type set out in Part II of Sched 6 entered into or subsisting at any time during the relevant period by the company or any subsidiary. These are:

(1) loans or other transactions or arrangements of any of the types described in s 330 (see 8.12) above for a person who is or was a director of the company or of its holding company at any time during the relevant period or connected with such a director; or

(2) other transactions with the company or a subsidiary in which a person who is or was at any time in the relevant period a director of the company had, directly or indirectly, a material interest, but excepting:

   (a) a service contract;

(b) a transaction or arrangement between the company and another company in which a director is interested solely as a director of the other company; and

(c) transactions excluded by Sched 6 paras 24 and 25 and s 344 (certain types of transactions etc where the aggregate values do not exceed specified amounts).

Subject to these exceptions, the disclosure requirements apply whether or not the transaction, arrangement or agreement was one prohibited by the Act. They apply to relevant companies (see 8.12.2) and other companies without distinction, and transactions etc with a person connected with a director are treated as ones in which the director is interested (Sched 6 para 17(1)), even where not so treated for the purposes of s 330.

The particulars to be given in the accounts are specified in detail in Sched 6 para 22.

There are modified requirements for recognised banks and their holding companies in relation to transactions, arrangements or agreements to which the bank is a party (see Sched 9, Part IV).

In the case of transactions referred to in s 330 by a recognised bank for directors of the bank or its holding company, no disclosure is required in the accounts of the bank or its holding company, but the bank or holding company must maintain a full record of matters which, would otherwise require to be fully disclosed in its accounts and (except in the case of a recognised bank which is a wholly-owned subsidiary of a company incorporated in the United Kingdom) make such record available for inspection (s 343 and para 2, Part IV, Sched 9).

It should be noted also that:

(1) The aggregate of the amounts outstanding under transactions etc in the nature of or relating to loans, quasi-loans, credit transactions, guarantees etc made by a company or a subsidiary for officers other than directors and the numbers of officers concerned must be disclosed in the accounts of the company or group accounts as the case may require, but the officers need not be identified (Sched 6 para 29). However, if the amount outstanding in respect of any officer does not exceed £2,500 his case can be omitted.

(2) For the purposes of the disclaimer requirements summarised above, shadow directors are treated as directors.

(3) No machinery is provided whereby a company or its directors can ascertain whether any person is connected with a director of the company or its holding company or is a shadow director; but

nonetheless liabilities, including penal liabilities, may fall on the company and its directors for infringements of the substantive prohibitions and of the disclosure requirements; and it cannot be assumed that ignorance is a good defence.

8.15 Information to be given by Directors

In order that the company may be in a position to comply with the various statutory requirements, it is the duty of directors to supply the company with certain information concerning themselves and their activities as follows:

(1) Any person who is appointed or proposed to be appointed director of a company subject to s 293 (see 8.4) at a time when he has attained any retiring age applicable to him under the Act or the company's Articles must give notice of his age to the company (s 294). However this section does not apply on reappointment on the termination of a previous appointment as director.

Since the register of directors and secretaries must show the ages of directors of companies which are subject to s 293, all such directors may be required to disclose their ages to the company to enable the register to be completed.

(2) It is the duty of a director to give notice to the company of such matters relating to himself as may be necessary to enable the company to comply with the following requirements:

> (a) the completion of the register of directors and secretaries (s 288(4)—see 8.8.1);
> (b) the completion of the register of directors' holdings (ss 324(1) and 328(3)—see 8.9.1);
> (c) the inclusion in accounts of particulars as to directors' salaries, pensions, etc, and waivers of emoluments (s 232(3) and Sched 6, Part I—see 7.4.6).

In the case of the information required by s 324 the notice must be in writing and be expressed to be given in fulfilment of the obligation imposed by that section (s 324(1) and (5)).

The information needed to enable the company to satisfy the requirements under (c) above must be given also by persons who are or have been at any time during the preceding five years officers of the company (ibid).

(3) Directors and other officers of a company must provide true and accurate information to the auditors of the company in their capacity as such (s 389A(2), and see 9.6.2).

Chapter 9

Auditors

9.1 Qualifications of Auditors

References in 9.1 of this chapter to a section or Schedule are, unless the context otherwise requires, to a section or Schedule in the Companies Act 1989.

The Companies Act 1989 has introduced a detailed régime of rules designed to secure that only persons who are properly supervised and appropriately qualified are appointed as company auditors, and that audits by persons so appointed are carried out properly and with integrity and with a proper degree of independence.

In order to be appointed as a company's auditor the auditor must be a member of a recognised supervisory body and be eligible for appointment under the rules of that body. The detailed requirements for a person to become a recognised supervisory body are set out in Sched 11 to the 1989 Act and require such a body to have rules which will ensure, for example, technical competence and professional integrity. At present the following are recognised supervisory bodies: the Institute of Chartered Accountants in England and Wales, the Institute of Chartered Accountants in Scotland, the Association of Certified Accountants and the Institute of Chartered Accountants in Ireland.

Furthermore, neither an individual nor a firm may be a company auditor unless (in the case of an individual) he holds an appropriate qualification and (in the case of a firm) the individuals responsible for company audit work hold an appropriate qualification and the firm is controlled by qualified persons (Part II, Sched II). A person holds an 'appropriate qualification' if he: (i) by virtue of membership of those professional bodies referred to above was qualified to act as an auditor immediately before 1 January 1990 and before 1 October 1991; or (ii) holds a recognised professional qualification obtained in the UK granted by a qualifying body which complies with the standards set out in Sched 12; or (iii) holds an approved overseas qualification and satisfies any additional educational requirements which the Secretary of State may impose in accordance with s 33(4) for ensuring that such persons have an adequate knowledge of the law and practice in the UK relevant to the audit of accounts. In exercising this power, the Secretary of State is able to take into account the eligibility of UK qualified auditors to practice in the relevant country. It is intended that those professional bodies which are 'recognised' bodies will also apply to be qualifying bodies for the purpose of granting a recognised professional qualification.

No person who is an officer or employee of the company, or who is a partner or employee of an officer or employee of the company or a partnership of which such person is a partner, may be its auditor or an auditor of any company in the group (s 27). A body corporate may be a companys's auditor and the circumstances in which a body corporate is to be ineligible to act as the auditor are to be set out in regulations to be made by the Secretary of State.

By s 28(1), no person shall act as an auditor at a time when he knows that he is disqualified for appointment, and if an auditor becomes disqualified he shall thereupon vacate office and notify the company that he has by reason of such disqualification vacated office.

9.2 Appointment of Auditors

One or more auditors must be appointed for the purpose of preparing the auditors' report already mentioned (see 7.6). A private company is able to elect to dispense with the annual appointment of auditors (see 6.10) and where this is the case the following provisions are not relevant.

Unless a private company has elected to dispense with the laying of accounts (see 6.10.3), the first auditors may be appointed by a resolution of the directors at any time before the first general meeting at which the duty to lay accounts before the company is complied with pursuant to s 241; and auditors so appointed shall hold office until the conclusion of that meeting (s 385(3)). If the directors fail to make such appointment, the company in general meeting may do so (s 385(4)).

At each general meeting at which accounts are laid before the company pursuant to s 241 the company in general meeting must appoint an auditor or auditors to hold office from the conclusion of that meeting until the conclusion of the next general meeting at which accounts are laid (s 385(2)).

If no auditor is appointed or reappointed when the company is required to appoint one then it is required to give notice of that fact within one week to the Secretary of State who may appoint a person to fill the vacancy (s 387).

The directors, or the company in general meeting, may fill any casual vacancy in the office of auditor, but while any such vacancy continues the surviving or continuing auditor or auditors (if any) may act (s 388(2)). Section 250 enables a private company which (i) is not required to prepare group accounts, (ii) falls within the exemption for individual accounts conferred by s 246 and (iii) is dormant, to dispense by special resolution with the requirement to audit accounts. For this purpose a company is to be regarded as dormant for any period during which no significant accounting transaction occurs (s 250(3)).

Where a private company has elected to dispense with the laying of accounts in general meeting then:

(i) the first auditors may be appointed by the directors at any time before the end of the 28 day period commencing on the day on which copies of the company's first annual accounts are sent to members under s 238 (see 7.2.4) (the '28 day period') or, if a shareholder requires a meeting to be held in accordance with s 253(2) (see 6.10.3) then the appointment has to be made before the beginning of the meeting; and

(ii) subsequently, auditors are to be appointed in general meeting before the end of the 28 day period or if notice is given under s 253(2), the conclusion of the meeting.

Auditors who are in office when any election to dispense with the laying of accounts in general meeting is made continue in office until the end of the time for appointing auditors for the next financial year (unless the shareholders determine othewise) and auditors holding office when the election ceases to have effect shall continue to hold office until the conclusion of the next general meeting at which accounts are laid (s 358A).

9.3 Duties of Auditors

There are a number of reported cases dealing with the general duties of auditors (see eg *Re London and General Bank Ltd (No*

2) [1895] 2 Ch 673, *Re Kingston Cotton Mill Co* (No 2) [1896] 2 Ch 279 and *Re Thomas Gerrard & Son Ltd* [1968] Ch 455) but discussion of these does not fall within the scope of this work. It should be noted, however, that two recent cases have held that auditors would not generally be held liable for losses to third party purchasers of a company's shares, whose decision to buy was based on negligently audited accounts (*Capro Industries v Dickman* [1990] 2 WLR 358 and *Morgan Crucible Company v Hill Samuel Bank* [1991] Ch 259). The statutory duties imposed by s 237 (auditors' report to state any non-compliance with Sched 6—see 7.6.2 and 8.14.2) and s 235(3) (under which the auditors have a duty to check the consistency of the directors' report with the accounts) should however be noted.

9.4 Removal of Auditors

A company may by ordinary resolution remove an auditor before the expiration of his term of office. Notice of the passing of a resolution to remove an auditor must be given to the Registrar on Form 386 within 14 days of the meeting at which the resolution was passed (s 391(2)).

Special notice (see 6.4.3) must be given of a resolution proposed to be passed at a general meeting of a company appointing as auditor a person other than a retiring auditor, or removing an auditor before the expiration of his term of office (s 391A(1)). On receipt of special notice of such an intended resolution the company shall forthwith send a copy of the resolution to the person proposed to be removed or, as the case may be, appointed and to the retiring auditor. The retiring auditor or the auditor proposed to be removed has the right to make written representations to the company (not exceeding a reasonable length), and to request that they be notified to the members, in which case, if they are not received too late, the notice to the members must state that such written representations have been received, and a copy thereof must be sent to every member to whom the notice is sent (whether before or after the receipt of the representations); and, if the representations are not so sent, the auditor may (without prejudice to his right to address the meeting) require that they are read at the meeting (s 391A(3) and (4)). The representations need not be sent to members or read out at the meeting if, on application by any person claiming to be aggrieved, the court is satisfied that the procedure is being abused to secure needless publicity for defamatory matter (s 391A(5)).

Where an auditor ceases for any reason to hold office, he is required to deposit at the company's registered office a statement indicating whether there are any circumstances which ought to be brought to the attention of members. If the statement does contain a statement of such circumstances then the procedure set out under 9.5 must be followed.

9.5 Resignation of Auditors

By s 392, an auditor may resign by written notice of resignation to the company deposited at the registered office, such notice being effective as from the date of deposit or, if later, the operative date specified in the notice. Such notice will not, however, be effective unless it contains a statement either (a) that there are no circumstances connected with his resignation which he considers should be brought to the notice of the members or creditors of the company or (b) setting out such circumstances. The statement must be deposited, where the auditor is not seeking reappointment, not less than 14 days before the end of the time allowed for appointing auditors and in any other case, not later than the end of the period of 14 days from the date he ceased to hold office (s 394(2)). If such notice contains a statement of the circumstances referred to in (b) above, the company must within 14 days of the deposit of the statement either send a copy to every person entitled to receive copies of the company's accounts or apply to the court. Unless the auditor is notified within 21 days of the deposit of the statement he must within a further seven days send a copy to the Registrar. If the company applies to the court and it is satisfied that such notice is being used by the auditor to secure needless publicity for defamatory matter, it may order that copies of the notice need not be sent out and order that the auditor pay the company's costs. The company must within 14 days of the court's decision, send to each person entitled to receive copies of the company's accounts a statement setting out the effect of the court order (if such an order is made) or (if no such order is made) a copy of the notice containing the statement of circumstances connected with the auditor's resignation and must notify the auditor of the court's decision. The auditor is required within seven days of such notification to send a copy of the statement to the Registrar.

Where the auditor's notice of resignation contains a statement of circumstances that should be brought to the attention of members and creditors, the auditor is entitled (s 392A) to deposit with the notice a signed requisition calling on the directors of the company forthwith to convene an extraordinary general meeting of the company for the purpose of receiving and considering such explanation of the circumstances connected with his resignation as he may wish to place before the meeting. The auditor may request the company to circulate to the members a statement (not exceeding a reasonable length) of the circumstances connected with his resignation. Unless such statement is received too late (or the court considers that the procedure is being abused to secure needless publicity for defamatory matter), the company must state in every notice of the meeting that the statement has been made and must send a copy to every member to whom the notice is or has been sent. The directors must convene a meeting, to be held not more than 28 days after the date of the notice, calling it within 21 days from the date of the deposit of the auditor's requisition. The auditor may, without prejudice to his right to be heard orally, require that his statement be read out at the meeting. Every director who fails to take all reasonable steps to secure the convening of such a meeting is liable to be fined.

9.6 Right of Auditors to Information etc

9.6.1 Access to books etc

Every auditor has a right of access at all times to the books and accounts and vouchers of the company, and is entitled to require from the officers of the company such information and explanation as he thinks necessary for the performance of his duties (s 389A(1)). The auditors of a company are entitled to attend any general meeting of the company, and to receive all notices of, and other communications relating to, any general meeting which any member of the company is entitled to receive, and to be heard at any general meeting which they attend on any part of the business of the meeting which concerns them as auditors (s 390(1)). In addition, auditors are entitled to receive copies of written resolutions to be passed pursuant to s 381A (see 6.6.3).

A subsidiary undertaking and its auditors are under a duty to give to the auditors of the parent undertaking such information and explanation as the latter may reasonably require for the purposes of their duty as auditors of the parent undertaking. In the case of a subsidiary undertaking which is not a body corporate incorporated in Great Britain, the auditors of the parent undertaking can require the holding company to take such steps as are reasonably open to it to obtain from the subsidiary such information and explanation as the auditors of the parent undertaking may require (s 389A(4)).

9.6.2 False statements to auditors

An officer of a company is liable to be fined or imprisoned if he knowingly or recklessly makes a statement which is misleading, false or deceptive in a material particular and such statement is made to the auditors of the company (whether orally or in writing) conveying or purporting to convey any information or explanation which such auditors require or are entitled to require as auditor of the company (s 389A(2)).

9.7 Remuneration of Auditors

Where an auditor is appointed by the directors or the Board of Trade, the appointor(s) may fix his remuneration. In other cases, it is fixed either by the company in general meeting or in such manner as the company in general meeting may determine (s 390A(1)). Expenses paid to an auditor are deemed to be part of his remuneration (s 390A(4)).

Chapter 10

Charges and Debentures

10.1 Power to Borrow

The Memorandum almost invariably empowers a company to borrow money and to give security for loans, while the Articles usually state the manner in which and the extent to which this power may be exercised. Even in the absence of such a provision in the Memorandum, however, a trading company has implied power to borrow and give security (*General Auction Estate and Monetary Co v Smith* [1891] 3 Ch 432) although not, normally, to give guarantees, or provide collateral security, for obligations of third parties.

A company which has power to borrow also has implied power to charge its assets as security, unless the power is excluded by the Memorandum or Articles. In general, any of the assets may be charged, including uncalled capital; but in no circumstances may a charge be created over a reserve liability (*Re Mayfair Property Co Ltd, Bartlett v Mayfair Property Co Ltd* [1898] 2 Ch 28); or the liability of the members of a company limited by guarantee (*Re Pyle Works Ltd* (1890) 44 Ch D 534).

In the majority of cases borrowing powers will be exercisable by resolution of the board (which must act bona fide in the best interests of the company, and for a proper purpose). It is not unusual for the Articles to contain a limit on the aggregate amount which may be borrowed (by reference for example to a multiple of the company's share capital and reserves) but it should be noted that Table A does not contain such a limit.

An express borrowing power in the Memorandum must be exercised for the purposes of authorised objects: it cannot be treated as an independent object even though there is provision in the Memorandum for each sub-clause to be read separately (*Introductions Ltd v National Provincial Bank Ltd* [1970] Ch 199). The third party will be entitled to enforce the loan if he can establish the application of s 35A (see 1.3.2).

10.2 Forms of Borrowing

10.2.1 General

All methods of borrowing which are available to individuals may be employed by a company, with the addition of the method involving the issue of a debenture or debentures.

10.2.2 Types of debentures

Although a number of provisions in the Act are concerned with debentures, and s 744 contains a definition of it, it is generally recognised that there is no complete and comprehensive statement of what, in law, constitutes a debenture. However for present purposes it is taken to be a formal written instrument creating or acknowledging loan indebtedness of the company. Debentures can be:

(1) unsecured or 'naked' debentures, which give no security to the lender but involve merely a promise by the company to repay the indebtedness with or without interest;

(2) secured debentures, which give security for the indebtedness by way of mortgage or charge on the company's assets. The security in such cases may take either or both of the following forms:

(a) a *fixed charge* on specified assets; or
(b) a *floating charge* on the whole of the assets or on certain classes of assets.

This chapter is principally concerned with secured debentures.

A company cannot dispose of assets which are the subject of a *fixed charge* except subject to the charge and/or to the extent provided by the terms of the charge which usually requires the consent of the chargee. This should be contrasted with a *floating charge* which permits a company freely to dispose of the assets subject to the charge until the charge crystallises, which will generally be when the company goes into liquidation or a receiver is appointed pursuant to the terms of the charge.

Debentures may be either payable to bearer, or payable to the registered holder. Further, they may be either redeemable at a specified date or on demand, or irredeemable, in which case a repayment of the loan can be claimed only in the event of a default or liquidation; but the precise effect of these debentures depends upon the terms of issue (and see s 193).

By s 744 'debenture' includes debenture stock, which is borrowed money consolidated into one amount and constituted and, if applicable, secured, by means of a trust deed. Lenders receive a debenture stock certificate entitling them to repayment of a specific sum, being their entitlement of stock, upon and subject to the terms of the trust deed, which contains the legal contract between the company and the trustees for the stockholders. The use of a trust deed enables action to be taken by the trustees on behalf of all stockholders without delay occurring. The expression 'debenture stock' normally indicates stock secured by a floating charge; where a fixed charge is given as security the stock will normally be called a 'mortgage debenture stock', and where there is no security an 'unsecured loan stock'.

No stamp duty is payable on the creation or issue of debentures and/or charges.

10.2.3 Issue of debentures

The procedure to be employed on an issue of debentures (including debenture stock) varies with the circumstances.

Where a single debenture is issued to a single creditor, as where a loan is made by the company's bank, there is little to be done beyond the sealing and registration of the necessary documents pursuant to the relevant board resolution. But where a series of debentures is to be issued or an issue of debenture stock is to be made to secure a loan made by a number of persons, a number of other administrative acts must be performed.

If the debentures are to be offered to the public, a copy of the listing particulars or prospectus must be filed (see 3.4 to 3.7). In such a case applications and allotments will be dealt with much as if an issue of shares were being made; but no return of allotments is required.

Frequently, where a series of debentures is issued, the debentures are supported by a trust deed. This deed appoints trustees in whom are vested the assets which form the debenture-holders' security, and states, inter alia, the circumstances in which a receiver may be appointed. Where a single debenture secured by a floating charge has been issued before the creation of a series of debentures, notice of the creation of the series should be given to the holder, who should be supplied with a copy of the trust deed. As to priority of charges, see 10.2.7.

Except where otherwise provided by the terms of issue, debentures or certificates for debenture stock must be issued within two months after allotment (or lodgement of a transfer) (s 185(1)).

Debentures may be issued at a discount, and where issued by a banking or insurance company must be shown in the balance sheet until finally written off (Sched 9 Pt I para 3(e)). The terms of issue may also provide for a premium on redemption. As to the position regarding the timing of debenture issues see 3.12.

Particulars of issues of debentures, and the reasons for the issue, during any financial year, must be stated by way of note to a company's accounts for the financial year (Sched 4 para 41(1)).

A contract to take up and pay for debentures may be enforced by specific performance.

10.2.4 Register of debenture holders

Where a register of debenture holders is kept (ie where debentures payable to the registered holders thereof are issued), the rules laid down for the register of members (see 4.2) apply also to the register of debenture holders (s 190, Form 190).

The rules set out in the Companies (Inspection and Copying of Registers, Indices and Documents) Regulations (SI 1991 No. 1998) apply to the register of debenture holders. Accordingly, the company has to make the register available for inspection for not less than two hours between 9 am and 5 pm on each business day and any person inspecting the register is able to take notes or transcribe the available information.

The register may be inspected free of charge by any registered holder of debentures or shares. Persons other than debenture holders or shareholders may inspect the register on payment of a fee of £2.50 for each hour or part thereof during which the right of inspection is exercised.

A copy of the register of debenture holders or of any part thereof may be obtained by any person on payment of a fee of £2.50 for the first 100 entries, £20 for the next 1,000 and £15 for every subsequent 1,000 entries. Copies of debenture trust deeds may also be demanded by debenture holders (s 191(3)) at a fee of 10p per 100 words or part thereof.

The form of a register of debenture holders is not laid down by the Act, but it usually follows closely that of the register of members. A register in non-legible form is permitted (Companies (Registers and other Records) Regulations (SI 1985 No 724)). It may therefore be in computerised form. Where the debenture instrument provides that the company shall not be obliged to enter in the register notice of any trust to which the debentures are subject, the company is nevertheless not entitled to disregard such notice as it is in the case of shares (*Re Palmer's Decorating & Furnishing Co Ltd* [1904] 2 Ch 743).

10.2.5 Transfer of debentures

A transfer of debentures payable to the registered holder thereof is effected in the manner prescribed by the debenture instrument or by a stock transfer in accordance with the Stock Transfer Act 1963. The procedure prescribed is usually similar to that employed in transferring shares; but the directors do not usually have the right of rejecting a proposed transfer. No stamp duty is payable on transfers of loan capital (which is defined to include debenture stock) (s 108, Finance Act 1990).

Debentures are sometimes issued payable to bearer. In which case they may be transferred by mere delivery of the instrument without the knowledge of the company.

A registered debenture is not a negotiable instrument, and is transferable subject to equities (*Athenum Life Assurance Society v Pooley* (1858) 3 De G & J 294 and *Re Rhodesia Goldfields Ltd* [1910] 1 Ch 239), unless the debenture conditions provide otherwise, as they will normally do.

10.2.6 Reissue of debentures

Section 194 allows a company to reissue redeemed debentures, unless:

(1) the Articles or any contract entered into by the company forbid this; or

(2) the company has by resolution or some other act manifested an intention that the debentures shall be cancelled.

As upon the reissue of redeemed debentures the holders have the priorities they would have enjoyed if the debentures had not previously been redeemed, the power to reissue may be of considerable value, but it will be lost if a memorandum of satisfaction is registered, or if a clause in any subsequent debenture prohibits the reissue. It is not, however, necessary to keep redeemed debentures alive by transferring them to a nominee pending reissue.

Where debentures have been deposited to secure an overdraft, the fact that the company's account is temporarily in credit is not treated as a redemption of the debentures so deposited.

Particulars of any redeemed debentures which the company has power to reissue must be included in the balance sheet or notes thereto (Sched 4, Pt III, para 41(2) and Sched 9, para 2(*d*)).

10.2.7 Priority rights of debenture holders

Where debentures are issued in a series it is usual to insert a provision that the holders shall rank pari passu for repayment but, if no such provision is inserted, the debentures rank (*a*) in the order in which they are numbered where they are issued simultaneously, or (*b*) in the order of issue where they are issued at different times (*Gartside v Silkstone and Dodsworth Coal and Iron Co* (1882) 21 Ch D 762).

As regards the priorities enjoyed by the holders of two or more single debentures or two or more distinct series of debentures, much depends upon the terms of issue and the nature of the charges created thereby.

In general, fixed charges take priority in the order in which they were created; but a subsequent fixed charge takes priority over a floating charge created previously (*Wheatley v Silkstone Haigh Moor Coal Co* (1885) 29 Ch D 715). A clause in a debenture secured by a floating charge prohibiting the creation of subsequent fixed charges does not prevent this rule from operating unless the holder of the fixed charge has notice of the clause (*English and Scottish Mercantile Investment Co v Brunton* [1892] 2 QB 700); and, though the registration of the floating charge gives constructive notice of the charge, it does not, in England at any rate, necessarily give constructive notice of the terms thereof (*G & T Earle Ltd v Hemsworth Rural District Council* (1928) 140 LT 69). It is common practice, therefore, to register particulars of the relevant prohibition: this is accepted by the Registrar and is assumed to put holders of subsequent fixed charges on constructive notice, but the position has never been tested before the courts.

Where two or more debentures or series of debentures each create a floating charge they rank, in general, in the order in which they are created, but the first debenture may expressly authorise the company to create subsequent debentures with priority over or ranking pari passu with the first debenture. In such a case, power to create a subsequent 'mortgage' with priority does not enable the company to give priority to a subsequent floating charge (*Re Cope (Benjamin) and Sons Ltd* [1914] 1 Ch 800); but power to create a 'mortgage or charge' will do so (*Re Automatic Bottle Makers Ltd* [1926] Ch 412).

As regards the priority rights attaching to reissued debentures, see above.

The holder of a single debenture can set off a sum owing by him to the company against sums due to him in respect of his debenture; but no such set-off can be made by the holder of one of a series of debentures ranking pari passu inter se (*Re Brown & Gregory Ltd* [1904] 1 Ch 627).

Where in the case of a company registered in England a receiver is appointed on behalf of debenture holders secured by a charge which was, when created a floating charge, or possession is taken by or on behalf of the debenture holders of any property subject to such a charge, then, if the company is not being wound up, the debts which would be entitled to preferential payment were the company being wound up (see 11.2.16) are to be paid out of any assets coming into the hands of the receiver or person taking possession before payments are made to the holders of the debentures. The periods in respect of which preferential treatment can be claimed are calculated from the date of the appointment of the receiver or the taking possession, as the case may be: but any payments so made to the preferential creditors may be recouped out of the assets available for the unsecured creditors (s 196 and s 40 Insolvency Act 1986, and see *IRC v Goldblatt* [1972] Ch 498). It should be noted that it is the nature of the charge *when created* that is relevant for establishing the priority of preferential claims. This differs from the position prior to the Insolvency Acts 1985 and 1986 (see for example *Re Woodroffes (Musical Instruments) Ltd* [1985] WLR 543).

10.3 Trustees for Debenture Holders

Where there is a debenture trust deed, this must be consulted for the purposes of determining the rights of the debenture holders inter se and against the trustees appointed under the deed; but as a general rule, any provision in the trust deed or in any contract with debenture holders, where there is such a deed or contract, is void in so far as it would have the effect of exempting a trustee from or indemnifying him against liability for breach of trust where he fails to show the degree of care and diligence required of him as a trustee (s 192). This general rule is subject, however, to the modifications stated in s 192(2) and (3).

The trustees are not entitled to any remuneration, unless there is provision in the trust deed (*Re Accles Ltd* (1902) 46 SJ 686). Where they are entitled to remuneration, the deed usually provides that their claim thereto shall take priority over the claims of the debenture holders (*Re Locke & Smith Ltd* [1914] 1 Ch 687); but, unless the deed otherwise provides, their right to remuneration ends when a receiver is appointed (ibid).

10.4 Registration of Charges

10.4.1 General

The 1989 Act makes a number of amendments to the law relating to company charges which it is intended will be introduced in mid-1993. A summary of the principal charges to be introduced by the 1989 Act is set out in 10.4.6.

The provisions relating to registration of charges are contained in ss 395 to 424 of the Act. Sections 395 to 409 are concerned with the registration of charges created by or over property acquired by English companies or companies incorporated outside Great Britain with a place of business in England. Sections 410 to 424 (Part XII, Chapter II) contain equivalent provisions in relation to Scottish companies or companies incorporated outside Great Britain with a place of business in Scotland (registration in such cases being with the Registrar of Companies in Edinburgh).

10.4.2 Registration of charges created by companies

Section 395 of the Act provides for the registration with the Registrar of Companies in Cardiff of particulars of the following charges if created by a company registered in England:

(1) a charge securing an issue of debentures.
(2) a charge on uncalled capital.
(3) a charge created by an instrument which, if executed by an individual, would require registration as a bill of sale.
(4) a charge on any land (wherever situate) or on any interest therein, but not including a charge for any rent or other periodical sum issuing out of land.

(5) a charge on book debts.
(6) a floating charge on the company's undertaking or property.
(7) a charge on calls made but not paid.
(8) a charge on a ship or aircraft or any share in a ship.
(9) a charge on goodwill, patents, licences under patents, trade marks, copyrights or licences under copyrights (s 396).

A 'book debt' means a debt (including a future debt) which would or could be entered in the books of the company in the ordinary course as a debt even if not so entered (*Independent Automatic Sales Ltd v Knowles & Foster* [1962] 1 WLR 974). An assignment by way of charge of money when it becomes due at a future date can be registrable as a charge on future book debts (*Re Brush Aggregates Ltd, The Times*, 11 February 1983; cf *Paul & Frank Ltd v Discount Bank (Overseas) Ltd* [1967] Ch 348). It was held in *Re Brightlife Limited* [1986] 3 All ER 673 that the credit balance on a company's bank account did not fall within the term 'book and other debts' used in the debenture because this was not the meaning usually accorded to the term by businessmen or accountants, who would describe such a balance as cash at bank. *Re Charge Card Services Limited* [1986] 3 WLR 697 went one step further and held that it is not possible for a company to charge in favour of a bank any of its credit balances held by that bank. However, the Registrar has announced in a Practice Direction of 25 March 1988 that, despite the *Charge Card* case, he will continue to register securities created by an account holder in favour of its banker.

Only the forms of charges mentioned in the appropriate section have to be registered with the Registrar. It is not necessary to register eg an absolute assignment of a book debt (*Ashby, Warner & Co Ltd v Simmons* [1936] 2 All ER 697) or an absolute bill of sale (*Stoneleigh Finance Ltd v Phillips* [1965] 2 QB 537); nor a deposit of shipping documents; nor an assignment of a hire-purchase agreement (*Re George Inglefield Ltd* [1933] Ch 1).

The consequences of failure to comply with the registration provisions are severe. The charge will be void against a liquidator or creditor of the company, although it will still be enforceable against the company. If a charge becomes void due to failure to comply with the registration requirements the money secured by the charge becomes immediately repayable (s 395).

The charges which do require to be registered must be registered within 21 days after the date on which they were created by the company, the Form 395 or Form 410 (Scot) being accompanied by the instrument, if any, by which the charge is created or evidenced. In the case of a charge created outside the United Kingdom comprising property outside the United Kingdom, a verified copy of the instrument creating or evidencing the charge is sufficient, and the time for registration is within 21 days after the date on which such a copy would be received in the United Kingdom in the ordinary course of post assuming that it had been posted with due diligence (ss 398(2) and 411(1)). As to charges created by a company registered in England on property in Scotland or Northern Ireland, see s 398(4).

Great care must be taken in completing Form 395 or Form 410 (Scot). It was previously the Registrar's practice to register a charge if the Form was sent within the 21 day period, even though the particulars in the Form as presented were defective. The Form would be returned to the applicant for amendment and the charge registered on re-submission even though the 21 day period had expired. This procedure has been held invalid by the High Court and the Court of Appeal and a Form 395 re-submitted after the 21 day period held to be ineffective (*R v Registrar of Companies, ex parte Esal (Commodities) Ltd (in liquidation)* [1985] 2 WLR 447).

The Registrar has announced that his practice following the Court of Appeal judgment in the *Esal Case* will be as follows:

(1) except as provided by ss 398 (verification of charge on property outside UK), and 400 (charges existing on property acquired) copy instruments will not be accepted; the original charging instrument must accompany the appropriate form. Oversea companies should state in a covering letter where their place of business is within England and Wales, or in appropriate circumstances state that they have no such place of business.

(2) with the agreement of the presentor the Registrar will amend either within or outside the 21 days errors in the company number and the company name, and any other minor clerical or typing error that appears in the words or figures that have been entered on the submitted Form 395 that differ from the accompanying instrument submitted by the presentor.

(3) all other errors or omissions, for example omitting reference to 'all other monies' in the section headed 'Amount secured by the Mortgage or Charge' or referring only to a fixed charge where a floating charge is also created, which the Registrar

highlights within the 21 days will require to be rectified by the submission of an amended Form 395 within the 21 day period.

(4) if any error or omission other than those stated at (2) above is discovered by the Registrar after the 21 days or if an amended Form 395 is not returned within the 21 days in relation to (3) above then it will be necessary to obtain a s 404 Court Order. There are no exceptions to this rule.

It is therefore necessary to ensure that all the required particulars have been accurately and comprehensively completed and that Form 395 is submitted as early as possible (ideally on the same day as the charge is created) thereby assisting the Registrar in returning a defective form within the 21 day period. The Registrar has indicated that he will try to notify presentors of apparently defective particulars as soon as he can but he does not undertake to do this before the end of the 21 day period.

All the relevant information must be on the Form 395 itself which must be signed and dated. It is not sufficient merely to cross refer to the instrument or other documents creating the mortgage or charge expressly or by implication (and see also the Registrar's Practice Direction of 29 May 1987).

Sections 395 and 410 apply only to charges created by the company; but ss 400 and 416 provide that, where a company acquires property which is subject to any of the charges listed in s 396(1) or s 410(4) respectively, the charge must be registered within 21 days after the property has been acquired. For this purpose Form 400 or Form 416 (Scot) should be employed, accompanied by a certified copy of the instrument creating or evidencing the charge; but if the property is situated, and the charge was created, outside Great Britain, the time for filing is extended to within 21 days of the date on which the copy would be received in the United Kingdom in the ordinary course of post.

Section 409 applies the provisions of ss 395 to 408 to charges on property in England which are created, and to charges on property in England which is acquired, by a company incorporated outside Great Britian which has an established place of business in England. Section 424 applies the provisions of ss 410 to 423 to charges on property in Scotland which are created, and charges on property in Scotland which is acquired, by a company incorporated outside Great Britain which has a place of business in Scotland. It will thus sometimes be necessary to register the same charge in both England and Scotland.

An oversea company having a place of business in England or Scotland must file particulars of charges within 21 days under ss 409 and 424 whether or not it has registered under Part XXIII of the Act (*NV Slavenburg's Bank v Intercontinental Natural Resources Ltd* [1980] 1 WLR 1076). Whether an oversea company has established a place of business in England or Scotland will often be difficult to determine. The test laid down in *Re Oriel* [1985] BCLC 343 is that the company must have a permanent location in England or Scotland, not necessarily owned or leased by it, but at least associated with the company and from which habitually or with some degree of regularity business is conducted.

Copies of instruments requiring to be verified or certified under s 398(1) (or 410(1)) or s 400 (or 416) should be verified or certified to be a correct copy under the hand of the person delivering the copy to the Registrar or an officer of the company creating the charge (SI 1985 No 854 reg 7).

The duty of registering the necessary particulars is imposed on the company, and directors or secretaries who are knowingly parties to a default are liable to be fined; but since, if the registration is not effected within the prescribed period, the charge will become void as against a liquidator or creditors of the company, such registration may be effected on the application of any person interested therein (ss 399 and 415) and is frequently effected by or on behalf of the chargee. Such a person is entitled to recover from the company the fees paid by him for the registration. It is only a charge created by the company which is rendered void by failure to register within the prescribed period. Non-registration under s 400 or s 416 of a charge on property acquired by the company will not have this effect.

10.4.3 Particulars to be registered

In the case of a *single mortgage or charge*, the following particulars must be registered on Form 395 or 410 (Scotland) (ss 401 and 417):

(1) the date of creation, if created by the company, or the date of acquisition, if created before the company acquired the property charged.
(2) the amount secured.
(3) short particulars of the property charged.
(4) the persons entitled to the charge.

(5) in the case of a floating charge created by a company registered in Scotland a statement of the restrictions, if any, on the power of the company to grant further securities ranking in priority to, or pari passu with, the floating charge, or which vary or regulate the order of ranking of floating charges in relation to subsisting securities.

The rate of interest need not be stated.

In the case of a *series of debentures*, the holders of which are entitled pari passu to the benefit of the mortgage or charge, Form 397 or Form 413 (Scot) will be employed including the following particulars (ss 397 and 413(2)):

(1) the total amount secured by the series.
(2) the date of the resolution authorising the issue.
(3) the date of the covering deed (if any) which creates or defines the security.
(4) a general description of the property charged.
(5) the names of the trustees (if any).
(6) in the case of a floating charge created by a company registered in Scotland, a statement of the restrictions, if any, on the power of the company to grant further securities ranking in priority to, or pari passu with, the floating charge or which vary or regulate the order of ranking of floating charges in relation to subsisting securities.

Where more than one issue of debentures in a series is made, particulars of the date and amount of each issue must also be sent to the Registrar (Form 397(a) or Form 413(a) (Scot)) but failure to do this will not invalidate the debentures issued (ss 397(1) and 413(2)).

In the case of a series of debentures, slight variations exist according to the presence or absence of a trust deed. The following points should be noted:

(1) Where a trust deed is employed (a) registration must be effected within 21 days of the execution of the deed; and (b) the deed itself must accompany the registration form.
(2) Where there is no trust deed (a) registration must be effected within 21 days of the first execution of any debenture of the series; and (b) one of the debentures of the series must accompany the form.

A trust deed for debenture stock is often executed some weeks after allotment of the stock constituted and secured thereby and, in such cases, an equitable stock is frequently registered against the company to cover the interim period.

If any commission, allowance or discount has been paid or made, whether directly or indirectly, in consideration for a subscription or agreement to subscribe for debentures, or for procuring or agreeing to procure subscriptions, the particulars to be registered must include particulars of the amount or rate per cent of the commission, allowance or discount (ss 397(2) and 413(3)).

A copy of the certificate of registration issued by the Registrar must, if the company is registered in England, be endorsed on every debenture or certificate of debenture stock secured by the charge so registered which is issued after the creation of the charge (s 402). This is usually printed on the back of the debenture or stock certificate. The certificate of registration is conclusive evidence that the prescribed particulars have been delivered to the Registrar (*Re Mechanisations (Eaglescliffe) Ltd* [1966] Ch 20) and that the requirements of the Act have been complied with (*Re Eric Holmes (Property) Ltd* [1965] Ch 1052 and *Re C L Nye Ltd* [1971] 1 Ch 442). Section 401(2) precludes evidence being adduced before a court to challenge the Registrar's certificate but the Registrar's decision may be subject to judicial review (*R v Registrar of Companies, ex parte Esal (Commodities) Ltd (in liquidation)* [1985] 2 WLR 447; (1985) *Financial Times*, 16 August.

10.4.4 Registration of memorandum of satisfaction

Since the registration with the Registrar of charges on the company's assets affects the credits of the company, the Act makes provision for enabling the Registrar to record the fact that any registered charge has been satisfied (ss 403 and 419). Form 403a or Form 419a (Scot) should be employed where the charge has been wholly satisfied. It must be accompanied by a statutory declaration. Where, however, it is desired to keep debentures alive with a view to their reissue (see 10.2.6), a memorandum of satisfaction should not be registered.

A memorandum may be registered to the effect that the charge has been partly satisfied or that part of the assets charged has been released from the charge or has ceased to form part of the company's property (Form 403b or Form 419b (Scot)).

There is no legal requirement on the company to file a memorandum of satisfaction but it is good practice even if often overlooked.

The court may order rectification of the register of charges (ss 404 and 420) (*Watson v Duff, Morgan & Vermont (Holdings) Ltd* [1974] 1 WLR 450).

As to the registration of the appointment of a receiver, see s 405 and 10.5.1.

10.4.5 Register of charges

In addition to the duty of registering certain kinds of charges with the Registrar, every limited company must keep at its registered office a register of charges in which must be entered particulars of all charges specifically affecting the company's property and of all floating charges on the undertaking of or on any property of the company (ss 407 and 422). This register must contain a short description of the property charged, the amount of the charge, and the names of the persons entitled thereto (except in the case of securites to bearer) (ibid).

It must be noted that it is necessary to record in this register all charges specifically affecting the company's property and all floating charges, whether or not particulars have to be registered with the Registrar. No time limit is laid down within which entries must be placed in the register; but a penalty is imposed for failing to register.

A copy of every instrument creating a mortgage or charge which requires registration with the Registrar must be kept at the registered office (ss 406 and 421). These instruments and the register of charges may be inspected free of charge during business hours by any creditor or member of the company (ss 408 and 423). The register of charges may also be inspected by any other person on payment of a fee of not more than 5p. The company in general meeting may restrict the period during which inspection may be demanded to not less than two hours per day.

10.4.6 The Companies Act 1989

Introduction   The 1989 Act makes a number of amendments to the law relating to company charges, which it is intended will be introduced in mid-1993. The new law is not retrospective in effect and, accordingly, the existing law will continue to apply to charges created prior to the introduction of the relevant sections of the 1989 Act. References in this paragraph to section numbers are to the Act as amended by the 1989 Act.

Definition of charge   The 1989 Act (unlike the existing law) contains a definition of a charge. It is defined in 'any form of security interest (fixed or floating) over property [see below] other than an interest arising by operation of law' (s 395(2)). The extent to which this amends the existing law is not clear. Although it is arguable that this extends the definition of registrable charges to include, for example, retention of title clauses (ie where the seller retains title in goods until payment), a number of commentators have suggested that a security interest will only arise where there is a transfer of ownership or an appropriation of property for satisfaction of a debt. Accordingly, where something is done merely to enhance the creditor's right to payment it will not constitute a security interest.

Property is defined as including future property (s 395(2)) and it is immaterial where the property subject to a charge is situated (s 395(3)). Accordingly, where an English company creates a charge over property located abroad it will have to be registered if it falls within the list of charges specified in s 396.

There are a number of minor amendments to the list of registrable charges. In particular, partial floating charges are expressly included and a shipowners' liens over sub-freights has been excluded (overruling *Re Walsh Irish Ferries Ltd* [1986] Ch 471). It should be noted that the Secretary of State is able to amend a list by way of statutory instrument giving a degree of much needed flexibility.

The registration procedure   The 1989 Act will make a number of important amendments to the registration procedure:

(1) It will be no longer necessary for the original charging instrument to be submitted with the appropriate particulars and, accordingly, the Registrar will not check the accuracy of the particulars against the charge (s 398).

(2) The Registrar will only be required to keep on file a copy of the particulars which have been submitted and there will no longer be any obligation to include the information currently required by s 401.

(3) The Registrar is required to send to the company *and* any person appearing to be the chargeholder (whether or not he actually filed the particulars) a copy of the relevant particulars and a note as to the date on which the particulars were filed. The reason for the Registrar being required

to send a copy of the particulars to the chargeholder is that he may be prejudiced by any inaccuracy contained in them.

The Registrar's certificate   A certificate will no longer be issued by the Registrar as a matter of course, it will have to be requested (s 397(3)). Furthermore, the certificate that is supplied is conclusive evidence that the particulars were delivered to the Registrar no later than the date stated in the certificate and it is presumed, unless the contrary is proved, that they were not delivered earlier than that date (s 397(5)). A chargeholder will, therefore, be able to attempt to show that the particulars were delivered earlier than the date shown on the certificate.

This is a significant departure from the existing law whereby the certificate is no longer considered conclusive evidence that the statutory requirements as to registration by the fact that the Registrar will not be able to check the accuracy of the filed particulars.

A consequential amendment is made as to the effect of defectively registered particulars. Section 402(1) provides that where the registered particulars of a charge are not complete and accurate the charge is void to the extent that rights are not disclosed by the registered particulars that would be disclosed if they were complete and accurate. The persons against whom the charge is void as regards undisclosed rights are an administrator, liquidator or a person acquiring an interest in or right over the charge property. Accordingly, for example, if the registered particulars state the debenture is to secure £500 whereas in reality it is for £5,000 the debenture holder will only be able to claim priority over a subsequent charge held to the extent of £500. Accordingly it is essential that only the chargee prepares the particulars or checks the ones prepared by the company. The court is, however, able to order that the charge is effective against a person acquiring an interest in or right over property subject to a charge if it is satisfied that such person did not rely on the particulars in deciding to make the acquisition (s 402(5)). Thus a potential chargeholder should always be advised to make a company search in order to avoid any possible claim under this section. Similarly, the court is able to order the charge effective against an administrator or liquidator if it can be shown that the deficiency is not likely to have misled any unsecured creditor or that no person became an unsecured creditor of the company at a time when the registered particulars were deficient (s 402(4)).

Constructive notice The 1989 Act, in effect, consolidates the existing common law. Section 416(1) provides that a person taking a charge over a company's property is to be taken to have notice of any matter requiring registration and disclosed on the register at the time the charge is created. Otherwise a person is not deemed to have notice of it being disclosed on the register. This general rule overrides the provisions set out in s 711A in respect of matters on the register relating to charges. Accordingly, it is likely that there will be no change in the existing practice whereby details of any negative pledge contained in a debenture are included on the registered particulars even though there is no place for such details. Persons will not have constructive notice of such clauses since these are not matters requiring registration but creditors who read the contents of the register will have actual notice of the clause.

Effect of failure to deliver particulars The effect of failure to register particulars is the same as under the existing law although it is expressed rather differently. Where particulars are not registered within 21 days of the creation of the charge it is void against an administrator or liquidator or any person who for value acquires an interest or right subject to the charge provided that, in both cases, a 'relevant event' occurs after the creation of the charge (s 399).

A 'relevant event' is defined as meaning, in relation to an administrator or liquidator, the onset of insolvency proceedings being the time when an administration or winding up order is made (ss 399(2)(*a*), 419(5)). In relation to a person acquiring an interest in the charge, the relevant event is the acquisition of that interest (s 399(2)(*b*). Furthermore, there is a presumption that where a relevant event occurs on the same day as a charge is created that it occurred after the charge was created unless the contrary is proved.

Late delivery of particulars The 1989 Act does away with the existing requirement to involve the court in authorising the registration of late particulars. This is, however, subject to the provision that the charge will be void against an administrator or liquidator if:

(1) At the time of the delivery of the particulars the company is unable to pay its debts (defined in s 123 of the Insolvency Act 1986) or subsequently becomes unable to pay its debts in consequence of the transaction under which the charge is created.

(2) Insolvency proceedings begin within two years if the charge is created in favour of a connected person (defined in s 249 of the Insolvency Act 1986), one year where a floating charge was created in favour of an unconnected person and six months in any other case (s 400).

Memorandum of Satisfaction   Notice that a charge ceases to affect a company's property may be given to the Registrar and it must be signed by both the company and the chargee. The Registrar is required to send a copy of the memorandum filed by him to the company and any other person appearing to be interested in the charge. If a memorandum is filed then the charge is void against an administrator or liquidator of the company or any person who for value acquires an interest in the property subject to the charge (s 403).

10.5 Receivers

10.5.1 Appointment of receiver

In the event of a default by the company in complying with the terms on which debentures are issued, various remedies are available to the debenture holders. A simple action for the recovery of any sum due may be commenced; but since more valuable rights are usually given by the debenture instrument, this remedy is rarely employed.

In most cases it will be found that the debenture instrument gives the debenture holders or their trustees power to appoint in writing a receiver or a receiver and manager (see *Cripps v Wickenden* [1973] 1 WLR 944) if certain specified events occur. A receiver's duty is to sell the assets of the company, the subject of the security, in order to repay the secured debt but, more usually, provision is made for the appointment of a receiver and manager: this enables the receiver to manage such assets pending sale, or other repayment of the secured creditor. It should be noted that the appointment of a receiver is totally separate from winding-up proceedings and whilst such proceedings may well follow receivership this will not necessarily be the case. It is possible that a company may be in both receivership and liquidation but once a receiver has been appointed neither the making of a winding up order nor the passing of any resolution to wind up displaces the receiver or terminates his power.

If the company is registered in England and the debentures are secured by a floating or a fixed charge and a receiver or manager is appointed, notice of the appointment must be given to the Registrar by the debenture holders or trustees within seven days of the appointment (s 405(1)) (Form 405(1)).

The appointment of a receiver or manager is not effective unless it is accepted by the person appointed before the end of the business day next following that on which the instrument of appointment is received by him or on his behalf. Such an appointment, if so accepted, is deemed to take effect at the time the instrument of appointment is so received (Insolvency Act 1986 s 33). Where it is discovered that an invalid appointment has been made the court has a discretion to order the person making the appointment to indemnify the 'receiver' (Insolvency Act 1986 s 34).

10.5.2 Administrative receiver

The Insolvency Act 1986 makes a distinction between an administrative receiver and other types of receivers. An administrative receiver is defined by s 29 of that Act as 'a receiver or manager of the whole (or substantially the whole) of a company's property appointed by or on behalf of the holders of any debentures of the company secured by a charge which, as created, was a floating charge, or by such a charge and one or more other securities'. It should be noted that only qualified insolvency practitioners may be appointed as administrative receivers and for any other person to act as an administrative receiver is a criminal offence (ss 388 and 389 Insolvency Act 1986).

10.5.3 Investigation of the company's affairs

An administrative receiver is required to comply with the following formalities:

(1) forthwith upon his appointment to give notice of his appointment to the company and publish a notice of his appointment in the prescribed manner in the *Gazette* and such other newspaper as he thinks appropriate for ensuring that it comes to the notice of the company's creditors (Insolvency Act 1986 s 46(1)(*a*) and Insolvency Rules 1986, r 3.2).

(2) forthwith upon his appointment require some or all of the categories of persons specified in the Act to give affidavit evidence relating to particulars of the company's assets, debts

and liabilities, names and addresses of its creditors, details of security held by any of them over the company's property and such further information as may be prescribed. The administrative receiver may require officers, previous officers, persons who have taken part in the company's formation (if the company was formed within the year prior to his appointment), current employees and previous employees (employed within the last year) to provide him with a statement in the prescribed form. Failure to comply with the administrative receiver's request renders the person in default liable to a fine (s 47 *ibid*).

(3) within 28 days of his appointment to send a similar notice to all the company's creditors (so far as he is aware of their addresses) (s 46(1)(*b*) *ibid*).

(4) within 3 months of his appointment he must (unless the court sanctions an extension) send to the Registrar of Companies, to any trustee for secured creditors of the company and all such other creditors a report detailing:

    (*a*) the events leading up to his appointment, so far as he is aware of them;

    (*b*) the disposal or proposed disposal by him of any property of the company, and the carrying on or proposed carrying on by him of any business of the company;

    (*c*) the amounts of principal and interest payable to the holder of the charge by virtue of which he was appointed and the amount payable to preferential creditors;

    (*d*) the amount (if any) likely to be available for the payment of other creditors (s 48(1) *ibid*).

(5) Within 3 months of his appointment (unless the court sanctions an extension) either send a copy of his report to all unsecured creditors or publish a notice in the prescribed manner stating the address from which copies of the report can be obtained free of charge. A copy of the report is to be laid before a meeting of the unsecured creditors summoned on not less than 14 days' notice. Such a meeting may establish a committee of creditors before which the administrative receiver may be required to attend and provide it with such information as it may reasonably require (s 48(2) *ibid*).

The above provisions, which impose on an administrative receiver the duty of giving the company notice of his appointment and on the company the duty of submitting a statement of affairs, do not apply where an administrative receiver is appointed to act with an existing administrative receiver or to take the place of an administrative receiver dying or ceasing to act, unless the receiver dying or ceasing to act has not fully complied with the requirements (s 46(2) Insolvency Act 1986). But the requirements must be complied with where the company is being wound up, notwithstanding that the receiver is also the liquidator of the company (s 46(3) ibid).

10.5.4 Appointments by the court

Upon the application of a debenture holder or a trustee for debenture holders, a receiver or manager may be appointed by the court whether or not the debenture instrument gives power to make such an appointment in writing without the aid of the court. The court will generally appoint a receiver where it is necessary to enable persons who possess rights over property to obtain the benefit of those rights in circumstances where ordinary legal remedies are defective or where the appointment is necessary to protect property from some danger which threatens it.

10.5.5 Filing of returns

A receiver (other than an administrative receiver) must file within one month after the period of 12 months from the date of his appointment and thereafter in every subsequent period of six months receipts and payment accounts (s 38 Insolvency Act 1986).

When a receiver or administrative receiver ceases to act he must file a notice to that effect (s 405(2) and s 45(4), Insolvency Act 1986: Form 405(2)) and give notice of his resignation in the prescribed manner.

10.5.6 Powers and status of receiver

A debenture instrument usually confers extensive powers on a receiver as regards dealing with and disposal of the company's property and management of its business. The Insolvency Act 1986 expressly provides that an administrative receiver is deemed to have all the powers specified in Schedule 1 to the Act provided that such powers are not inconsistent with the terms of the debenture (s 42). These powers are very wide and include the power to manage the business and establish subsidiaries.

Furthermore, this Act gives the administrative receiver a power with the sanction of the court, to sell property free from fixed charges or securities to which it is subject, provided that the sale of such property would be likely to promote a more advantageous realisation of the company's assets than would otherwise be the case, and the price obtained for the property is an amount which would be obtained on a sale in the open market by a willing vendor. The net proceeds for sale have to be applied towards the sums secured by the fixed charges or securities in accordance with their respective priorities (s 43 Insolvency Act 1986). A notice of any such order made by the court has to be filed with the Registrar of Companies.

An administrative receiver is deemed to be the company's agent unless and until the company goes into liquidation (s 44(1)(b) ibid) and a debenture will usually provide that other types of receivers will likewise be deemed to be the agent of the company. Notwithstanding such provisions, administrative receivers and receivers appointed out of court are, to the same extent as if they had been appointed by the court, personally liable on any contract entered into by them in the performance of their functions, except in so far as the contract otherwise provides (ss 37(1)(a), 44(1)(b) Insolvency Act 1986). Such receivers are, however, entitled to an indemnity out of the assets in respect of such liability (ss 37(1)(b), 44(1)(c) Insolvency Act 1986). Any such agency usually ceases on liquidation of the company (and is expressly provided so to do in the case of administrative receivers), though an express power to convey property as agent may continue (*Sowman v Samuel (David) Trust Ltd* [1978] 1 WLR 22). Where the agency ceases, personal liability cannot be excluded, but the right of indemnity out of the assets remains available.

A receiver appointed by the court is an officer of the court, not an agent of the company, appointed to assume possession of and, if the order so authorises, to sell the property which forms the debenture holders' security, to collect the rents and profits of such property, and to apply them for the benefit of the debenture holders. Where the debentures are secured by a floating charge, he is usually given power to take over the management of the company's business and undertaking. A court-appointed receiver is personally liable on any contract entered into by him but he is entitled to an indemnity out of the assets of the company (*Burt v Burt* [1895] 1 QB 276, *Strapp v Bull & Sons* [1895] 2 Ch 1).

10.5.7 Other effects of receiver's appointment

The appointment of a receiver with power to take over and manage the company's business may affect adversely the employees of the company. If the appointment is made by the court, or if it is made out of court and the receiver is not an administrative receiver and the debenture instrument does not provide that the receiver shall be deemed to be the agent of the company, the appointment terminates all contracts of employment; but it will not have this effect if the receiver appointed out of court is deemed to be the company's agent whether expressly provided for in the debenture instrument or by virtue of the receiver being an administrative receiver (*Reigate v Union Manufacturing Co (Ramsbottom)* [1918] 1 KB 592 and *Griffiths v Secretary of State for Social Services* [1974] QB 468). Continuation of employment will not be presumed where the employment is inconsistent with the role or functions of the receiver or unless any new agreement which the receiver enters into with him has the effect of superseding the old contract. In the case where termination of employment is not automatic, it is usual for the receiver to dismiss those not needed and to inform the others that their employment by the company will be continued on the same terms, the receiver paying their wages as part of the receivership expenses.

Where the appointment does terminate contracts of employment, since such termination usually has the effect of a dismissal without notice, the employees may be entitled to damages for wrongful dismissal against the company; but they will rank only as unsecured creditors in respect of these damages. Certain debts of the company within specified limits, including wages, salary and accrued holiday pay of employees, and advances from a lender used in payment thereof, are required to be paid out of assets comprised in a floating charge (as distinct from a fixed charge) before anything is paid to the debenture holders (see 11.2.16).

Two other important effects of the appointment are that a floating charge crystallises and the assets subject thereto become assigned in equity to the debenture holder. If the company is not in the course of being wound up, the receiver is required to pay all preferential debts in priority to any claim for principal or interest in respect of the debentures (s 40 Insolvency Act 1986). Costs of a subsequent liquidation are probably not payable out of the receivership assets (*Re Christonette International Ltd* [1982] 3 All ER 227).

A receiver may be liable to the company or its liquidator or to a surety if he fails to take reasonable steps to obtain a proper price for the assets he sells, and the debenture holder too may be so liable if his interference with the receivership results in such sale (see *Cuckmere Brick Co Ltd v Mutual Finance Ltd* [1971] Ch 949; *Standard Chartered Bank Ltd v Walker* [1982] 3 All ER 938).

10.5.8 Letters, invoices etc

When an administrative receiver, or a receiver or manager has been appointed, every invoice, order for goods, or business letter bearing the name of the company must disclose the fact that such an appointment has been made (s 39(1) Insolvency Act 1986).

Chapter 11

Reconstruction and Winding-up

Note: references in this chapter to IA are references to the Insolvency Act 1986 and references to Rules are to the Insolvency Rules specified in 11.2.1

11.1 Reconstructions

There are various ways of effecting a corporate reconstruction (including here for this purpose arrangements with creditors) but the following are the principal methods generally met:

(1) By a scheme of arrangement pursuant to s 425 (see also 4.14) which, when sanctioned by the court and if provided for by the scheme, can be followed by an application to the court for a vesting order pursuant to s 427 which vests the assets and transfers the liabilities of one company (the transferor company) in and to either a new company or an existing company (the transferee company). A vesting order usually provides for the dissolution of the transferor company without a winding-up and directs the Registrar to consolidate the files of the two companies. Section 425 can also be utilised to effect a compromise or arrangement between a company and its creditors or any class of them (and see also 11.2.12).

(2) By means of a voluntary arrangement pursuant to ss 1–7 IA. Section 425 suffers from two major defects: the time taken to get the scheme approved which, because of the nature of the court's involvement, cannot be reduced to less than eight weeks and the difficulty in identifying separate classes of creditors. Accordingly, ss 1–7 were introduced to allow a company to come to an agreement with its creditors with less formality and with a correspondingly greater chance for the company to avoid liquidation. A proposal to the creditors of a company for a composition in satisfaction of its debts or a scheme of arrangement of its affairs ('voluntary arrangement') can be made by the directors or, if an administration order is in force, the administrator or,

if the company is being wound up, by the liquidator. Where the directors are making the proposal it will be necessary for them to appoint a nominee, a qualified insolvency practitioner and provide him with the information listed in Rule 1.2 including details of the proposed arrangement and, a list of assets and liabilities of the company. The nominee prepares a report on the proposal for submission to the court stating whether, in his opinion, meetings of the company and its creditors should be summoned to consider the proposal and if so when such a meeting should be held. The nominee then summons the meetings, indicated in his report, in order to approve the voluntary arrangement (with or without modifications). The meetings summoned may not, except with the consent of the creditors concerned, approve any proposal or modification which affects the right of a secured creditor to enforce his security or interferes with the priority of, or amount payable in respect of, preferential debts. The chairman of the meetings reports the result to the court and if the voluntary arrangement is approved it takes effect from the date of the creditors meeting and binds every person who had notice of, and was entitled to vote at that meeting. Where the company is being wound up, or is subject to an administration order the court may stay the winding-up proceedings or discharge the administration order or make such direction as it thinks fit for facilitating the implementation of the approved voluntary arrangement. The nominee (or liquidator or administrator, as the case may be) together with any creditor, member or contributory of the company may challenge the decision of the meetings, within 28 days of the chairman's report, by application to the court on the grounds that:

    (*a*) the voluntary arrangement unfairly prejudices the interests of a creditor, member or contributory;

    (*b*) there has been some material irregularity at or in relation to either of the meetings.

(3) By means of a voluntary winding-up pursuant to s 110, IA (and see further 11.2.13 below). Where this method is employed, a company goes into voluntary liquidation and a liquidator is appointed. The liquidator, with the sanction of a special resolution of the company if a member's voluntary winding-up, or the court or the liquidation committee if a creditor's voluntary winding-up, then contracts to sell the goodwill and assets of the company to a new company, accepting as consideration shares in the new company instead of cash. It is advisable for the resolutions to wind up and to approve the sale to be considered at the same meeting,

thus avoiding the situation where the company is in liquidation but the proposed sale does not receive the necessary approval. The shareholders of the company are nominated by the liquidator as allottees of the shares in the new company in accordance with the scheme agreed upon, and arrangements are made with the company's creditors who, if they do not agree to look to the new company, must be paid off. When this has been done, the liquidator summons a final meeting of the old company and makes the necessary returns to the Registrar. This, in due course, brings about the dissolution of the old company. Section 111, IA gives dissentient shareholders power to require the liquidator to abstain from carrying the resolution into effect or to be bought out for cash. For this reason professional advice should, and usually will, be sought by the secretary where a reconstruction of this type is contemplated.

It is not, however, essential for reconstructions to involve the winding-up or dissolution of an existing company. A reconstruction involving an amalgamation of two or more companies is frequently effected by the formation of a holding company to acquire the shares of the companies to be amalgamated in exchange for shares of the holding company leaving the constituent companies to continue trading as formerly.

In a reconstruction, relief from payment of ad valorem stamp duty may under certain circumstances be obtained under the provisions of s 75 et seq, Finance Act 1986; but great care must be taken to comply with the technical requirements to enable relief to be claimed and the company's solicitors should be consulted.

11.2 Winding-up

11.2.1 Introduction

The Insolvency Act 1985 introduced a number of important and far-reaching changes into insolvency law. This Act was repealed by the Insolvency Act 1986 which consolidated the law relating to liquidation and receivership and was supplemented by the Insolvency Rules 1986 (SI 1925) as amended by the Insolvency (Amendment) Rules 1987 (SI 1919). It is neither appropriate nor practical to summarise in detail all the provisions of the 1986 Act and Rules: indeed, no secretary can be a liquidator unless he is a qualified insolvency practitioner (see 11.2.2). Accordingly, this chapter provides only a broad overview of insolvency law, highlighting those areas to which the Secretary has to have specific regard.

11.2.2 Insolvency practitioners

Only persons who are authorised under the Act may act as a liquidator, provisional liquidator, administrator (see 11.2.3) or administrative receiver (see 10.5.2) (ss 390–392, IA). The Act requires the insolvency practitioner to be a fit and proper person, to have received the educational standards and practical training laid down in the Rules and to provide security for the proper performance of his functions. A person who acts as an insolvency practitioner when he is not qualified to do so is liable to imprisonment and/or a fine.

11.2.3 Administration order

The 1985 Act introduced a new concept into English insolvency law: the administration order.

(1) This new procedure is designed to assist companies in financial difficulties by empowering the court to make an administration order. Such an order places the affairs of the company in the hands of an administrator and imposes a moratorium on the enforcement of its debts during the period of the administration order and on any winding-up proceedings in respect of the company (s 10, IA). It is particularly designed for cases where there is no charge over substantially the whole of the undertaking and assets of the company, or where there is such a charge but the chargee is unwilling to appoint an administrative receiver. An administration order should provide a breathing space to enable the company's fortunes to be restored or its assets to be realised in an orderly fashion.

(2) An application for an administration order is made by petition and may be presented by the company, its directors or creditors or by a combination of any of these parties. In addition, a clerk of a magistrates' court can apply for such an order where the company has unpaid fines. For the court to make an administration order it must be satisfied that the company is or is likely to become unable to pay its debts, and that the effect of the order will be:
- (a) to secure the survival of the company as a whole or in part; or
- (b) to secure a more advantageous realisation of the company's assets than would be the case in a winding-up; or
- (c) to enable a composition of its debts or a scheme of

compromise or arrangement to be effected whether under
s 425 or a voluntary arrangement under s 1, IA.

The most important limitation on the court's power to make
such an order is that it must normally refuse the order where it
is satisfied that an administrative receiver (see 10.5.2 above) has
been appointed unless the person by whom or on whose behalf
the administrative receiver was appointed has consented, or any
security pursuant to which the receiver was appointed would be
liable to be set aside under normal insolvency rules (s 9(3), IA).
Where an application for an administration order has been made
on grounds (a) or (b) above, the courts, in order to prevent parties
unjustifiably obtaining the protection of an administration order,
require an independent auditor's report to show that the order
is likely to result in survival of the company or a more advantageous
realisation of its assets.

(3) *Consequences of the application*   The making of the application has the effect of 'freezing' the position of the company with
the following consequences:

   (a) no resolution can be passed or order made for the winding-
       up of the company;
   (b) no steps can be taken to enforce any charge on or security
       over the company's property, or to repossess goods in the
       company's possession under any hire-purchase or retention
       of title agreement, except with the leave of the court and
       subject to such terms as the court may impose; and
   (c) no other proceedings and no execution or other legal process
       can be commenced or continued against the company or
       its property except with the leave of the court and subject
       to such terms as aforesaid (s 10, IA).

(4) *Consequences of the order*   Once an administration order is
made then, in addition to the consequences mentioned above, any
petition for the winding-up of the company is to be dismissed and
no administrative receiver may be appointed and to the extent that
one has already been appointed he shall vacate office (s 11, IA).

(5) *Powers of an administrator*   If the application is successful
the administrator takes over, from the date of the order, responsibility for the management of the company's business. The administrator takes into custody all the company's property and exercises
and the powers conferred and the duties imposed on the directors
by the Companies Act 1985 or by the Memorandum or Articles
of Association can be performed only with his consent. An administrator is expressly given the power to do all such things as may

be necessary for the management of the affairs, business and property of the company and, like the administrative receiver, has all the powers specified in Sched 1 to the Act. In addition, the administrator has power to remove any director and appoint any person to be a director and to call a meeting of shareholders or creditors (ss 14 and 17, IA).

(6) *Administrative requirements*   There are a number of administrative requirements arising from the appointment of an administrator. In particular once an order is made the administrator is required forthwith to send a notice of the order to the company and publish a copy of the notice in the *London Gazette* and such newspapers as he thinks most appropriate for ensuring that the order comes to the notice of the company's creditors (Rule 2.10), and within 14 days send a copy to the Registrar of Companies (s 21, IA). Within 28 days of the order, the administrator is to give notice of the order to all creditors; and within three months (or such longer period as the court may allow) of the making of the order the administrator is required to send to the Registrar of Companies, creditors and members of the company a statement of his proposals for the company's survival or realisation of assets, and to lay the proposal before a creditors' meeting held on not less than 14 days' notice. The contents of the statement of affairs to be provided to the administrator and the persons who are required to provide the administrator with the necessary information to prepare the proposal are the same as the provisions for the administrative receiver (ss 22 and 23, IA and see 10.5.3).

After the creditors' meeting, the administrator is to report the result of the meeting to the court and the Registrar of Companies. If the meeting does not approve the scheme, the court may discharge the order or make any other order it thinks fit. If the scheme is approved it becomes the duty of the administrator to manage the affairs, business and property of the company in accordance with the proposals.

Furthermore every invoice, order for goods or business letter on which the company's name appears and which is issued on behalf of the company or the administrator must also contain the administrator's name and a statement that the affairs, business and property of the company are being managed by an administrator (s 12, IA).

(7) *Liability on contracts and powers of sale*   An administrator, like an administrative receiver, is deemed to be the agent of the company and is not personally liable on any contract entered into

or adopted by him (except insofar as the contract provides otherwise). An administrator may dispose of assets free from existing charges in the same manner as an administrative receiver where the sale is likely to promote the purposes set out in the administration order (see s 15, IA and 10.5.6). Court approval is required where the property is subject to a fixed charge but not where it is subject to a floating charge. Where court approval is not required, the remedy of the holder of the charge would be to rely on the safeguards referred to below.

(8) *Safeguards*   Creditors and, to a lesser extent, members are provided with certain safeguards during the currency of an administration order. In particular a creditor or member may make an application to the court on grounds analagous to a s 459 claim (see 4.16.1) ie that the company's affairs are being or have been managed by the administrator in a manner unfairly prejudicial to the interest of its creditors or members generally or a part thereof or any actual or proposed act or omission of the administrator would be so prejudicial. (s 27, IA). The court is given wide powers to remedy any such prejudice.

11.2.4 *Types of winding-up*

There are three statutory procedures for winding-up:

(1)   *Members' voluntary winding-up* which is available only to a company which is solvent and the liquidation is commenced by a special or extraordinary resolution and the directors must make a statutory declaration that the company will be able to pay its debts in full within 12 months of the winding-up;

(2)   *Creditors' voluntary winding-up* which is similar to a members' voluntary winding-up except that, as the company is insolvent, the creditors carry out the principal supervisory functions;

(3)   *Compulsory liquidation* which is liquidation by the order of the court and is the only method available to a creditor. A winding-up petition can be presented by any creditor, the directors, the company or (in certain circumstances) a shareholder or the Secretary of State for Trade and Industry. The petition to the court has to be on one of the grounds set out in s 122 IA of which the most common is that the company is unable to pay its debts by failing to pay within

21 days a statutory demand for at least £750. Compulsory liquidations are outside the scope of this book.

11.2.5 Voluntary winding-up

A voluntary liquidation is commenced by resolution of the company, the type of resolution required varying with the circumstances (s 84, IA). Thus:

(1) an ordinary resolution will suffice if the liquidation is sought because the period fixed by the Articles for the company's duration has expired, or an event has occurred as a result of which the Articles require the company to be dissolved;

(2) an extraordinary resolution is necessary if liquidation is sought because the company cannot continue its business by reason of its liabilities, and this fact must be stated in the resolution; this is an insolvent, or creditors' voluntary winding-up;

(3) a special resolution is necessary in any other case, ie when the company is solvent and the members wish to bring its existence to an end, whether as part of a reconstruction or otherwise.

Whichever type of resolution is passed for winding up the company, notice of it must be advertised in the *Gazette* within 14 days of the passing of the resolution (s 85, IA), and within 15 days a copy of the resolution must be filed with the Registrar (s 84(3), IA). The resolution sent for insertion in the *Gazette* must be signed and, unless the person signing it is a solicitor, accountant or chartered secretary, attested by a person who is.

Where the winding-up is for reconstruction purposes, it is advisable at the meeting at which the resolution to wind up is passed to pass resolutions (*a*) appointing the liquidator, and (*b*) (i) authorising the liquidator to sell the business for shares in the new company (see 11.1) and (ii) (if the company is solvent and the Articles contain a clause similar to reg 117 of Table A) to divide among the members in specie or kind the whole or any part of the assets of the company (in accordance with that clause). Resolution (*a*) may be an ordinary resolution but resolution (b)(i) must be a special resolution and resolution (b)(ii) an extraordinary resolution. The various resolutions may be expressed to be interdependent as appropriate but a conditional *winding-up* resolution will not be valid. The alternative is to make all the resolutions part of one composite *special* resolution. The notice convening the meeting should provide for these resolutions.

11.2.6 Commencement of a members' voluntary winding-up

Before a resolution that a company shall be wound up voluntarily is passed it is necessary, if it is to be a *members'* winding-up, that at a meeting of directors the directors or, in the case of a company having more than two directors, the majority of the directors should make a statutory declaration that in their opinion the company will be able to pay its debts in full together with interest at the official rate within the period (not exceeding twelve months from the commencement of the winding-up) specified therein. The declaration must be made within the five weeks immediately preceding the date of the passing of the resolution for winding-up the company or on that date but before the passing of that resolution, and must embody a statement of the company's assets and liabilities as at the latest practicable date before the making of the declaration. It must be filed with the Registrar not later than 15 days after the day on which the winding-up resolution is passed by the company in general meeting (s 89, IA). The declaration should be signed by the directors at their meeting.

Great care should be taken in making such a declaration, for if it be made and the company is not able to pay its debts within the specified period it is presumed, until the contrary is shown, that the directors making it did not have reasonable grounds for their opinion, and if they do not prove the contrary, they may be liable to serious penalties (s 89(5), IA). Moreover the figures shown in the statement of assets and liabilities have later to be compared with the amounts realised as shown in the liquidator's final account.

The general meeting of the company which is to pass the winding-up resolution is summoned in the ordinary way in accordance with the rules which govern the summoning of meetings of the company. The company in general meeting must appoint a liquidator (s 91, IA) but it is advisable that this be done at the meeting at which the winding-up resolution is passed. Notice of the meeting need not be given to the creditors.

The procedure which a liquidator has to follow if a members' voluntary winding-up becomes a creditors' voluntary winding-up is contained in s 95, IA.

11.2.7 Commencement of a creditors' voluntary winding-up

Where a declaration of solvency cannot be made or filed in accordance with the above requirements, the winding-up commenced by a winding-up resolution will rank only as a creditors' voluntary winding-up (s 90, IA). In such a case the resolution is almost invariably an extraordinary resolution in the terms of s 84(1)(c), IA, although it can also be a special resolution in the terms of s 84(1)(b), IA if the requirement as to the longer period of notice is complied with (see 11.2.5). In addition to the winding-up resolution, the company may also pass an ordinary resolution appointing a liquidator and members (up to five) of a liquidation committee (s 101(2) IA).

The company must summon a meeting of creditors to be held not later than the 14th day after the day on which the meeting of the company at which the resolution to wind up is to be proposed (s 98, IA). In addition, the company must give creditors at least seven days' notice of the creditors' meeting by post and must be advertised in the *Gazette* and in two local papers circulating in the district in which the company's registered office or principal place of business is situated. The notice must be accompanied by general and special forms of proxy.

The directors are required to prepare a full statement of the position of the company's affairs on affidavit together with a list of creditors which is to be laid before a meeting of the creditors. As soon as a liquidator has been appointed the directors are to give a copy of the statement to the liquidator who is to deliver it, within seven days of receipt, to the Registrar of Companies (Rule 4.34(3)).

At the meeting of creditors the chair is to be taken by a director appointed by the directors of the company (s 99(1)(c), IA). A quorum consists of at least one creditor entitled to vote (Rule 12.4A). Resolutions are passed by a majority in value of those present personally or by proxy and voting (Rule 4.63(1)). A secured creditor who does not intend to surrender his security may not vote unless he lodges at the registered office before the meeting a statement giving particulars of the security, the date when it was given and the value at which he assesses it. His vote is limited to the amount by which his debt exceeds the value at which he assesses his security (Rule 4.67(4)). Minutes and a list of creditors present must be made (Rule 4.71). The chairman may in his discretion adjourn the meeting and shall adjourn it if the meeting so resolves (Rule 4.65(3)).

The primary function of the meeting is to enable the creditors, if they so wish, to appoint a liquidator and appointees (up to five) of a liquidation committee, in either case whether in substitution for or addition to any person or persons appointed by the members. A statement of affairs together with a list of creditors of the company is presented by the directors and the creditors have an opportunity to ask for explanations thereon before they vote on any resolution (s 99, IA). If the creditors do not appoint a liquidation committee any appointment of such a committee made by the members lapses.

11.2.8 Appointment of a liquidator

In a *members'* winding-up, the liquidator is appointed by ordinary resolution of the members (s 91, IA). This resolution is usually passed at the meeting at which the company resolves to wind up.

In a *creditors'* winding-up, the liquidator may be appointed by resolutions of the company and creditors (s 100, IA). If no person is nominated by the creditors, the nominee of the company is liquidator, but if different persons are nominated, the creditors' nominee is liquidator, subject to the right of any director, member or creditor of the company to appeal to the court. In order to avoid a liquidator nominated by the members acting to the creditors' detriment before the creditors have the opportunity to meet and appoint their own liquidator, it is provided that a liquidator nominated by the company shall not, without the sanction of the court, exercise any of the powers prior to the creditors' meeting except insofar as it is necessary to protect the company's assets (s 166, IA). The remuneration of the liquidator in a creditors' winding-up is fixed by the liquidation committee, or, where there is no committee, by the creditors (Rule 4.127(5)).

Both in a *members'* and a *creditors'* winding-up, the liquidator must give notice of his appointment to the Registrar within 14 days on Form 4.27 (s 109, IA). This form must be filed in addition to the copy of the resolution to wind up, even if the latter resolution also includes the appointment of the liquidator. He must also advertise his appointment in the *Gazette* (ibid) and in such newspaper as he thinks most appropriate for ensuring that this appointment comes to the notice of the company's creditors and contributories (Rule 4.106). If a sheriff is in possession, notice should be given to him immediately; he should already have been given notice of the general meeting of the company at which the winding-up resolution is to be proposed.

In a *members'* winding-up, a vacancy in the office of liquidator may be filled by resolution of the company, subject to any arrangement with the creditors (s 92, IA).

In a *creditors'* winding-up, vacancies may be filled by the creditors, unless the original liquidator was appointed by the court (s 104, IA).

In either type of winding-up the court may, on cause shown, remove a liquidator and appoint another liquidator and, where from any cause whatsoever there is no liquidator acting, appoint a liquidator (s 108, IA).

11.2.9 *Effect of winding-up resolution*

As soon as a resolution to wind up is passed, the company ceases to carry on its business except as required for the beneficial winding-up thereof, and, thereafter, no transfer of shares may be made except with the sanction of the liquidator or any alteration made in the status of a member (ss 87 and 88, IA).

The appointment of the liquidator terminates the powers of the directors except in so far as their continuance is sanctioned (*a*) by the company in general meeting or the liquidator in a *members'* winding-up, or (*b*) by the liquidation committee or the creditors in a *creditors'* winding-up (ss 91 and 103, IA). The liquidator becomes the agent of the company (*Stead, Hazel & Co Ltd v Cooper* [1933] 1 KB 840).

The liquidator has the powers specified in Sched 4 to the Insolvency Act, and the powers contained in Parts II and III of that Schedule together with those contained in s 165(4), IA, may be exercised without obtaining any sanction. The liquidator may, among other things, settle a list of the contributories, make calls, summon meetings of the company, carry on the business for the purpose of the winding-up, borrow money, bring legal proceedings, sell the assets of the company for cash and, adjust the rights of contributories among themselves. He may also, when necessary, use the company's seal.

The liquidator cannot, however, without sanction (*a*) pay any class or creditor in full (*b*) make compromises with creditors, contributories, or debtors (s 165 and Part I of Sched 4 to the IA) or (*c*) sell the business of the company for shares in another company (s 110, IA). Even though the company is solvent, there is no power to pay statute-barred debts without the consent of the contributories

(*Re Art Reproduction Co* [1952] Ch 89). The sanctions required are set out in 11.2.12.

The powers of the liquidator may be limited or augmented by proceedings under s 112 IA, which authorises the liquidator, or any creditor or contributory, to apply to the court to determine any question arising in the winding-up, and empowers the court, where any such application is made, to exercise any of the powers it may exercise in a winding-up by the court.

The following further effects of a winding-up should be noted:

(1) The court may stay actions and proceedings against the company (ss 112, 126 and 130, IA and s 17 Companies Consolidation (Consequential Provisions) Act 1985).

(2) Various provisions aimed at setting aside recent execution and distress proceedings become applicable (ss 112, 126, 128, 130, 183, 184, 185, IA).

(3) Certain antecedent transactions entered into by the company can be called into question as can also the past conduct of the company's officers and others in relation to the affairs of the company (see ss 212 (misfeasance), 1A, 213 (fraudulent trading), 214 (wrongful trading), 239 (preferences) and 245 (floating charge), IA).

(4) The period of limitation ceases to run against a creditor in relation to his claim (*Re General Rolling Stock Co* (1872) 7 Ch App 646).

(5) The contracts of employment of employees are automatically terminated, at least where the company is insolvent or the winding-up is followed by cessation of trading (*Measures Bros Ltd v Measures* [1910] 2 Ch 248).

(6) The authority of all agents is automatically determined except that a power of attorney expressed to be irrevocable and granted by the company to secure a proprietary interest of or an obligation owed to the donee survives (Powers of Attorney Act 1971, s 4).

(7) All the liabilities of the company, which are notionally discharged, fall to be ascertained as at the date of the winding-up and are replaced by a statutory scheme for the distribution of its assets and a statutory right for the creditor to receive a dividend (see *Lines Bros Ltd* [1981] 2 WLR 1010 CA). The rules as to distribution among the creditors are mandatory and no contracting out is possible (*British Eagle International Airlines v Compagnie Nationale Air France* [1975] 2 All ER 390). The interest payable on debts proved in a winding-

up is the higher of the rate specified in s 17, Judgments Act 1838 on the day on which the company went into liquidation and the rate applicable to that debt which would otherwise be payable (s 189, IA).

(8) The company ceases to be the beneficial owner of its assets. This may have important tax implications (see *IRC v Olive Mill Ltd* [1963] 1 WLR 712; *Ayerst v C & K Construction Ltd* [1975] 3 WLR 16).

(9) Every invoice, order for goods or business letter is to contain a statement that the company is being wound up.

11.2.10 Transactions liable to be avoided

The Insolvency Act has strengthened the previous provisions enabling the court to set aside certain transactions made by an insolvent company. The three main provisions are as follows:

(1) Section 238 IA provides that an administrator or liquidator, as the case may be, may apply to the court for any transaction which the company at the relevant time entered into with any person at an undervalue to be set aside. A transaction at an undervalue means a transaction under which the consideration received by the company is nil or significantly less than the consideration provided by it thereunder. The section is expressed not to apply to any transaction which was entered into by the company in good faith for the purpose of carrying on its business and at the time the transaction was entered into there were reasonable grounds for believing that the transaction would benefit the company. Application to the court may be made only in respect of transactions which have been entered into within two years ending with the onset of insolvency, which is the commencement of the winding-up. Where this section applies because an administration order has been made or liquidation occurs immediately after the discharge of such an order, an application may be made in respect of a transaction entered into within two years of the date of the presentation of the administration order or petition. In addition, the liquidator or administrator must show that at the time of the transaction the company was unable to pay its debts or became unable to pay its debts because of the transaction. The burden of proof is reversed if the transaction was entered with a 'connected person' defined as a director or shadow director or an

associate of either (which broadly includes a wide range of relatives) or an associate of the company (ss 249 and 435 IA).

(2) Section 239, IA provides that a liquidator or administrator, as the case may be, may apply to the court for any preference made by an insolvent company to be set aside. A preference is defined as any action by the company in favour of any of its creditors, sureties or guarantors whereby, if the company goes into insolvent liquidation, the creditor will be in a better position than he would have been if the company had done nothing. The company must also be shown that in giving the preference it was influenced by a desire to achieve a preference and this is deemed to be the case where the preference is given to a connected person (other than by reason only of being its employee). The application to the court must be made within six months of the onset of insolvency or, where the preference was given to a connected person, within two years. The same considerations relating to the company's inability to pay its debts at the time of preference apply as in s 238 IA.

(3) Section 245, IA provides that a floating charge to the extent that new consideration is not provided in respect thereof created within 12 months ending with the onset of insolvency, or within 24 months if the charge is created in favour of a connected person may be set aside by the court. Where the charge is not made to a connected person the requirement regarding the company's ability to pay its debts must be shown as in s 238, IA.

11.2.11 *Personal liability of directors*

Fraudulent trading The liquidator of a company may apply to the court for an order that anyone who was knowingly a party to the company carrying on business with intent to defraud creditors is liable to make such contributions to the company's assets as the court thinks fit (s 213, IA). It is necessary to show that the company has been incurring debts when the directors knew that there was no real prospect of their ever being repaid. The requirements of the section are very difficult to establish in practice and consequently few applications have been made under this section or its predecessors.

Wrongful trading In this case the liquidator of the company may make an application to the court for an order that a director or former director is liable to make such contribution to the company's assets as the court thinks proper (s 214, IA). In order for a director to be liable for wrongful trading it must be shown that the company is in insolvent liquidation and at some time before the commencement of the winding-up the director knew or ought to have concluded that there was no reasonable prospect that the company would avoid going into insolvent liquidation. No declaration or contribution will be made if the court is satisfied that after he reached or should have reached this conclusion he took every step with a view to minimising the potential loss to the company's creditors as he ought to have taken. For these purposes the facts which a director ought to know or ascertain, the conclusions which he ought to reach and the steps which he ought to take are those which would be known, reached or taken by a reasonably diligent person with the general knowledge, skill and experience that may reasonably be expected of a person carrying out the same functions carried out by that director in relation to the company and with the general knowledge skill and experience that that director has (s 214 (4), IA). In a recent case *Re Produce Marketing Consortium Ltd* (No 2) [1989] BCLC 520 the directors were held liable to contribute to the assets of a company pursuant to s 214 on the basis that although the amounts were not available for some 15 months after the year and the directors were taken to know information which they would have known if the obligations of the Companies Act 1985 had been complied with (ie the accounts should have been prepared within ten months of the year end).

In addition the court may also make a disqualification order against the director (s 10, Company Directors Disqualification Act 1986).

11.2.12 Making compromises

The creditors of a company in voluntary liquidation are legally entitled to be paid what is owing to them out of the company's assets before any payment is made to the shareholders, and, where a company is being reconstructed, they are not bound to look to the new company for payment. In the majority of cases where the company in liquidation is solvent, there is little difficulty in making arrangements for the discharge of the outstanding liabilities out of cash in hand, but where the liquidator proposes to pay a *class* of creditors in full or to make compromises with any creditors, or with debtors, or with any contributories, he must first obtain sanction.

In a *members'* winding-up, the payment or compromise must be authorised by extraordinary resolution of the company. In a *creditors'* winding-up, it must be authorised by resolution of the liquidation committee (or if there is no such committee the creditors) or by order of the court (s 165, IA).

A compromise with a class of creditors or contributories may also be made under s 425 (see 4.14 and 11.1) or under ss 1–7 IA (see 11.1).

11.2.13 *Selling the company's business for shares*

Although, where a company goes into voluntary liquidation for reconstruction purposes, a sale of the business for shares in the new company may be contemplated, the liquidator cannot effect such a sale unless he is authorised to do so by a special resolution of the company (s 110, IA and see 11.1); and, in a creditors' winding-up, he must also obtain sanction from the court or the liquidation committee.

The special resolution may be passed either before or concurrently with the resolution to wind up, and, when it is passed, all members of the company are bound by the arrangement; but any dissentient member who did not vote in favour of the resolution may, within seven days of the passing of the resolution, serve upon the liquidator written notice of dissent, requiring him either to abstain from carrying the resolution into effect, or to purchase the dissentient's interest in the company at a price to be determined by agreement or by arbitration (s 111, IA). This notice must be addressed to the liquidator at the registered office of the company, and nothing in the Articles can take away the dissentient's right to have his interest purchased or the resolution disregarded (*Payne v Cork Co Ltd* [1900] 1 Ch 308); and if a price cannot be agreed upon, the dissentient may insist on arbitration, notwithstanding that the Articles make provision for the valuation of his shares (*Baring-Gould v Sharpington Pick and Shovel Syndicate* [1899] 2 Ch 80). Finally, where the liquidator elects to purchase the dissentient's interest, he must obtain directions by special resolution of the company as to the manner in which the money is to be raised, and must pay the money to the dissentient before the company is dissolved (s 111(3), IA).

11.2.14 Duties of the liquidator

A winding-up for reconstruction purposes is usually completed within the space of a few weeks; but, where a winding-up is not completed within one year, it is the duty of the liquidator to summon certain meetings and to make returns to the Registrar of Companies.

In a *members'* winding-up, a meeting of the company must be summoned to receive the liquidator's accounts within three months after the expiration of each period of twelve months (s 93, IA). These meetings must be summoned and conducted in accordance with the provisions of the Articles as to general meetings of the company.

In a *creditors'* winding-up, a meeting of creditors must be summoned annually in addition to a meeting of the company (s 105, IA). Twenty-one days' notice of such meetings must be given, and notice sent by post to every person appearing from the company's books to be a creditor. The notice must specify a time and a date, not more than four days before that fixed for the meeting, identifying the place at which proxies are to be lodged (Rule 4.54). The chair must be taken by the liquidator or his nominee who must be an insolvency practitioner (Rule 4.56); but in other respects the procedure at such meetings of creditors is similar to that observed at the first meeting of creditors (see 11.2.7).

In a *members'* winding-up, it is not normally necessary for the liquidator to summon meetings of creditors; but if the liquidator is at any time of the opinion that the company will not be able to pay its debts in full (together with interest at the official rate) within one year, he must forthwith, and, in any event, within 28 days, summon a meeting of creditors in the same manner as provided in s 98, IA and lay before the meeting a statement of the company's assets and liabilities (s 95, IA), and in such a case annual and final meetings of the creditors must be summoned as if it were a *creditors'* winding-up. However, if the creditors' meeting is held three months or less before the end of the first year of winding-up the liquidator is not required to summon a meeting of the creditors at the same time as that of the members (s 105(4), IA).

Both in a *members'* and a *creditors'* winding-up which are not completed within one year, the liquidator must make returns on Form 4.68 (s 192) to the Registrar of Companies in duplicate (s 192, IA). The first of these returns showing the liquidator's receipts and payments must cover the period from the first appointment of a liquidator to the end of the 12 months following the commencement of the winding-up, and must be sent to the Registrar within 30 days after the expiration of that year (Rule 4.223). Subsequent returns must be made at intervals of six months, and a final return when the assets of the company have been fully realised and distributed.

The liquidator may apply to the court for directions in relation to any particular matter arising under the winding-up (s 112, IA).

11.2.15 Final meetings and dissolution

In a *members'* winding-up, the liquidator must summon a final meeting of the company as soon as the affairs of the company are fully wound up, to receive and consider an account showing how the winding-up has been conducted and the property of the company disposed of (s 94, IA); and, in a *creditors'* winding-up, a final meeting of the creditors must likewise be summoned (s 106, IA). A meeting of creditors must also be held in a *members'* winding-up if the liquidator has found the company insolvent (s 95, IA).

It may not strictly be necessary to send notices of these meetings to the members or creditors but such notices are desirable. In any event notice specifying the time, place and object of the meeting must be advertised in the *Gazette* one month at least before the date of the meeting. The procedure is otherwise as in the case of a general meeting of the company or the first meeting of creditors.

Within one week after the date of the final meeting or meetings, the liquidator must file with the Registrar a return of the holding of the meeting (or, if no quorum is present, a return to that effect) and a copy of his account (ss 94 and 106, IA).

The company is deemed to be dissolved at the expiration of three months after the Registrar has registered the liquidator's final account and return of the final meeting (s 201, IA).

11.2.16 Distribution of assets

The assets of the company, after payment of or provision for the costs of the winding-up (including the liquidator's remuneration), fall to be distributed in the following order:

(1) Preferential creditors (s 175, IA).
(2) (Subject to the rights of holders of floating charges) general creditors, other than (3) and (4) below (s 107, IA).
(3) Creditors claiming in their character of members eg in respect

of pre-liquidation dividends declared but remaining unpaid (s 74(2)(*f*), IA).

(4) Members in accordance with their rights unless the articles otherwise provide (s 107, IA).

Claims in each class rank pari passu, and abate rateably, with each other.

11.2.17 *Preferential creditors*

A list of these is contained in s 386 and Sched 6, IA. The debts are ascertained by reference to 'the relevant date' ie the date of the winding-up order or resolution or the appointment of a provisional liquidator or, where the company is not being wound up, the date of the making of the administration order or approval of the voluntary arrangements. Some of the most important types of preferential debt are dealt with below:

(*a*) The following rates and taxes:

(i) All sums due from the company on account of tax deductions for the twelve months preceding the relevant date (Sched 6, para 1) (and in particular under PAYE).

(ii) Any VAT payable by the company which is referable to the period of six months next before the relevant date (Sched 6, para 3).

(iii) The amount of any betting duty, bingo duty, car tax, gaming licence duty, general betting and pool betting duty (in certain circumstances) due from the company at the relevant date and having become due and payable within twelve months next before that date (Sched 6, paras 4 and 5).

(*b*) Any amount which is owed by the company to a person who is or has been an employee during the four months next before the relevant date and all wages or salary (whether payable for time or for piece work or not earned wholly or in part by way of commission) of any person in respect of services so rendered to the company subject to a maximum of an amount prescribed from time to time by the Secretary of State which is currently £800 per person (Sched 6, para 9). Certain entitlements of employees under the Employment Protection (Consolidation) Act 1978 are deemed to be wages for the purposes of Sched 6 para 9 (Sched 6, para 13).

(*c*) All accrued holiday remuneration in respect of any period of employment before the relevant date, to a person whose employment by the company has been terminated, whether before, on, or after that date (Sched 6, para 10).

(*d*) All amounts due in respect of contributions due from the company on account of Class 1 or Class 2 contributions under the Social Security Act 1975 during the twelve months next before the relevant date by the company as an employer. All sums which on the relevant date have been assessed on and are due from the debtor on account of Class 4 contributions under that Act (Sched 6, paras 6 and 7).

(*e*) Subrogated rights

(i) The Secretary of State is subrogated to the rights of an employee against the company in respect of any payments made to the employee pursuant to s 122 of the Employment Protection (Consolidation) Act 1978. To the extent that the employee's rights would have ranked as preferential claims, the Secretary of State is entitled to be paid in the winding-up 'in priority to any unsatisfied claim of the employee' against the company.

(ii) Where any payment has been made to an employee on account of wages, salary or holiday remuneration out of money advanced by some person for that purpose, such person is entitled to a preferential claim in respect of the money so advanced and paid to the extent to which the employee's preferential claim has been diminished by reason of such payment (Sched 6, para 11).

(iii) Preferential debts are a first charge on any assets distrained by a landlord within three months before the date of a winding-up order in a compulsory liquidation. To the extent that such claims are satisfied out of that charge, the landlord steps into the shoes of the claimants (s 176(2), IA).

11.2.18 *Return of capital*

Where in a winding-up there are surplus assets after all liabilities to creditors have been discharged in full, this surplus must be applied in accordance with the provisions of the Memorandum and Articles.

In general, it will be used in the first place to repay to the members of the company the amounts paid up on their shares. Where shares with preferential rights as to capital have been issued, the amounts paid up on these must be repaid before a payment is made to ordinary shareholders: and where more has been paid up on some of the ordinary shares than on others, this excess payment must, unless the Articles contain provisions to the contrary, be repaid before a general distribution of the surplus is made (*Ex parte Maude* (1870) 6 Ch App 51). If the realised assets are not enough to repay the preferential capital and such excess payments, the liquidator must make a call on the holders of any partly paid shares (*Re Anglo-Continental Corporation of Western Australia Ltd* [1898] 1 Ch 327) unless the Articles contain provisions to the contrary (*Re Kinatan (Borneo) Rubber Ltd* [1923] 1 Ch 124). As to the right of holders of preference shares to arrears of cumulative dividends, see 4.1.1.

Where there is a surplus after all the paid-up capital has been refunded, this must be distributed among the shareholders pari passu in proportion to the nominal value of their holdings. But if on the true construction of the Memorandum and Articles the rights of the preference shareholders are exhaustively defined, and no express right to share in surplus assets is thereby given, such shareholders are not entitled to share in surplus assets (*Scottish Insurance Corporation v Wilsons and Clyde Coal Co Ltd* [1949] AC 462). The Memorandum or Articles may, moreover, be phrased in such a manner as to exclude a class of shareholder from participation, and great care should be exercised in making such a distribution (see, for example, *Re Fraser & Chalmers Ltd* [1919] 2 Ch 114; *Re National Telephone Co* [1914] 1 Ch 755; and *Dimbula Valley (Ceylon) Tea Co Ltd v Laurie* [1961] Ch 353).

Chapter 12

Unlimited, Guarantee and Oversea Companies

12.1 Unlimited Companies

Unlimited company status (see s 1(2)(*c*)) is normally adopted where the proprietors of a company do not wish it to file accounts (see below) or where corporate status is desired but not limited liability (as where the rules of a professional body permit its members to incorporate but not to limit their liability).

In the case of unlimited companies, the provisions of the Acts which apply to limited companies having a share capital are modified in certain respects. In particular:

(1) The directors of an unlimited company are not required to deliver accounts to the Registrar in respect of any accounting reference period unless at any time during such accounting reference period the company was an undertaking or parent undertaking of a limited company or had been carrying on business as the promoter of a trading stamp scheme within the meaning of the Trading Stamps Act 1964 (s 254).

(2) Section 135 does not apply, and an unlimited company may purchase its own shares without restriction; and

(3) Articles of Association must be registered with the Memorandum (s 7(1)) which must be in the form set out in accordance with Table E or as near to that form as circumstances permit (SI 1985 No 805).

12.2 Companies Limited by Guarantee

The Act defines a company limited by guarantee as 'a company having the liability of the members limited by the Memorandum to such amount as the members respectively thereby undertake

276

to contribute to the assets of the company in the event of its being wound up' (s 1(2)(*b*)).

In the case of such companies which have no share capital (see s 1(4)), the provisions of the Acts which apply to companies having a share capital are modified in certain respects including the following:

Memorandum and Articles   Articles must be registered with the Memorandum (s 7(1)), which must be in the form set out in accordance with Table D or as near to that form as circumstances permit (SI 1985 No 805). Any provision in the Memorandum or Articles or in any resolution giving any person a right to participate in divisible profits otherwise than as a member is void (s 15(1)).

Annual return   Companies not having a share capital need not include the information set out in s 364A relating to particulars of share capital and shareholders.

Meetings   Subject to any contrary provision in the Articles, not less than five per cent in number of the members may call a meeting, and every member has one vote (s 370). Section 372, which gives a statutory right to vote by proxy, does not apply where the company has no share capital.

12.3 Oversea Companies

12.3.1 General

Oversea companies are companies incorporated outside Great Britain which have a place of business within Great Britain (s 744). Within one month of the establishment of such a place of business in Great Britain, the oversea company must (s 691) deliver to the Registrar for registration:

(*a*) a certified copy of the charter, statutes or Memorandum and Articles of the company, or other instrument constituting or defining the constitution of the company, and, if the instrument is not in the English language, a certified translation thereof;

(*b*) a list of the directors and the secretary of the company containing the particulars detailed in s 691(2) (Form 691);

(*c*) the names and addresses of some one or more persons resident in Great Britain authorised to accept on behalf of the company service of process and any notices required to be served on the company (s 691(1)(*b*)) (Form 691);

(*d*) a list of the documents delivered for registration (Form 691); and

(*e*) a statutory declaration stating the date on which the place of business was established (s 691(1)(*b*)) (Form 691).

Particulars of alterations in the charter, statutes, Memorandum and Articles or other governing instrument (Form 692(1)(*a*)), the corporate name (Form 692(2)), the directors or secretary, or the particulars registered in respect thereof (Form 692(1)(*b*)), or the names or addresses of the persons authorised to accept service on behalf of the company (Form 692(1)(*c*)) must be registered with the Registrar (s 692). The time period for registration is 21 days where change of a person authorised to accept service is made and, in all other cases, 21 days after the date on which notice of the alteration could have been received in Great Britain in due course of post (if despatched with due diligence).

12.3.2 Accounts

Every oversea company must in respect of each accounting reference period (determined in accordance with s 701) prepare accounts similar to those required from companies registered in Great Britain and must deliver copies (accompanied where necessary by a certified translation) to the Registrar (s 700) within 13 months of the end of the relevant accounting reference period although where the accounting reference period is the company's first and is more than 12 months, the 13 month period runs from the first anniversary of the company establishing a place of business in Great Britain (s 703, which also lays down penalties for non-compliance). Notice to the Registrar of its accounting reference date is given by an oversea company on Form 701(2). The rules applicable to altering an accounting reference period apply as set out in ss 223 to 225 (see 7.2.2). The Secretary of State has power to prescribe for oversea companies exceptions to the strict accounts requirements under the Acts: certain exceptions have been prescribed—see SI 1990 No 440.

12.3.3 Prospectuses

An oversea company which issues a prospectus in Great Britain must comply with the requirements of ss 72 to 79 (until superseded by Part V of the Financial Services Act 1986 (see 3.4)) or in the case of listed securities the relevant provisions of the Financial Services Act 1986 (see 3.5).

12.3.4 Name

The name of the company and the country in which it is incorporated must be conspicuously exhibited on every place where it carries on business, and must be stated in legible characters in all billheads, letter-paper, notices and other official publications of the company (s 693).

The Secretary of State has powers, similar to those under s 26 et seq (see 2.1) in relation to companies incorporated in Great Britain, under which he can prohibit the use of the corporate name as the name under which an oversea company may carry on business in Great Britain (see s 694). Where use of the corporate name is prohibited, the oversea company may deliver to the Registrar for registration a statement, on Form 694(*a*), specifying in place of its corporate name another name approved by the Secretary of State under which it proposes to carry on business in Great Britain; such name may thereafter be altered by notice to the Registrar, on Form 694(*b*). The name so registered is deemed for all purposes to be the corporate name of the oversea company (s 694).

12.3.5 Names of directors

Unless the place of business was established in Great Britain before 23 November 1916, the requirements of s 305 (see 8.8.1) must be complied with (s 305(2)).

12.3.6 Limited liability

If the liability of members is limited, the fact must be stated in legible characters in every prospectus and in all billheads, letter-paper, notices and other official publications in Great Britain, and on every place of business (s 693)).

12.3.7 Charges on property in England

These must be registered with the Registrar of Companies to the same extent as if the company were incorporated in England (s 409).

12.3.8 Branch registers of dominion companies

See Sched 14 Part III.

12.3.9 Companies incorporated in the Channel Islands or the Isle of Man

All the provisions of the Act as to the filing of documents apply to such companies if they have a place of business in England or Scotland (s 699).

Appendix 1

Secretarial Programmes

The following programmes are designed to serve as brief summaries, or check lists, for secretaries in relation to certain of the duties or procedures in the main text. The treatment accorded is not exhaustive and will have to be adapted to the specific circumstances of each case. In particular, the Articles should be consulted upon each point which arises.

In these programmes, as elsewhere in this work, the word 'file' is often used in place of the more cumbersome 'deliver to the Registrar of Companies for registration'.

1.1 Formation of a private company

(1) Consider, in relation to proposed name, the provisions of s 26 (see 2.1) and search at Companies Registry to check similar names.

(2) Arrange for the drafting, printing, signing and witnessing by subscribers of the Memorandum and Articles of Association.

(3) Prepare and have signed by or on behalf of the subscribers to the Memorandum a statement of particulars to be delivered on application for registration (Form 10) containing the names and relevant particulars of the first directors and secretary and a consent to act signed by each person named as a director or secretary and specifying the intended situation of the company's registered office on incorporation.

(4) Prepare and have signed a declaration of compliance with the requirements of the Acts on application for registration of a company (Form 12).

(5) File the above documents and pay registration fee of £50.

(6) A certificate of incorporation will then be issued. *This entitles a private company to commence business.*

(7) File a return of allotments (on Form 88(2) or 88(3)) within one month of each allotment (s 88 and NB s 80 and ss 89 to 95 see 3.1).

1.2 Duties immediately subsequent to formation

As soon as the above preliminary steps have been taken, the following requirements must be complied with:

(1) The register of members must be opened, and, if it is not kept at the registered office, notice of the place at which it is kept (Form 353) must be filed (ss 352 and 353).

(2) The register of directors and secretaries must be opened (s 288).

(3) The register of directors' holdings must be opened (s 325).

(4) The register of charges must be opened (s 407 or s 422).

    NB In practice in the case of small companies the above registers are frequently contained in a 'combined register'.

(5) If any of the charges listed in s 396 or s 410 has been created, or property has been acquired subject to such a charge, the prescribed particulars (on Form 395 or 410) must be filed within 21 days of creation or acquisition (see ss 395(1), 400(2), 410(2) and 411(1) see 10.4).

(6) The important first meeting of directors must be held (see Programme 9).

(7) A return of allotments (on Form 88(2) or 88(3)) must be filed within one month of any allotment made at this meeting (s 88).

1.3 Conversion of a private company to a public company

(1) Convene an extraordinary general meeting to pass a special resolution:

    (*a*) altering the company's Memorandum to state that it is to be a public company; and

    (*b*) making any other necessary alterations in the company's Memorandum and Articles of Association.

NB The relevant capital requirements for a public company must be met at the time when the resolution is passed and the company's name must be changed so that it ends with the words 'public limited company' or 'plc' (or their Welsh equivalent)—see 2.3 and 2.9.

(2) Prepare and file an application for re-registration in the prescribed form (Form 43(3)) accompanied by the following documents required by s 43:

    (*a*) A printed copy of the Memorandum and Articles as amended by the resolution;

    (*b*) A copy of a company balance sheet made up to a date not more than seven months previously, with an unqualified auditor's report thereon;

    (*c*) A written statement from the auditors in relation to the net assets position shown in the balance sheet;

    (*d*) A valuation report on any shares allotted for a non-cash consideration since the balance sheet date;

    (*e*) A statutory declaration in the prescribed form (Form 43(3)(*e*)) as to the passing of the resolution; the nominal value of the issued capital and the amount paid up thereon; allotments for non-cash consideration; and the net assets position as at the date of application.

(3) Obtain from the Registrar a certificate of incorporation stating that the company is a public company.

1.4 Conversion of a public company to a private company

(1) Convene an extraordinary general meeting to pass a special resolution:

    (*a*) altering the company's Memorandum so that it no longer states that the company is to be a public company;

    (*b*) making any other necessary alterations in the company's Memorandum and Articles of Association. (NB the company's name must be changed so that it no longer ends with the words 'public limited company' or 'plc' (or their Welsh equivalent)).

(2) Prepare and file an application for re-registration in the prescribed form (Form 53), signed by a director or secretary, together with a printed copy of the Memorandum and Articles as amended.

(3) Obtain from the Registrar after the expiration of 28 days from the passing of the resolution a new certificate of incorporation:

the company will become a private company on the issue of the certificate. NB Dissentient shareholders can apply to the Court for cancellation of the special resolution within 28 days of the passing thereof (ss 53–54).

2   Declaring a dividend

(1)   Assuming that the board have resolved to recommend a dividend or declare an interim dividend, the necessary dividend cheques/warrants should be ordered and stamped.

(2)   Where share warrants to bearer have been issued, the declaration should be advertised in the press.

Note. As it is usual to close the transfer books for a short time before the declaration of a dividend, a notice to this effect is usually included in the advertisement.

(3)   Prepare list of dividends and check carefully.

(4)   Examine file of requests to pay dividends to persons other than the registered holder.

(5)   Obtain necessary signatures to cheques/warrants.

(6)   The company's bankers should be advised of the dividend.

Note. It will sometimes be found convenient to transfer the net total of the dividends to a dividend account in which only the numbers of the warrants need be entered.

(7)   Despatch warrants (following passing of company resolution, if applicable).

(8)   Collect paid cheques/warrants from bankers and mark off on dividend lists.

A form of resolution to be passed by the board for the declaration of an interim dividend and the closing of the transfer books is given below:

'That an interim dividend of .... per share in respect of the year ending .... 19...... is hereby declared, to be payable on .... 19...... to shareholders on the register on .... 19......
That the share transfer books of the company be closed from .... 19...... to .... 19...... inclusive.'

3.1   Making a call

(1)   Procure passing of requisite board resolution. A form of resolution to be passed by the board is given below:

'That a call of .... per share be made on .... shares numbered .... to ...., to be payable on the .... day of .... 19...... to the company at [its account with .... Bank Ltd at ....]'

(2)   The Articles should be examined in order to ascertain the mode of service of notice, etc.

(3)   Prepare and despatch notice to all the members concerned.

(4) Upon receipt of particulars of payments from the bankers, a list of calls unpaid should be prepared.
(5) Letters reminding dilatory members should be despatched.
(6) Payment of the calls must be recorded in the register.
(7) If calls still remain unpaid, the board should be consulted as to the course to be taken.

3.2 Forfeiture of shares

(1) Assuming that the board decide to forfeit shares if calls remain unpaid, the Articles should be consulted as to the method to be employed.
(2) Despatch a letter to the shareholder warning him to expect forfeiture if call and interest is not paid by a certain date.
(3) Prepare agenda of forfeiture for next board meeting.
(4) After obtaining resolution of forfeiture from board, despatch letter to the shareholder informing him of the forfeiture.

A form of resolution for forfeiture is given below:

'That ...., the holder of .... shares of ...... each, upon which...... per share has been paid, having failed to pay the call authorised by the board on .... 19......, due on . 19......, and having failed to comply with the notice served upon him on . 19......, the aforementioned shares are hereby declared forfeited.'

(5) Make necessary adjustments in the register of members and index (if any).

4 Death of a member

(1) Inspect carefully the copy of probate or letters of administration submitted by the personal representative. If thought necessary, call for the relevant share certificate(s).

    Note. The personal representative cannot be compelled to produce the original grant of probate or letters of administration, notwithstanding anything in the Articles to the contrary (s 187) but the copy should be an official copy.

(2) Note in register name of personal representative, particulars of title, date of grant and date noted.
(3) If the personal representative wishes to be registered as holder of shares, the old certificate must be surrendered, a letter of request for registration obtained, and a new certificate issued.
(4) In this latter case a new account in the name of the personal representative must be opened in the register. In this account he should not be described as a personal representative.
(5) The letter of request should be dealt with as a transfer.
(6) Adjust the index (if any) to the register.

5 Bankruptcy of a member

Upon receiving notice of a receiving order, a note should be made in the register and the name of the trustee entered upon his appointment.

6 Increase of authorised capital

(1) Assuming that the board have resolved to recommend an increase of authorised capital, the Articles should be consulted in order to discover what resolution of the company is necessary. (See 4.12).

(2) Summon meeting of company necessary to pass resolution on appropriate notice. Consider necessity or desirability of resolutions under ss 80 and 89 to 94 (see 3.1) being put to same meeting.

(3) Having obtained the necessary sanction, prepare copy of resolution(s) for filing, with notice of increase on Form 123.

(4) File resolution(s) and notice within 15 days of resolution (s 123).

(5) Prepare copies of resolution for supplying to members with copies of Memorandum and Articles or on demand.

A form of resolution for an increase of authorised capital to be passed by the company in general meeting is given below:

'That the share capital of the company be increased from .... to .... by the creation of an additional .... shares of .... each.'

7 Reduction of capital

The procedure in the case of a reduction of share capital (other than a reduction of unissued capital—see 4.12.2) will necessitate legal assistance. The following points may, however, require the attention of the secretary:

(1) Summon general meeting to pass special resolution to amend the Articles (if required) and to reduce capital (s 135).

(2) File copy of resolution (s 380).

(3) If an inquiry as to creditors is directed (see 4.12.2)–

    (*a*) prepare list of creditors to assist the court in settling a list of those entitled to object (s 136); and

    (*b*) prepare to notify creditors of the proposed reduction and the date of the application to the court as directed by the court.

(4) Upon the making by the court of an order confirming the reduction and approving the minute scheduled thereto, file same with Registrar (s 138).

(5) See that a copy of the minute is embodied in every copy of the Memorandum subsequently issued (s 138).

(6) If the words 'and reduced' have to be added to the company's name, attend to alteration of stationery, name plate, seal, etc.

(7) Amend copies of Memorandum and Articles of Association in hand and particulars of capital on unissued share certificates.

8 Holding the Annual General Meeting

(*Note.* Items referred to in *italics* will be relevant only if the annual general meeting is intended to be the general meeting at which the requirements of the Act as to the laying of accounts before the company are to be complied with. As to the ordinary business of an annual general meeting see 6.2.)

(1) Make certain that the date on which it is intended to hold the meeting is within the statutory period (s 366) *and within the period allowed for laying and delivering accounts for the relevant accounting reference period (s 244).*

(2) Obtain from a meeting of directors authority to despatch notices to members.

(3) *See that copies of the statutory accounts are ready for despatching with the notices (s 238 and s 241).*

(4) Prepare and despatch notice of meeting *with copies of accounts* and, if required, proxy forms.

(5) Remember to send notice to the auditors.

(6) Prepare agenda for the meeting.

(7) As and when proxies are lodged, particulars thereof should be entered in a voting list.

(8) See that the register of members, register of directors' holdings, directors' service agreements, accounts, auditors' report, and minute book are ready to be placed before or, as the case may be, available for the meeting.

   Note. Do not overlook the notice summoning the meeting which is often read at the meeting although this is not essential.

(9) Check provisions of Articles relating to polls and prepare a summary of these, and of the procedure to be followed if a poll should be properly demanded, to be available for the chairman at the meeting. Prepare (or ensure that the company's registrars or professional advisers will provide) voting cards for use in the event of a poll.

(10) Take notes of proceedings at the meeting sufficient to enable the minutes to be written up.

(11) Within 15 days after the meeting file with the Registrar copies of any resolutions requiring registration (s 380 and s 122).

   Note. In the case of large companies it may be thought advisable to send out admission cards with the notices and to have scrutineers at the doors to see that no unauthorised persons attend the meeting.

9 Draft minutes of first meeting of directors .... Limited

Minutes of the First Meeting of the Board of Directors held at
on   day, the   day of   , 19 .
   Present: [The first directors appointed pursuant to s 13(5)].
   In attendance: [The first secretary appointed pursuant to s 13(5)]
      [The additional director[s] mentioned in item 1].

(1)   There was laid on the table:
    (*a*)   the Certificate of Incorporation of the company dated ......
        ...... 19.......
    (*b*)   a print of the Memorandum and Articles of Association.
    (*c*)   a copy of the statement (Form 10) required under s 10 of
the Companies Act 1985 signed by or on behalf of the
subscribers to the Memorandum of Association containing:
        (i) particulars of the first director or directors of the company
and the first secretary of the company and their respective
consents to act in the relevant capacity; and
        (ii) particulars of the intended situation of the registered
office of the company.
    (*d*)   [It was reported that on the   day of   19   the
following persons had been appointed as additional directors
of the company:

        and the following person as secretary of the company:
            and there was laid on the table the resignations
of the first director(s) and secretary.]
There [was] [were] laid on the table [a] letter[s] from [the
first director(s)] offering to resign with immediate effect and
IT WAS RESOLVED that [each] such resignation be accepted.
[The directors being of the opinion that the said
was a person with the necessary knowledge and experience
to discharge the duties of secretary of the company, being
[here insert one or more of the qualifications specified in
s 286(1)(*a*) to (*e*)]. IT WAS RESOLVED that his appointment
as secretary be confirmed [on the terms of the [letter] [draft
service agreement]] produced to the meeting and signed for
identification by   and that   be authorised
to execute on behalf of the company a service agreement with
the said   [embodying the said terms] [on
terms to be agreed between him and   on
behalf of the company]].
(2)   [It was resolved that the secretary be ordered to obtain the relevant
particulars and consent[s] under s 288 to 290, Companies Act 1985
and to complete, sign and deliver Form 288 to the Registrar of
Companies in respect of the foregoing appointment(s) and
resignation(s).]
(3)   Each of the directors laid upon the table:
    (*a*)   a list of other directorships held by him and of companies
or firms of which he was a member and which might in the
future enter into contracts or arrangements with the company
and declared in accordance with s 317 of the Companies Act
1985 that he was to be regarded as interested in any contract
thereafter made with any such company or firm;
    (*b*)   written particulars of the interests of himself, his wife and
children in shares and debentures for inclusion in the Register

of Directors' Interests to be kept for the purposes of s 324 of the Companies Act 1985.

(4)   It was resolved that

be appointed chairman to hold that office until otherwise resolved.

(5)   It was resolved that

of

be appointed auditors of the company to hold office until the conclusion of the first general meeting of the company at which the requirements of the Companies Act 1985 as to the laying of accounts before the company are complied with.

(6)   It was resolved that the accounting reference date of the company be   in each year and accordingly that the first accounting reference period of the company be the period ending on   . The secretary was instructed to complete and sign 'Notice of accounting reference date' (Form 224) for delivery to the Register of Companies. [IT WAS FURTHER RESOLVED that the Register of Interests in shares required by s 211 Companies Act 1985 for the purposes of ss 198 to 202 of the Companies Act 1985 be kept with the Register of Directors' Interests and that the Secretary be instructed to include in the register particulars of interests notified to him pursuant to the provisions of Part VI of such Act] (only necessary in the case of a public company).

(7)   It was resolved that the registered office of the company be situated at   and that the Register of Members, Register of Directors' Interests and copies or memoranda of Directors' Service Agreements referred to in s 318 of the Companies Act 1985 be kept thereat. The secretary reported that such address had [not] been specified in the statement referred to above as the intended situation of the company's registered office on incorporation [and accordingly the secretary was instructed to complete and sign 'Notice of change of registered office' (Form 287) specifying such address as the situation of the company's registered office for delivery to the Registrar of Companies].

(8)   It was resolved that the seal of which an impression is affixed in the margin of these minutes be adopted as the common seal of the company. [Only necessary if the company wants to use a physical seal—see 2.7]

(9)   It was resolved that, so long as all the issued and fully paid ordinary shares of the company ranked pari passu in all respects, distinguishing numbers for the ordinary shares should not be maintained.

(10) It was resolved to allot and issue one ordinary share of to each of the subscribers to the Memorandum of Association (and   further ordinary shares of   each in accordance with applications received), as set out below, payment having been made in cash in full at par:

Name of Allottee   Number of Shares allotted

The sealing of certificates in respect of the shares so allotted was authorised and the secretary was instructed to complete and sign 'Return of allotments of shares' (Form 88(2)) for delivery to the Registrar of Companies.

(11)   It was resolved that the under-mentioned transfers of ordinary shares be approved and registered [subject to their being duly stamped and presented for registration in accordance with the provisions of the Articles of Association]:

Name of Transferor   Name of Transferee   Number of
                                                    Shares

The sealing of the necessary new certificates, following cancellation of the existing certificates covering the shares concerned, was authorised.

(12)   [*Here insert the form of resolution required by the company's bankers for the opening of a bank account.*]

(13)   It was agreed:
That the next meeting of the directors shall be held on 19......
at ......m.
[That meetings of the directors be held on the first day in each month.]
[That the chairman [secretary] be authorised to call a meeting of the directors at such time as he thinks fit.]

10   Bonus or Capitalisation issue

(1)   Check Articles to ensure bonus issues are permitted. If not amend Articles by special resolution.

(2)   Check authorised share capital. If insufficient follow the procedure set out in programme (6).

(3)   Convene extraordinary general meeting (or include the proposed resolution as special business at the annual general meeting).

(4)   Despatch share certificates for new shares (renounceable if desired). ·

(5)   File return of allotment within one month of the allotment and agreement (if any) entered into between the company and some person (usually the secretary) on behalf of the members concerned in accordance with the Article (see eg reg 110(*d*)).

Appendix 2

Redemption and Purchase of Own Shares
Permissible Cases Under the Act

Moneys payable on redemption	May come from		
	Either	Or	Or
Up to the nominal amount of the shares being redeemed	Distributable profits (s 160(1)(a), first limb, and (b))	Fresh issue (s 160(1)(a), second limb)	Fresh issue (s 160(1)(a) second limb)
Premium (if any) on their issue		Distributable profits (s 160(1)(b))	Fresh issue, but must come from share premium account (including premium on new shares) not from nominal amount of new shares (s 160(2)(b))
Additional premium (if any) on redemption			Distributable profits (s 160(1)(b))

Notes

1   References above and in these notes to redemption by a company of its shares include purchase of its own shares.
2   Fresh issue means a fresh issue of shares made for the purposes of the redemption.
3   References to the first limb and the second limb of s 160(1)(a) are respectively to the words 'redeemable shares may only be redeemed out of distributable profits of the company ...' and 'redeemable shares may only be redeemed ... out of the proceeds of a fresh issue of shares made for the purposes of the redemption'.
4   In the case of preference shares issued before 15 June 1982 which could have been redeemed under the Companies Act 1948 s 58 any premium on redemption may be paid wholly or partly from share premium account (s 180(2)).
5   The diagram does not deal with the provisions of s 171 which permit private companies to redeem shares out of capital.

Appendix 3

Registers to be Maintained by a Company Secretary

1   Register of members (s 352) with index if necessary (s 354).
2   Register of debenture holders (not specifically required by statute but needed if the debentures are to be registered).
3   Register of applications and allotments (not obligatory).
4   Register of transfers (not obligatory).
5   Register of directors and secretaries (s 288).
6   Register of interests of directors and their families in the shares and debentures of the company and certain related companies (s 325).
7   If a public company, register of information notified in respect of interests in the company's voting shares (s 211) with separate part containing information received pursuant to a request by the company (s 213). Both the basic register and any such separate part must have indices unless they constitute indices in themselves.
8   If a company has the status of a recognised bank or the holding company of a recognised bank, register of transactions and arrangements described in s 330 (or agreements therefor) with directors and persons connected with directors which would but for such status have to be disclosed in its accounts (s 343).
9   Register of charges (s 407) (and NB if a register of debenture holders (which is not mandatory—see 2 above), is maintained, the provisions of s 190 should be observed).
10 Minutes of all proceedings of general meetings, directors' meetings and managers' meetings (s 382).

Appendix 4

Special, Extraordinary and Elective Resolutions

The following are the cases in which a special, extraordinary or elective resolution is required. For all other purposes an ordinary resolution suffices. In particular, an ordinary resolution suffices to remove a director from office notwithstanding anything in the company's Articles or in any agreement between it and the director (s 303).

1 Special resolution

A special resolution is needed to:
(1) Change a company's name (s 28).
(2) Alter the objects in the Memorandum (s 4).
(3) Alter the Articles (s 9).
(4) Alter any provision in the Memorandum which could lawfully have been in the Articles (s 17).
(5) In the case of a company whose registered office is in Wales, alter the Memorandum to provide that the registered office is to be situated in Wales (s 2(2)).
(6) Re-register an unlimited company as limited (s 51).
(7) Re-register a private company as public (s 43).
(8) Re-register a public company as private (s 53).
(9) Disapply the pre-emption rights in respect of allotment of equity securities given by s 89 (s 95).
(10) Reduce the company's capital (subject to confirmation by the court) (s 135).
(11) Approve the giving of financial assistance by a private company in certain circumstances in connection with the acquisition of shares in itself or its holding company (s 155).
(12) In connection with the purchase of a company's own shares, authorise the terms of:
    (a) a contract for an off-market purchase (s 164);
    (b) a contingent contract (s 165); or
    (c) an agreement for the assignment or release by a company of rights of purchase of its own shares (s 167).

(13) Approve the purchase or redemption of a company's own shares out of capital (s 173).

(14) In the case of a dormant company, resolve that auditors not be appointed (s 250).

(15) Resolve that a company be wound up by the court (s 122(1)(*a*), IA) or voluntarily (s 84(1)(*b*), IA).

(16) In a members' voluntary winding-up, sanction the acceptance of shares as consideration for the sale of property (s 110, IA).

Rarer matters needing a special resolution are to:

(17) Determine that uncalled capital shall be called only in a winding-up (s 120).

(18) Alter Memorandum to render liability of directors or managers or any managing director unlimited (s 307).

(19) Approve assignment of the office of director (s 308).

(20) In the case of a company registered under Part XXII, substitute a Memorandum and Articles for a deed of settlement (s 690).

2 Extraordinary resolution

An extraordinary resolution is needed to:

(1) Resolve that a company cannot by reason of its liabilities continue its business and that it is advisable to wind up (s 84(1)(*c*), IA).

(2) Sanction in a members' voluntary winding-up the exercise of certain powers by the liquidator (s 165(2)(a), IA).

(3) Sanction in a winding-up the division of assets among members in specie (reg 117).

(4) Do anything else which by a company's Articles requires an extraordinary resolution (other than something for which the Act requires a special resolution or the removal of a director under s 303 as to which see the introductory wording at the beginning of this Appendix).

Variation of the rights of a class of shares also usually requires the passing of an extraordinary resolution at a separate meeting of shareholders of that class (s 125).

3 Elective resolution

An elective resolution is needed to enable a private company to:

(1) Enable s 80 authority to be given for any fixed period exceeding five years or for an indefinite period of time (s 80A).

(2) Dispense with the requirement to hold annual general meetings (s 366A).

(3) Dispense with laying of accounts and reports before general meeting (s 252).

(4) Dispense with the annual appointment of auditors (s 386).

(5) To reduce the number of members required to consent to short notice for the holding of general meetings from 95 per cent of members to a lesser percentage not less than 90 per cent (s 369).

Appendix 5

Forms

Forms l, m, n, w, and x are published by the Solicitors' Law Stationery Society PLC and are reproduced here by its kind permission.

a Form of application for shares

To the Directors,

Limited ('the Company')

I/We hereby apply for   shares of   each in the Company at a price of
each and enclose a cheque for £   .

I/We agree to take such shares subject to the Memorandum and Articles of Association of the Company and request you to enter my/our name in the Company's register of members as holder of such shares.

Dated   19

Signature:

Name:

Address:

Editors' note
This is a simple form of application suitable for use when specific investors agree to take shares in a company. A form of application used on a public issue or offer for sale of shares will be much more complex and should be drafted by the relevant professional advisers.

b Renounceable letter of allotment

X Limited
(Registered in England No 123456)

Registered Office:

To:

[Date]   19   .

ALLOTMENT LETTER

Dear Sir or Madam,

Issue of   **Ordinary Shares of £1 each at £1.50 per share**

In response to your application the Directors have allotted to you   Ordinary Shares of £1 each, fully paid, subject to the Memorandum and Articles of Association of the Company.

The procedure for renouncing all or part of this allotment is explained below. If you wish all the shares comprised in this allotment letter to be registered in your name, you need take no action and a share certificate in respect of them will be sent to you on 19   . The share certificate can be obtained earlier in exchange for this allotment letter on application to me, the Secretary, X Limited, [address].

If you wish to renounce all the shares comprised in this allotment letter in favour of one person (or several persons as joint holders) you should date and sign the form of renunciation below and pass this letter to the person(s) in whose favour you renounce it, who should complete the registration application form below and send it to me, the Secretary, X Limited, [address] to arrive not later than   19   .

If you wish some of the shares comprised in this allotment letter to be registered in your name but to renounce the remainder, or you wish to renounce all such shares but not all to the same person(s), this allotment letter should be split. To do this you should sign the form of renunciation below and send the letter to me, the Secretary, X Limited, [address] stating the number of split letters required and the number of shares to be included in each. I will then send you the split letters.

Surrender of this allotment letter to the Company purporting to have been signed in accordance with these instructions shall be conclusive evidence in favour of the Company of the title of the person(s) surrendering the same to deal with it and to receive a share certificate and/or split letters. Split letters and share certificates will be sent through the post at the risk of the person(s) entitled thereto.

Yours faithfully,

Secretary

continued overleaf

Form of Renunciation

the Directors of X Limited

I/We hereby renounce my/our right to the shares comprised in the above letter of allotment in favour of the person(s) named in the registration application form below.

Dated   19   .

....

Registration Application Form

To the Directors of X Limited

I/We hereby request you to register the shares comprised in the above letter of allotment in my/our name(s), subject to the Memorandum and Articles of Association of the Company.

Dated   19   .

Signature(s): ....

Name(s):   ....

Address(es):   ....

               ....

               ....

Editors' note
This is a simple form of renounceable letter of allotment (in fully paid rather than partly paid form). It is not suitable for use when the shares concerned are to be quoted: a more elaborate, standardised form will then be needed.

c Notice of Annual General Meeting

[LIMITED] [PLC]

Notice of Meeting

Notice is hereby given that the Annual General Meeting of   [Limited]
[PLC] will be held at   on   day,   19
      at   am/pm for the following purposes:

1   To consider and adopt the Company's accounts and the reports of the Directors and Auditors for the year ended   19   .

2   To declare a dividend.

3   To [elect] [re-elect] the following as Directors:
           (a) J Smith
           (b) D Jones.

4   To [appoint] [reappoint]   as Auditors of the Company to hold office until the conclusion of the next general meeting at which accounts are laid before the Company.

5   To authorise the Directors to fix the remuneration of the Auditors.

6   As special business, to consider and, if thought fit, pass the following resolution(s), which will be proposed as [a] [an] [Special] [Extraordinary] [Ordinary] Resolution(s):

      A member entitled to attend and vote is entitled to appoint a proxy (or proxies) to attend and, on a poll, vote instead of him. A proxy need not be a member of the Company.

By order of the Board,

Secretary.

[Date]   19   .

Registered office:

Notes:

1   A form of proxy is enclosed. The appointment of a proxy will not prevent you from subsequently attending and voting at the meeting in person.

2   To be effective the instrument appointing a proxy, and any power of attorney or other authority under which it is executed (or a duly certified copy of any such power or authority), must be deposited at the Company's registered office not less than 48 hours before the time for holding the meeting.

---

continued overleaf

3 [No Director of the Company has a contract of service with the Company or any of its subsidiaries.]

OR

[Copies of all contracts of service under which Directors of the Company are employed by the Company or any of its subsidiaries are available for inspection at the Company's registered office during business hours on any weekday (Saturdays and public holidays excluded) from the date of this notice until the conclusion of the Annual General Meeting and will also be available for inspection at the place of the meeting from fifteen minutes before it is held until its conclusion.]

Editors' notes

1   In the case of a private company a member will not usually be allowed to appoint more than one proxy: in that case delete '(or proxies)' in the last paragraph of the notice.

2   Note 3 above applies to listed companies and is included to comply with a requirement of the Stock Exchange *Yellow Book*.

d Notice of Extraordinary General Meeting

[LIMITED] [PLC]

Notice of Meeting

Notice is hereby given that an Extraordinary General Meeting of
[Limited] [PLC] will be held at   on   day,
          19   at   am/pm to consider and, if thought fit, pass the
following resolution(s), which will be proposed as [a] [an] [Ordinary] [Special] [Extraordinary]
Resolution(s):

A member entitled to attend and vote is entitled to appoint a proxy (or proxies) to attend
and, on a poll, vote instead of him. A proxy need not be a member of the Company.

By order of the Board,

Secretary.

[Date]   19   .

Registered office:

Notes:

1   A form of proxy is enclosed. The appointment of a proxy will not prevent you from
     subsequently attending and voting at the meeting in person.

2   To be effective the instrument appointing a proxy, and any power of attorney or other
     authority under which it is executed (or a duly certified copy of any such power or authority),
     must be deposited at the Company's registered office not less than 48 hours before the
     time for holding the meeting.

Editors' note

In the case of a private company a member will not usually be allowed
to appoint more than one proxy : in that case delete '(or proxies)' in
the last paragraph of the notice.

e Form of consent to short notice of a general meeting and/or special resolution

I/We consent to the meeting above-mentioned being held on the date specified in the above notice [and to the resolutions [set out above] [numbered 1 and 2] being proposed and passed as special resolutions at such meeting] notwithstanding that the notice given of such meeting [and resolutions] has been shorter than required by the Companies Act 1985 or the Company's Articles.

[Date]   . . . .

Editors' notes

1   The wording of the above form assumes that it will be added at the end of the notice of meeting. If it is to be a separate document alter 'the meeting above-mentioned being held on the date specified in the above notice' to 'the [Annual] [Extraordinary] General Meeting of X Limited called by a notice of meeting dated
    being held on   ' and if special resolutions are involved refer to them as 'the resolutions set out in such notice of meeting' or 'the resolutions numbered 1 and 2 in such notice of meeting'.

2   The notice requirements for meetings and those for special resolutions are distinct (see eg ss 369 and 378 respectively). An extraordinary resolution as such (as distinct from the meeting at which it is to be considered) will not, unless the Articles contain unusual provisions, require a particular period of notice. Although the wording of s 369 and of most Articles does not stipulate a period of notice for a meeting (as opposed to the resolution) if it is called to consider a special resolution and is not the annual general meeting, the inclusion in the above form of consent of the wording relating to the holding of the meeting does no harm.

3   If required, add at the end of the above form of consent the following wording relating to the sending of balance sheets and documents required to be annexed:
    'and I/we agree that copies of the documents referred to in Section 238 of the said Act to be laid before the Company at such meeting shall be deemed to have been duly sent notwithstanding that they were sent less than 21 days before the date of such meeting'.

f Form of proxy

XYZ [LIMITED] [PLC]

I/We
of   being a member(s) of the above-named
Company hereby appoint the chairman of the meeting or
as my/our proxy to vote for me/us and on my/our behalf at the [Annual] [Extraordinary]
General Meeting of the Company to be held on   19   and at every
adjournment thereof. I/We request such proxy to vote on the following resolutions as indicated
below:

Resolutions	FOR	AGAINST
1 To adopt the Company's accounts and the reports of the Directors and Auditors for the year ended 19	☐	☐
2 To declare a dividend	☐	☐
3 (a) To elect Mr J Smith a director (b) To re-elect Mr D Jones a director	☐	☐
4 To reappoint Messrs as Auditors of the Company until the conclusion of the next general meeting at which accounts are laid before the Company	☐	☐
5 To authorise the Directors to fix the remuneration of the Auditors	☐	☐
6 [Other resolutions]	☐	☐

etc

Names of joint holders (if any) . . . .

Signed this . . . . day of . . . . 19 . . . .

Signature . . . .

Notes:

1   Please indicate with an 'X' in the appropriate boxes how you wish the proxy to vote.
The proxy will exercise his discretion as to how he votes or whether he abstains from
voting:

   (a)   on any resolution set out above if no instruction is given in respect of that resolution;
   and

   (b)   on any business or resolution considered at the meeting other than the resolutions
   set out above.

2   If you wish to appoint someone other than the chairman of the meeting as your proxy
please delete the words 'the chairman of the meeting' and insert the name of the person
you wish to appoint. A proxy need not be a member of the Company.

3   To be effective this form, and any power of attorney or other authority under which it
is executed (or a duly certified copy of any such power or authority), must be deposited
at [the Company's registered office] not less than 48 hours before the time for holding
the meeting.

continued overleaf

4 Where the member is a corporation this form must be under its common seal or signed by an officer, attorney or other person duly authorised by the corporation.

5 In the case of joint holders only one need sign this form, but the names of the other joint holders should be shown in the space provided. The vote of the senior holder who tenders a vote, whether in person or by proxy, will be accepted to the exclusion of the votes of the other joint holders. Seniority will be determined by the order in which the names of the holders appear in the register of members in respect of the joint holding.

Editors' notes

1 The resolutions included above are of the type likely to appear in the business of an annual general meeting and are included merely by way of example.

2 The exact wording of notes 3, 4 and 5 above will depend on the wording of the company's Articles or (if applicable) regs 55 and 62.

g Resolutions by a corporation appointing representative(s) to act at meetings of companies

A—Appointment of one representative in relation to a specific company

---

XYZ INVESTMENTS PLC

Copy of resolution of the Directors passed on   , 19

'IT WAS RESOLVED that John Smith be authorised in accordance with Section 375 of the Companies Act 1985 to act as the representative of XYZ Investments PLC at any meeting of The Eastern Steam Packet Company, Limited.'

I certify that the above is a true copy of a resolution of the Directors of XYZ Investments PLC which was duly passed on the above-mentioned date.

. . . .
Secretary
XYZ Investments PLC

B—Appointment of several representatives to act generally

XYZ INVESTMENTS PLC

Copy of resolution of the Directors passed on   , 19

'IT WAS RESOLVED that John Jones, John Smith, Thomas Green and John Thompson each be authorised in accordance with Section 375 of the Companies Act 1985 to act as the representative of XYZ Investments PLC at any meeting of the members or creditors (or any of them) of any company of which XYZ Investments PLC may from time to time be a member or creditor (the expression creditor herein including a holder of debentures).'

I certify that the above is a true copy of a Resolution of the Directors of XYZ Investments PLC which was duly passed on the above-mentioned date.

. . . .
Secretary
XYZ Investments PLC

---

h Copy of resolution for filing

No. . . . .

The Companies Act 1985

COMPANY LIMITED BY SHARES

[LIMITED] [PLC]

Special Resolution passed on   19

AT [the Annual] [an Extraordinary] General Meeting of the Company held on
19   the following resolution was duly passed as a Special
Resolution:

. . . .
[Director]   [Secretary]

Editors' Note
If the resolution is an ordinary or extraordinary one rather than a special
resolution, alter 'Special' to 'Ordinary' or 'Extraordinary'. Adapt as
necessary if more than one resolution is involved.

i Notice of appointment of alternate director

To the Directors,
XYZ Limited

I,   , a director of the Company, hereby give you notice, in accordance
with [Regulation 68 of Table A of the Companies Act 1985] * of the appointment of
                 as my alternate director. This appointment shall take effect forthwith.

Signed: . . . .

Dated: . . . .

* Where relevant, insert appropriate Article number

j Notice of resignation of auditors of a company

To the Directors
XYZ Limited

We hereby resign as auditors of the company and confirm that there are
no circumstances connected with our resignation which we consider should
be brought to the notice of the members of creditors of the company
pursuant to section 390 Companies Act 1985.

Dated: . . . .

. . . .

k Tax voucher to accompany dividend cheque

THE EASTERN STEAM PACKET COMPANY, LIMITED

Security code
0-123-456

Dividend no	Reference no	TAX VOUCHER	1st April 1992
123	456		

[Final] Dividend on Ordinary Shares at 5p per share for year ended 31 December 1991 to shareholders registered on 15 March 1992.

I certify that Advance Corporation Tax of an amount equal to that shown below as tax credit will be accounted for to the Collector of Taxes. This voucher should be kept. It will be accepted by the Inland Revenue as evidence of tax credit in respect of which you may be entitled to claim payment or relief.

J SMITH, Secretary

Number of shares	Tax Credit	Dividend Payable
200	£2.50	£10.00

JOHN JONES
1 HIGH STREET
BARCHESTER
BARSET

Notice of any change of address or any correspondence about this dividend should be sent, quoting the reference number given above, to The Registrar, The Eastern Steam Packet Company, Limited, 200 Gresham Street, London EC2A 2AB.

Editors' notes

1   For further details of the way in which a dividend warrant and its accompanying tax voucher should be laid out, see the specification published by the British Standards Institution.

2   The box in the top right corner giving the security code applies only to listed securities; the code is the number given against the name of the security in The Stock Exchange Daily Official List.

For Company's use only

1 Request for payment of interest or dividends

Name of Undertaking	

Insert name and address of Company

To : The Secretary or Registrar   Date_____

Please forward, until further notice, all Interest and Dividends that may from time to time become due on any Stock or Shares now standing, or which may hereafter stand in my (our) name(s) or in the name(s) of the survivor(s) of us in the Company's books to :-

Full name and address of the Bank, Firm or Person to whom Interest and Dividends are to be sent

or, where payment is to be made to a Bank, to such other Branch of that Bank as the Bank may from time to time request. Your compliance with this request shall discharge the Company's liability in respect of such interest or dividends.

This form must be signed by ALL the Registered Holders, Executors or Administrators as the case may be

(1) *Signature*_____   (3) *Signature*_____

*Name in full*_____   *Name in full*_____
(BLOCK CAPITALS)   (BLOCK CAPITALS)

*Address*_____   *Address*_____

Any change of address may be notified by quoting former and present address

(2) *Signature*_____   (4) *Signature*_____

*Name in full*_____   *Name in full*_____
(BLOCK CAPITALS)   (BLOCK CAPITALS)

*Address*_____   *Address*_____

NOTE   (i)   Directions to credit a particular account MUST be given to the Bank direct and NOT INCLUDED in this form.

          (ii)   Where the stock is in the name of a deceased Holder, instructions signed by Executor(s) or Administrator(s) should indicate the name of the deceased.

Where the instructions are in favour of a Bank, this form should be sent to the Bank branch concerned for the insertion of the following details:-

Bank's Reference Numbers and Details:-

STAMP OF BANK BRANCH

(1)   Sorting Code No._____

(2)   Name of Bank and Title of Branch_____

(3)   Account Number (if any)
      (Please quote all digits including zeros)

Companies DM1

Published by Stat-Plus Limited Stat-Plus House Prince George's Road London SW19 2PU   Telephone: 081 646 5500

ZF0218   **STAT·PLUS**
                Stat-Plus Group PLC

1H1

m Letter of request:
Form Con 41A

LETTER OF REQUEST	
	above this line for Registrar's use only

REQUEST BY EXECUTORS OR ADMINISTRATORS OF A DECEASED HOLDER TO BE PLACED ON THE REGISTER AS HOLDERS IN THEIR OWN RIGHT.

Please complete in type writing or in block capitals

* A separate Letter of Request should be used for each class of security

Full name and address of undertaking	TO THE DIRECTORS OF		
*Full description of security			
Number or amount of shares, stock or other security and, in figures column only, number and denomination of units if any	WORDS		FIGURES
			(units of)
Full name of deceased	.... Deceased		
	late of		

I/We, the undersigned, being the personal representative(s) of the above-named deceased, hereby request you to register me/us in the books of the Company as the holder(s) of the above-mentioned Stock/Shares now registered in the name of the said deceased.

Dated this.. day of ....19..........

Signature(s) of Personal Representative(s)

....

....

....

Full name(s) and full postal address(es) (including post code(s) of the personal representative(s) in the order in which they are to be registered

Please state title, if any, or whether Mr., Mrs. or Miss

IF AN ACCOUNT ALREADY EXISTS IN THE ABOVE NAME(S) IN THE SAME ORDER THE ABOVE-MENTIONED HOLDING WILL BE ADDED TO THAT ACCOUNT. UNLESS INSTRUCTIONS ARE GIVEN TO THE CONTRARY.

The Certificate(s) in the name of the deceased if not already with the Company's Registrars must accompany this form No stamp duty is payable on this form in the case of a company registered in England; in the case of a company registered in Scotland stamp duty may be payable	Stamp or name and address of person lodging this form.

This form must be returned to:

The Registrar

.... (Name of Company)

.... (Address)

....

Miscellaneous 4 : Letter of Request   *(Form approved by the Institute of Chartered Secretaries and Administrators)*
Stat-Plus Limited, Stat-Plus House, Greenlea Park, Prince George's Road, London SW19 2PU
STAT-PLUS Stat-Plus Group PLC   EHE/H

n Indemnity for lost certificate:
Form Cos 5B

**INDEMNITY
FOR LOST
CERTIFICATE**

(above this line for Registrar's use only)

To the Directors of ....

....

The original certificate(s) of title relating to the undermentioned securities of the above-named Company has/have been lost or destroyed.

Neither the securities nor the certificate(s) of title thereto have been transferred, charged, lent or deposited or dealt with in any manner affecting the absolute title thereto and the person(s) named in the said certificate(s) is/are the person(s) entitled to be on the register in respect of such securities.

I/We request you to issue a duplicate certificate(s) of title for such securities and in consideration of your doing so, undertake (jointly or severally) to indemnify you and the Company against all claims and demands (and any expenses thereof) which may be made against you or the Company in consequence of your complying with this request and of the Company permitting at any time hereafter a transfer of the said securities, or any part thereof, without the production of the said original certificate(s).

I/We undertake to deliver to the Company for cancellation the said original certificate(s) should the same ever be recovered.

PARTICULARS OF CERTIFICATE(S) LOST OR DESTROYED

Particulars of Certificate	Amount and Class of Securities	In favour of

Dated this .... day of .... 19 ....

Signature(s) ....

*We ....

hereby join in the above indemnity and undertaking.

....
*Bank, Insurance Company or Guarantee Society.

oyez The Solicitors' Law Stationery Society Ltd., Oyez House, 27 Crimscott Street, London SE1 5TS

4.90 F16752
5017107
* * * * *

Companies 5B

o Declaration of trust and power of attorney

DECLARATION OF TRUST AND POWER OF ATTORNEY

To: . . . .

. . . .

1   I/WE . . . .

. . . .

HEREBY DECLARE that the share(s) specified in the Schedule hereto, the certificate(s) for which has/have been or will be delivered to you, is/are now and has/have at all times since the said share(s) became registered in my/our name(s) been held in trust for you absolutely.

2   I/WE HEREBY UNDERTAKE to transfer or otherwise deal with the said share(s) as you may from time to time direct and to account to you for all dividends or other moneys paid to me/us on or in respect of the said share(s) and to exercise my/our voting powers and other rights in respect of the said share(s) in such manner as you shall from time to time direct.

3   TO secure the performance of the above undertaking I/WE HEREBY IRREVOCABLY APPOINT YOU my/our Attorney at your cost and expense in all respects:

(a)   to sign in my/our name(s) and on my/our behalf any instrument(s) of transfer of the said share(s) (or to complete any necessary particulars in any instrument(s) of transfer in respect of the said share(s) executed by me/us in blank and delivered to you at any time) and any dividend mandate or form of proxy or consent to short notice of any meeting or resolution in writing or requisition or notice of any resolution or proposal or other document whatsoever (whether of the foregoing description or not) which may in your opinion be necessary or desirable and which as the holder(s) of the said share(s) I/we have power to sign; and

(b)   generally in my/our name(s) and on my/our behalf to execute and do all such instruments and things as you may think fit for the purpose of obtaining or exercising any and all rights and powers of and incidental to the holding or ownership of the said share(s).

[4*   [REFERENCES herein to the said shares shall where the subject or context permits or requires include references to any of the said shares.]

THE SCHEDULE above referred to

Name of Company   Particulars of Share(s)

[Insert details]

IN WITNESS whereof these presents have been executed as a Deed by me/us this
          day of   19   .

†   SIGNED AS A DEED by
    me the said   }

    in the presence of:

‡   THE COMMON SEAL of   }

    was hereunto affixed in the presence
    of:

    or
    SIGNED AS A DEED by
    ACTING BY   }
    A DIRECTOR AND [A DIRECTOR] [THE
    SECRETARY]

*   Insert clause 4 if the declaration relates to more than one share.
†   Use this form of words if the declaration is made by an individual.
‡   Use this form of words if the declaration is made by a company.

Editors' note

This form may be used where eg, to comply with the requirement that a company has more than one member, one or more shares in a wholly-owned subsidiary are registered in the name of a nominee of the holding company. This is no longer necessary where the shareholder complies with the requirements of the Companies (Single Member Private Limited Companies) Regulations 1992, see 1.4.2.

p Resolutions for the purposes of ss 80 and 89 (allotment of shares)

A—Resolution giving authority to allot relevant securities

THAT the Directors are hereby generally and unconditionally authorised in accordance with Section 80 of the Companies Act 1985 to exercise for a period of [five] year[s] from the date of the passing of this resolution all the powers of the Company to allot relevant securities up to the aggregate nominal amount of £   * and to make offers or agreements which would or might require relevant securities to be allotted after the expiry of the said period (provided that such allotments would fall within the limit aforesaid if made during the said period) and for the purposes of this resolution words and expressions defined in or for the purposes of the said Section shall have the same meaning herein.

*   The amount to be inserted here will generally be the amount of the Company's unissued share capital.

B—Special resolution disapplying s 89 generally

THAT:
(1) Section 89(1) of the Companies Act 1985 shall not apply to the allotment of equity securities which the Directors are authorised to allot pursuant to the authority conferred on them for the purposes of Section 80 of that Act [by the Ordinary Resolution already passed at this meeting];
(2) The Company may before the expiry of the power conferred by this Resolution make an offer or agreement which would or might require equity securities to be allotted after such expiry (provided that such allotments would fall within the limit provided for by the said authority if made before such expiry); and
(3) For the purposes of this resolution words and expressions defined in or for the purposes of the said Section 89 shall have the same meaning herein.

Editors' notes

1   An Ordinary Resolution suffices for A above.
2   Listed companies will generally require a more complicated version of B above, on which professional advice should be sought, in order to comply with the guidelines of certain bodies of institutional investors while retaining as much flexibility as possible.
3   B above is a general disapplication of the pre-emption rules in s 89 pursuant to s 95(1). Such pre-emption rules may also be disapplied (or modified) in relation to a specified allotment pursuant to s 95(2) but subject to the additional requirements in s 95(5).

q Special resolution under s 164 to approve a contract for off-market purchase by a company of its own shares

> THAT the terms of a proposed contract between
>
> of the one part and the Company of the other part providing for the purchase by the Company of certain of its own shares (a draft of which contract has been produced to this meeting and signed for identification by the Chairman thereof) are hereby approved and authorised for the purposes of Section 164 of the Companies Act 1985 and otherwise [but so that such approval and authority shall expire eighteen months after the date on which this resolution is passed].

Editors' notes

1   The words in square brackets are needed only in the case of a public company.

2   Attention is drawn to the detailed provisions of s 164, eg as to voting (subs (5)) and as to the requirement that a copy of a proposed contract (or a memorandum of its terms if it is not in writing) must be available for inspection (subs (6)).

r Resolution under s 166 to authorise market purchases by a company of its own shares

> THAT authority is hereby given for the purposes of Section 166 of the Companies Act 1985 for market purchases (as defined in the said Section) by the Company of any of its [own shares] [insert class or other description of shares to which authority is to extend] subject to the following restrictions:
>
> (1) The maximum aggregate number of shares to be so acquired is   .
>
> (2) The maximum and minimum prices to be paid for shares so acquired shall be respectively   and   .
>
> (3) This authority shall expire eighteen months after the date on which this resolution is passed but the Company may before such expiry make contracts for such purchases which would or might be executed wholly or partly after such expiry.
>
> (4) [Insert any other desired limitations or conditions].

Editors' notes

1   An ordinary resolution suffices.

2   The maximum and minimum prices may be specified by a formula (but without reference to any person's discretion or opinion) (s 166(6)).

s Special resolution under s 173 to approve payment out of capital by a company for the redemption or purchase of its own shares

> THAT approval is hereby given for the purposes of Section 173 of the Companies Act 1985 to the payment out of capital (within the meaning of Section 171 of the said Act) by the Company of £   [for] [towards the monies payable on] the [redemption] [purchase] by the Company of [number and brief description of the shares involved] in the Company's share capital.

Editors' note

Attention is drawn to the detailed provisions of ss 173–175, eg as to the timetable to be followed, as to voting (s 174(1)) and as to documents to be available for inspection (s 174(4)).

t Notice for publication under s 175 concerning payment out of capital by a company for the redemption or purchase of its own shares

> [Name of company]
>
> (registered in [England] No 123456)
>
> Proposed payment out of capital pursuant to
> Companies Act 1985, Section 171
>
> NOTICE is hereby given pursuant to Section 175 of the Companies Act 1985 that:
>
> (1)   ('the Company') has by a Special Resolution passed on   19   approved a payment out of capital for the purpose of acquiring by [redemption] [purchase] [number and brief description of shares] in its own share capital.
> (2) The permissible capital payment (as defined in Section 171 of the said Act) for such shares is £
> (3) The statutory declaration of the Company's directors and the report of the Company's auditors required by Section 174 of the said Act in respect of such payment out of capital are available for inspection by any member or creditor of the Company at the Company's registered office
>
>   during business hours on any day (except a Saturday, Sunday or public holiday) up to and including [insert date five weeks after the resolution].
> (4) Any creditor of the Company may at any time up to and including [insert date five weeks after the resolution] apply to the [High Court of Justice] under Section 176 of the said Act for an order prohibiting such payment out of capital.
>
> [Date]   . . . .
>   Secretary
> Registered Office:

Editors' note

A creditor's application to prohibit the payment of capital must be made to 'the court'. By s 744 this means the court having jurisdiction to wind up the company. Section 117 of the Insolvency Act 1986 specifies which courts have jurisdiction to wind up a company registered in England and s 120 of the Insolvency Act 1986 which courts have jurisdiction to wind up a company registered in Scotland.

u Notification under ss 198 to 200 as to an interest in relevant share capital of a public company

TO the Secretary of   Public Limited Company (hereinafter called 'the Company')

I,   of
hereby give the Company notice [in fulfilment of the obligation imposed by Section 198(1) of the Companies Act 1985][5] that:

(1) This notification relates to, and the expression 'the share capital' used below means, [the Company's whole share capital] [the part of the Company's share capital which is divided into [Ordinary Shares]].[6]

(2) The number of shares comprised in the share capital in which [I know that][7] I was interested[8] immediately after the time when my obligation to make this notification arose is   .

OR

(2) I no longer have an interest[8] [subject to the notification requirement under s 198 of the said Act] in shares comprised in the share capital.[9]

(3) [I am] [of[10]
          is] the registered holder of all the shares to which this notification relates.

OR

(3) The identities of the registered holders of the shares to which this notification relates and the numbers of those shares held by each of them are [, so far as known to me at the date of this notification,][7] as follows:

                    Identity   *Number*

    Name   *Address*[10]

[(4) [11]I am a party to an agreement to which Section 204 of the [said Act] applies. The names and, so far as known to me, the addresses of the other parties to that agreement are as follows:

                    Name   *Address*

[Insert number] [None] of the shares to which this notification relates are shares in which I am interested by virtue of the said Section 204.]

[(5) [11][I have] [of
          has] ceased to be a party to [the agreement referred to in paragraph 4 above] [an agreement to which [the said Section 204] [Section 204 of the said Act] applies made between[12]

                                                              ].]

Dated   199 .   . . .

Notes

(1) For the detailed requirements see Part VI of the 1985 Act.

(2) The obligation to make a required notification must be performed within the period of two days following that on which the obligation arises (s 202(1)) but see s 220(2) relating to Saturdays, Sundays and bank holidays.

(3) The notification must be in writing: s 202(1).

(4) The matters to be specified in a notification are set out in ss 202 and 210(2).

(5) These words should be included if the person making the notification is a director (s 210(2)) in order to distinguish this notification from a notification under s 324. Otherwise the words are optional. Where notifications are required by both the sections they can, if desired, be combined in one document but if this is done care should be taken to follow the distinct requirements of the respective sections.

(6) Note s 198(2).

(7) These words of qualification may be inserted if desired: see ss 199(5)(*a*) and 202(3).

(8) By ss 203(1) and (2), 204 and 205(1) a person is taken to be interested in shares if certain members of his family, certain bodies corporate or other parties to an agreement to which s 204 applies ('a concert party') and to which he is party are interested in them. Sections 208 and 209 specify certain interests to be taken into account for the purposes of ss 198 to 202 and certain interests to be disregarded. Since therefore:
   (i) a person is taken to be interested in shares in which the ordinary man would probably not regard himself as interested eg shares held by his wife; and
   (ii) there are to be disregarded shares in which the ordinary man would probably regard himself as having an interest, eg shares comprised in a settlement in which he has a life interest (s 209(1)(*e*) and (3));
it may be desired where such deeming provisions apply to insert after 'interested' in the first alternative for paragraph 2 or after 'interest' in the second alternative:
   '(within the meaning of Part VI of the [said Act])'.

(9) If the second alternative for paragraph 2 is used, delete both alternatives of paragraph 3.

(10) Addresses would not seem to be obligatory. Section 202 requires only the *identity* of the registered holder. Section 210 requires a notification to identify the person making it and give his address: from this it would appear that a person's name will normally suffice to identify him.

(11) Paragraphs 4 and 5 should be included only where applicable: see s 205(4) and (5).

(12) Insert names of parties to the agreement in order to identify it: some identification of the agreement would seem necessary as s 205(5) reads 'the notification shall include a statement that he or that other person has ceased to be a party to *the* agreement' rather than '*such an* agreement'. It would not seem necessary to include addresses.

(13) Note the continuing obligations in ss 202(4)(*a*) and (*b*) where the person making the notification later becomes aware of particulars of the registered ownership of shares in which he is interested or of any change in such particulars and the obligation to make a further notification if he ceases to have an interest subject to the notification requirement or the percentage level of his interest (rounded down if it is not a whole number to the next whole number) alters.

v Specimen notice to registered holder pursuant to s 212 requiring disclosure of interest in shares in public company (see 4.3)

To: [Registered Holder of
      Shares]

Disclosure of Interest in Shares

In accordance with the provisions of Section 212 of the Companies Act 1985 will you please provide to us in writing, within [seven]* days of the date hereof, the following details for all persons who, within your knowledge, have an interest in the shares of this company registered in your name [or have had such an interest during the three years preceding the date hereof].*

Name and address of person(s) having an interest	Particulars of interest	No of shares in which interest held

Please also indicate as required by Section 212(3) whether any of the persons interested in shares are or were parties to any agreement to which Section 204 of the Act applies (notification of interests of persons acting together) or to any agreement or arrangement relating to the exercise of any rights conferred by the holding of the shares.

Editors' note

Section 212(4) requires the relevant information to be provided within 'such reasonable time' as may be specified: the extent and nature of the request and the identity of the addressee will be taken into account by the court in determining what is reasonable. In exceptional cases the court has held that the two clear days notice was sufficient (*Lonhro v Edelman* (1989 5 BCC 68)). The notice can extend to other interests subsisting with that of the addressee during the preceding three years (s 212(2)(b)). These requirements, and the detailed provisions of s 212 generally, should be carefully considered in each case where a notice is to be served.

w Extraordinary resolution for voluntary winding-up of insolvent company

Number of Company } ....

The Companies Act 1985

COMPANY LIMITED BY SHARES

Extraordinary Resolution

(Pursuant to section 378 (1) of the Companies Act 1985 and section 84 (1) (C) of the Insolvency Act 1986)

Passed , 19 .

At an EXTRAORDINARY GENERAL MEETING of the above-named Company, duly convened, and held at

on the day of , 19 , the subjoined EXTRAORDINARY RESOLUTION was duly passed, viz.:—

RESOLUTION

"That is have been proved to the satisfaction of this meeting that the Company cannot by reason of its liabilities continue its business, and that it is advisable to wind up the same, and accordingly that the Company be wound up voluntarily, and that

of

be and he is hereby appointed Liquidator for the purposes of such winding-up."

Signature .... } To be signed by the Chairman, a Director or the Secretary of the Company.

....

*For the London Gazette the signature to this Notice must be attested in the space below by either a Solicitor of the Supreme Court, a member of any body of Accountants established in the United Kingdom and for the time being recognised by the Department of Trade for the purposes of section 389 (1) (a) of the Companies Act 1985, or a member of the Institute of Chartered Secretaries and Administrators, if the signatory is neither a Solicitor nor a member of any of the above bodies.

Attested by ....

Description ....

Name of signatory (in block capitals) ....

Section(1) of the Companies Act 1985 provides as follows:-

A copy of every resolution or agreement to which this section applies shall, within fifteen days after it is passed or made, be forwarded to the registrar of companies and recorded by him; and it must be either a printed copy or else a copy in some other form approved by the registrar.

* * * * *

Section 380(4) of the Companies Act 1985 provides (*inter alia*) as follows:-

This section applies to —

    (*a*) extraordinary resolutions;

    (*b*) resolutions or agreements which have been agreed to by all the members of a company, but which, if not so agreed to, would not have been effective for their purpose unless, as the case may be, they have been passed as special resolutions or as extraordinary resolutions; and

    (*c*) resolutions for voluntary winding-up, passed under section 84(1)(*a*) of the Insolvency Act 1986.

NOTE.—The Registrar of Companies is prepared to accept copy resolutions or agreements if produced by the following processes:-

    Letterpress, Gravure, Lithography, Stencil duplicating, Offset Lithography, "Office" Type-set, Electrostatic Photocopying, "Photostat" or similar processes properly processed and washed;

or if typed.

    No document will be accepted however, if, in general appearance, legibility, format or durability, it is unsuitable for publication and use on the Company's public file.

x Special resolution for voluntary winding-up of solvent company

Number of } ....
Company }

The Companies Act 1985
COMPANY LIMITED BY SHARES
Special Resolution

(Pursuant to section 378 (2) of the Companies Act 1985 and section 84 (1) (b) of the Insolvency Act 1986)

_____ *LIMITED*

Passed _____ , 19 .

At an EXTRAORDINARY GENERAL MEETING of the above-named Company, duly convened, and held at

on the   day of   , 19 , the subjoined SPECIAL RESOLUTION was duly passed, viz.:—

RESOLUTION

"That the Company be wound up voluntarily, and that

.

of

         be and he is hereby appointed liquidator for the purposes of such winding-up."

*Signature .... } To be signed by the Chairman, a Director or the Secretary of the Company.

*For the *London Gazette* the signature to this form must be attested in the space below by either a solicitor, a member of a body of accountants recognised by the Department of Trade for the purpose of section 389 (1) (a) of the Companies Act 1985 or a member of The Institute of Chartered Secretaries and Administrators if the signatory is neither a solicitor nor a member of any of the above bodies.

Witness to the above signature ....
Description ....
In order to prevent any possibility or error in printing the signature, the name of the signatory should be written below in block capitals.
*Name of signatory (in block capitals) ....

Section 380(1) of the Companies Act 1985 provides (inter alia) as follows:-

A copy of every resolution or agreement to which this section applies shall, within fifteen days after it is passed or made, be forwarded to the registrar of companies and recorded by him; and it must be either a printed copy or else a copy in some other form approved by the registrar.

         *   *   *   *

Section 380(4) of the Companies Act 1985 provides (*inter alia*) as follows:-

This section applies to —

     (*a*) special resolutions;

     (*b*) resolutions or agreements which have been agreed to by all the members of a company, but which, if not so agreed to, would not have been effective for their purpose unless, as the case may be, they have been passed as special resolutions or as extraordinary resolutions; and

     (*c*) resolutions for voluntary winding-up, passed under section 84(1)(*a*) of the Insolvency Act 1986.

NOTE.—The Registrar of Companies is prepared to accept copy resolutions or agreements if produced by the following processes:-

     Letterpress, Gravure, Lithography, Stencil duplicating, Offset Lithography, "Office" Type-set, Electrostatic Photocopying, "Photostat" or similar processes properly processed and washed;
or if produced by spirit duplicator, or if typed.

     No document will be accepted however, if, in general appearance, legibility, format or durability, it is unsuitable for publication and use on the Company's public file.

y Elective resolutions

Company Number [   ]

The Companies Act 1985
PRIVATE COMPANY LIMITED BY SHARES

Elective Resolutions of
[   ] Limited

Passed the [   ] *day of* [   ] *199* [   ]

At an EXTRAORDINARY GENERAL MEETING of the above-named Company, convened and held at

on the   day of   , 199   , the following resolutions were passed as elective resolutions:

'1 That pursuant to Section 379A and for the purposes of Section 366A of the Companies Act 1985 (as amended) the Company hereby elects to dispense with the holding of Annual General Meetings.

2 That pursuant to Section 379A and for the purposes of Section 252 of the Companies Act 1985 (as amended) the Company hereby elects to dispense with the laying of accounts and reports before the Company in general meeting.

3 That pursuant to Section 379A and for the purposes of Section 386 of the Companies Act 1985 (as amended) the Company hereby elects to dispense with the obligation to appoint auditors annually.

4 That pursuant to Section 379A and for the purposes of Section 369(4) of 378(3) of the Companies Act 1985 (as amended) the Company hereby elects that the latter two provisions shall have effect in relation to the Company as if for the references to 95 per cent there were substituted references to 90 per cent.

5 That pursuant to Section 379A and for the purposes of Section 80A of the Companies Act 1985 (as amended) the Company hereby elects that the provisions of Section 80A of the Companies Act 1985 (as amended) shall apply, instead of the provisions of Sections 80(4) and 80(5) of that Act, in relation to the giving or renewal, after this election, of an authority under that Section.'

Index